WITHDRAWN
NDSU

WARTIME ORIGINS OF THE BERLIN DILEMMA

TO MY MOTHER AND TO
THE MEMORY OF MY FATHER

Wartime Origins of the Berlin Dilemma

DANIEL J. NELSON

THE UNIVERSITY OF ALABAMA PRESS
University, Alabama

DD
881
N37

Maps facing pages 72, 80, and 118
were drawn by Richard Smythe

Library of Congress Cataloging in Publication Data

Nelson, Daniel J. 1938–
  Wartime origins of the Berlin dilemma.

  Bibliography: p.
  Includes index.
  1. Berlin question (1945–   ) I. Title.
DD881.N37   940.53'14   76-14876
ISBN 0-8173-4727-5

Copyright © 1978 by
The University of Alabama Press
All rights reserved
Manufactured in the United States of America

CONTENTS

Preface		vii
Foreword		ix
One	Berlin as a Problem of International Politics and Diplomacy	1
Two	The Establishment of the European Advisory Commission	10
Three	The Inheritance of EAC: Planning in 1943	24
Four	The First Round: EAC Negotiations in 1944	37
	MAP: EAC Protocol, 14 November 1944	facing page 72
Five	The Second Round: EAC Negotiations in 1945	75
	MAP: British Proposal, 1 March 1945	facing page 80
	MAP: Administrative Boundaries, July 1945	facing page 118
Six	The Special Problem of Access in Wartime and Postwar Negotiations	119
Seven	Post-mortem on the Work of EAC	140
Eight	The Berlin Negotiations and Wartime Alliance Diplomacy	155
Annexes		171

1. Draft Protocol on Military Occupation of Germany Submitted by British Delegation to EAC June 12, 1944 — 171
2. Draft of Text of Article 2 of Protocol on Occupation Submitted by British Delegation to EAC June 13, 1944 — 172
3. Redraft of Protocol on Military Occupation of Germany Submitted by American Delegation to EAC June 19, 1944 — 172
4. Redraft of Protocol on Occupation of Germany Submitted by Soviet Delegation to EAC June 29, 1944 — 173
5. Redraft of Berlin Section of Article 2 of Protocol on Occupation Submitted by British Delegation to EAC July 5, 1944 — 174
6-A. Redraft of Article 2 of Protocol on Occupation Submitted by American Delegation to EAC July 12, 1944 — 175

6-B.	Redraft of Article 5(a) of Protocol on Occupation Submitted by British Delegation to EAC July 12, 1944	176
6-C.	Redraft of Article 5(b) of Protocol on Occupation Submitted by British Delegation to EAC July 12, 1944	176
6-D.	Draft Paragraph for Inclusion in Covering Report to Protocol on Occupation Submitted by British Delegation to EAC July 12, 1944	176
7-A.	Protocol Between the United States, the United Kingdom, and the Soviet Union Regarding the Zones of Occupation in Germany and the Administration of "Greater Berlin," September 12, 1944	177
7-B.	Agreement Between the Governments of the United States of America, the United Kingdom, the Union of Soviet Socialist Republics, and the Provisional Government of the French Republic Regarding Amendments to the Protocol of September 12, 1944, on the Zones of Occupation in Germany and the Administration of "Greater Berlin," July 26, 1945 (Excerpt)	179
8.	Draft Agreement on Control Machinery in Germany Submitted by Soviet Delegation to EAC August 26, 1944	180
9.	Agreement on Control Machinery in Germany November 14, 1944	181
10.	Paragraph for Inclusion in Covering Report to Amending Agreement to Protocol on Zones of Occupation Submitted by French Delegation to EAC July 9, 1945	184
11.	Draft of Last Paragraph of Covering Report to Amending Agreement to Protocol on Zones of Occupation Submitted by Soviet Delegation to EAC July 11, 1945	185
12.	The Quadripartite Agreement on Berlin of September 3, 1971	185

Notes 192

Bibliography 207

Index 214

PREFACE

My interest in the problems of postwar Germany and Berlin dates from my early college years, though my knowledge of wartime and postwar Germany was substantially increased during my years in Germany from 1960 to 1962 as a Fulbright scholar at the Institut für Politische Wissenschaft of the University of Bonn under the guidance of Professor Karl Dietrich Bracher. The manuscript of this book was undertaken as an attempt to shed some light on the protracted postwar dilemma of the city of Berlin by reconstructing a full account of the wartime negotiations among the Four Powers which created the city's unique and difficult situation—a divided city within a divided country. Since no full account of these negotiations has heretofore been produced, it was felt that a study such as this might add a new dimension to our comprehension of the postwar Berlin question by increasing our knowledge of the wartime origins of the problem. In addition, it was hoped that the study might shed some light on some of the broader problems of international relations, such as the hazards of peace planning during times of emergency or war and the difficulties of diplomacy involving states with differing social systems and ideological foundations.

Acknowledgment of the people who aided in the completion of the manuscript is scarcely an adequate means of repaying the heavy debt I owe to all of them. My most immediate and deepest debt is to the late Professor Philip E. Mosely of Columbia University, who as statesman, teacher, and unrelenting critic made detailed comments on every single page of the manuscript. With his experience as a member of the European Advisory Commission, with his gift of near total recall of the events and personalities of the period, and with his compassion as a humanely civilized critic, he contributed his advice and counsel to the project so generously as to defy appraisal. A very special debt of gratitude is also owed to Dr. Arthur G. Kogan, Special Assistant to the Director of the Historical Office at the Department of State. Much of the research for chapters three through seven was carried out with full access to the State Department's decimal and lot files pertaining to the work of the American delegation to the European Advisory Commission. Dr. Kogan's bountiful help with the use of the files as well as his willingness to facilitate the research at every juncture contributed immeasurably to completion of the project. Professor Oliver J. Lissitzyn of Columbia University suggested the initial plan of the book and made many valuable suggestions. Professors Louis Henkin, Robert Paxton, and Zdenik Slouka, all of Columbia University, made many detailed and valuable suggestions on various portions of the manuscript. Much of my knowledge of the stuff and substance of international relations, reflected throughout the book, was acquired from Professor William T. R. Fox of Columbia University. A deep sense of obligation is felt to Professor Charles N. Fortenberry, Chairman of the Department of Political Science at Auburn University, for his constant encouragement and support through many months of labor. Mae Fortenberry contributed great expertise in editorial suggestions and the preparation of the index. And finally, acknowledgment must be made of the superb secretarial services of two of the most patient and remarkable women to be found anywhere, Mrs. Paula Eisman of New York and Mrs. John C. Ball, Jr. of Auburn, Alabama. Despite the encouragement and help from these and others, any errors of judgment or misinterpretation are solely the responsibility of the author.

New York City
September, 1972

DANIEL J. NELSON

FOREWORD

Only a generation after World War II are we beginning to see clearly how much the processes by which that war was brought to an end set the agenda for the international relations of Europe in the decades after 1945. Daniel J. Nelson's *Wartime Origins of the Berlin Dilemma* is the ripened version of an excellent Columbia University dissertation. In its contribution to our new understanding of the interplay of force and diplomacy in the war years it is in a class with Lynn E. Davis's *The Cold War Begins* (Princeton, N. J., Princeton University Press, 1975), by coincidence also a fully matured revision of a Columbia dissertation.

We may locate Dr. Nelson's *Wartime Origins of the Berlin Dilemma* in contemporary scholarship on international relations in another way. Detailed studies such as his of how the salient features of a new international order grow out of decisions made during the just previous war complement and give concrete meaning to recent efforts to state in more general terms how peace grows out of war. Among such efforts there are, for example, Robert F. Randle's *The Origins of Peace* (New York, The Free Press, 1973), Fred C. Iklé's *Every War Must End* (New York, Columbia University Press, 1971), and the November 1970 symposium of the *Annals* of the American Academy of Political and Social Science, "How Wars End."

For reasons which Professor Nelson's preface makes abundantly clear, the late Professor Philip E. Mosely would have been the ideal person to write this foreword. This balanced and judicious study, which sheds so much light on the workings of the European Advisory Commission in which Dr. Mosely was intimately involved, would, I am confident, have given him much satisfaction.

Institute of War and Peace Studies   WILLIAM T. R. FOX
Columbia University

WARTIME ORIGINS OF
THE BERLIN DILEMMA

All free men, wherever they may live,
are citizens of Berlin. And therefore,
as a free man, I take pride in the words,
"ich bin ein Berliner."

       President John F. Kennedy
       June 26, 1963

We are confident that history will
record Berlin not merely as a great
city but as a great principle in
the story of man's struggle for
freedom.

       Secretary of State Henry Kissinger
       May 21, 1975

ONE

BERLIN AS A PROBLEM OF INTERNATIONAL POLITICS AND DIPLOMACY

For well over thirty years the expression West Berlin has meant much more than the name of the proud city located in central Germany. Over the years West Berlin has become a graphic manifestation of the hopes and fears of the statesmen and citizens of the major nations of the Western World. To Western statesmen the maintenance of the viability and integrity of West Berlin has become a rather inflexible objective of foreign policy. To citizens in many Western nations West Berlin has become a symbol of the resilience of the human spirit. The determination of the population of West Berlin to resist communist encroachment and to preserve their freedom has served not only to inspire sentiments such as John Kennedy's "ich bin ein Berliner" in 1963 but also to commit the Western governments unalterably to the maintenance of the integrity of West Berlin as a foreign policy objective.

Berlin's Symbolic Significance

Berlin is much more than a city. It is a symbol as well: a symbol of the tensions of the Cold War, of the division of Germany, of East-West rivalry, and of the successes and failures of the foreign policies of both superpowers in the postwar order. Indeed the city is a symbol for, and a microcosm of, many of the problems of the postwar system of international relations. Nowhere can one observe as clearly as in Berlin the fragility of many of the assumptions made during the war years concerning the postwar international order. At the end of the war Germany became the testing ground of East and West, the place where the postwar zones of influence came together at the strategic and economic center of Europe. And the focal point of the entire cluster of problems surrounding Germany centered in Berlin.

In May of 1945 the once magnificent capital of the German *Reich* lay in ruins, a tragic symbol of the failure of Hitler's efforts to place all of Europe in the bondage of Naziism. Berlin as the symbol of German power was replaced by Berlin as the symbol and headquarters of the Allied occupation regime for defeated Germany. Amidst the desolation the Allied Kommandatura for Berlin began to function in July, 1945, and the Control Council for Germany in August. The initial stresses of East-West tension and the first faint rumblings of postwar rivalry between the Western Powers and the Soviet Union were felt most acutely in Berlin.

It was perhaps inevitable that Berlin would become one of the primary problems of international politics in the postwar period if the grand coalition which brought about the defeat of Germany failed to continue to function as a cooperative enterprise. The turbulent course of the city's history in the years following the war was in large measure dictated by two factors: the location of the city as an enclave within the Soviet zone of occupation, and the Four Power agreements which made Berlin a special area apart from the zones of occupation and divided the city into four separate sectors of occupation. The question has often been posed why the Allied Powers did not obviate the entire maze of problems surrounding Berlin by drawing up quite different arrangements for Germany in the Four Power agreements. Certainly another city could have been chosen as the headquarters of the occupation regime, a city more conveniently located on the boundary lines of the zones of occupation, or, alternately, perhaps the zonal boundaries could have been redrawn so as to converge upon Berlin, thus forestalling the problems associated with its geographical isolation. These and other suggestions will be discussed in succeeding chapters. One consideration, however, must be borne in mind: the significance of Berlin as a symbol was so great that it seemed almost inconceivable to locate the Allied control machinery anywhere else. As Berlin had once been the proud symbol of German power and Nazi domination, so it would represent the symbol of Allied victory in war and Allied objectives in Germany after the war. It seemed only natural that Berlin, power center of the *Reich*, would have to become Berlin, power center of Allied authority. Berlin's symbolic value as the capital of Germany seemed to demand that some special status be created for the city in the postwar occupation regime.[1] Consequently, it was in a sense inevitable that the success or failure of postwar Allied objectives in Germany and Europe would be tested most crucially and most immediately in Berlin.

For over a quarter of a century since the end of the Second World War, the great city of Berlin has played a crucial role in the fluid processes of international politics. As the focal point of Cold War politics, the city became an important barometer of East-West relationships and a testing ground for the strategies and policies of the superpowers. A city in constant tension and crisis, Berlin was in a sense the crucible of the Cold War. As the Cold War began to wane with the fragile development of a détente in the late 1960s and early 1970s, it seemed certain that eventually some new kind of East-West understanding on Berlin would have to be reached to reduce or at least moderate the smoldering tensions which had beset the city since 1945. The signature of the Quadripartite Agreement on Berlin on September 3, 1971, by the Four Allied Powers which had wrestled at times violently over the city's future for over twenty-six years marked an historic turning point in the history of the Cold War as well as the beginning of a new era of superpower relationships in Western and Central Europe. In a real sense this agreement represented a kind of *de facto* settlement of the unsatisfactory Berlin problem as it emerged from the Second World War.

Four Power talks on Berlin took place sporadically for over twenty-six years after the end of the war. Until the Quadripartite Agreement of September 3, 1971, however, the talks never achieved anything resembling a settlement or modification of the circumstances which defined the battleground between the Western Powers and the Soviet Union on the Berlin question, mainly because the major powers were not yet ready to compromise on any of their long established claims and objectives. The problem has its roots in the protocols and agreements on Germany and Berlin negotiated and signed by the Allied Powers even before the end of World War II. The agreements divided the historic German capital into four sectors of occupation as a special regime within the eastern or Soviet zone of occupation. The special regime envisioned for the city in the wartime agreements was in itself workable enough, given the assumptions of minimum East-West agreement, cooperation, and collaboration in the postwar European order which animated the work of the wartime negotiators in London. What made the agreements unworkable was the vicious rivalry which developed between the Soviet Union and the Western Powers in Germany at the end of the war. As the former members of the great wartime coalition began to differ seriously on a variety of postwar political issues, the situation in Berlin rapidly deteriorated. The eleven-month blockade of Berlin by the Russians from June, 1948, until May, 1949, represented a concerted effort by the Soviet Union to oust the Western Powers from Berlin completely. The effort, as is now well known, did not succeed largely due to the tenacity of the Western Powers in maintaining all their claims on the city, even to the extent of the massive and prolonged Berlin airlift. By the end of the blockade the administrative division of Berlin was complete, with separate city governments for East Berlin, the former Soviet sector, and for West Berlin, composed of the British, French, and American occupation sectors. In October, 1949, the Russians again violated the city's Four Power administration status by proclaiming Berlin the capital of the German Democratic Republic. Crisis after crisis punctuated the city's turbulent history throughout the 1950s culminating with Khrushchev's 1958 ultimatum to the Western Powers to remove all their troops from Berlin as a prelude to establishment of a "free city." In 1959, after four hectic months of negotiations in Geneva, the ultimatum was withdrawn. The most dramatic communist move in the protracted dispute came on August 13, 1961, when the East German regime sealed all the border crossings between East and West Berlin and began construction of the infamous Berlin Wall. The years following the Wall saw no improvement in the crisis atmosphere surrounding Berlin until the proposal by the Western Allies for a new series of talks to improve the situation in late 1969. On March 26, 1970, the talks began in the former Allied Control Council building in Berlin's Kleist Park. After seventeen months of delicate negotiations a new Quadripartite Agreement on Berlin was signed on September 3, 1971.

The signature of the Quadripartite Agreement represented a significant milestone in Berlin's turbulent history. The agreement was made possible by the fact that after twenty-six years of crisis and severe tension, the Four Powers were finally determined to make the fundamental political decisions needed for a settlement. These decisions rested upon assumptions about the postwar era in Germany and Berlin which were reflected in the wartime protocols and which should have but did not shape the actual policies of the Powers in the postwar period. The fundamental assumptions which were espoused by the wartime negotiators in London in 1944–1945 are in a real sense the assumptions to which the Four Powers returned in negotiating the Quadripartite Agreement of 1971: the assumption that the administration of the city must be a more or less cooperative enterprise by all Four Powers, the assumption that cooperation rather than conflict and hostility are the only possible cornerstones of a viable European order, and the assumption that any final restoration of Berlin as the true capital of postwar Germany must await a settlement of the German question as a whole including the restoration of a unified Germany to the status of peaceful great power participant in the counsels of world affairs. In a sense, then, the Quadripartite Agreement of 1971 vindicated at long last both the assumptions and the hopes of the wartime negotiators on the European Advisory Commission, despite the fact that for twenty-six years their work was eclipsed by the rivalry of the Great Powers in the Cold War.

Purpose of the Inquiry

The present study of the Berlin question turns the clock back many years to the dark days of 1943–1945 when the Allied Powers began making the basic decisions regarding the future of Germany and Berlin for the postwar period. It is a detailed inquiry into the Allied negotiations during the Second World War which determined the postwar situation of the city of Berlin—a divided city within a divided country. It retraces, step by step, all the decisions made in reference to Berlin's postwar status by the Allied Powers during the later stages of the war and shortly after its end. The major purpose is to create a new perspective from which to suggest answers to some of the troublesome questions which have so often been asked by statesmen and laymen alike since 1945: Why did the West conclude the war with Berlin as a divided city totally within the Soviet zone of East Germany? Why did the wartime negotiators produce a series of agreements on Berlin which worked only for a short period and eventually gave way to the creation of the greatest crisis point in world affairs for a protracted period of time? What were the successes and failures of the wartime negotiations on Berlin? Why did the negotiations not produce a viable settlement on Berlin for the postwar period?

It should perhaps be pointed out at the outset that this study overlaps the disciplines of history and political science. Basically it is an historical study, the careful reconstruction of one important thread of political history from 1943 to 1945. Obviously history is never written for its own sake; it is written primarily to provide answers to certain questions about the past which may be useful in giving us broader and deeper perspectives about the problems of the present and the future. In this study we shall be asking certain sets of politically related or political science related questions. Our assumption is, of course, that the answers to these historical questions may better equip us to analyze critically and deal with the intractable problems associated with the continuing Berlin problem, a problem modified but not yet settled by the Quadripartite Agreement of 1971.

That history and political science are overlapping disciplines should be utterly apparent. Both deal with the motivations of human behavior; both are social (not physical) and socially scientific disciplines in the sense of the application of empiricism and methodological rigor to social inquiry. History is in a sense the basic foundation stone of all the social sciences. Most especially, however, the political scientist needs the light of history to guide him in the analysis of contemporary political phenomena. It is indeed a strong bias of this writer that the best political scientists are those who possess, in addition to knowledge of sophisticated methods of analysis in behavioral science research, also a broad grasp of the political, social, and intellectual history of certain important periods. The political scientist who attempts to grapple with complex political questions with no knowledge of the history of how such problems emerged or the circumstances which gave rise to them is no political scientist at all.

It is with this general idea in mind that this study of the Berlin question has been written. From an historical standpoint we might point out that until now no satisfactory historical record of the Allied negotiations relating to Berlin during the war has been written. This study is, for one thing, an attempt to add to the completeness of volumes on recent contemporary history. But beyond that, as a political history of a series of intergovernmental decisions over a relatively short period of time, the study attempts to suggest tentative answers to certain questions which may contribute to our understanding of the Berlin question past, present, and future.

Asking the Right Questions

The questions which might be asked in a study such as this could perhaps be grouped into various sets of thematically related questions. One set of questions might concern East-West relationships. What were the divergent territorial and strategic interests between East and West which shaped the decisions on Berlin in 1944–1945? Were the seeds of postwar East-West conflict already to be seen in the wartime alliance in the Berlin negotiations? Did the decisions relating to Berlin diminish or exacerbate the incipient East-West conflict? Another set of questions might be woven around the theme of international diplomacy. What do the Berlin negotiations teach us about the techniques and procedures of diplomacy between Allies during times of great stress or emergency? More specifically, what special factors may have conditioned to some extent the success or failure of Western negotiations with the Russians at this time? What, if any, general observations might be made concerning the problems of Western negotiations with the Soviet government as seen in the light of the Berlin negotiations? A third set of questions might be structured around the general theme of peace planning during times of active hostilities. What preliminary observations on the problems of planning for peace during wartime might be made on the basis of a careful analysis of the Berlin negotiations? More specifically, what are the virtues as well as the disadvantages of a body such as the European Advisory Commission in the process of wartime peace planning? What general assumptions, mutually espoused by all negotiating partners, might be held to be indispensable to the successful work of an intergovernmental forum of negotiation such as the European Advisory Commission?

We shall, in the course of our inquiry, be concerned in some way with each of these sets of questions, as well as with many others. A segment of history is necessarily a whole piece of cloth from which no single strand of thread can be detached. The major theme of the book, however, revolves around the nexus of problems associated with the effort of an allied coalition to design fundamental alterations in the international order during times of war or general international breakdown.

Substantive and Procedural Aspects

In dealing with these questions we should be aware that there is a dual nature both in our focus and in our objective. On the one hand we are concerned with the Berlin question, i.e. the determination of Berlin's status at the end of the war; on the other hand we are studying the set of Allied negotiations during the war which in effect created the postwar Berlin dilemma. This dual focus could perhaps be seen in terms of the dichotomy between "substantive" and "procedural" matters that is often drawn in the social sciences. Insofar as the substantive-procedural division has any philosophical validity, we might posit that in this study the Berlin question is the subject of our substantive inquiry, while the Allied negotiations within the European Advisory Commission constitute the subject of our procedural inquiry. The former is body or structure, while the latter is instrument or medium. The two elements complement each other in much the same way as atoms and electrons in the study of physics. Hence the substantive inquiry illuminates the procedural questions, while the procedural inquiry, in reverse fashion, forms a backdrop for the substantive conclusions. The two types of inquiry are in a sense only reverse sides of the same coin, for they cannot be separated from each other in any coherent fashion. The substantive and procedural elements in any historical inquiry are necessarily intertwined to a great extent. Consequently, our concentration on the process of negotiation within the European Advisory Commission in this study alternates with and complements our attention to the emergence of a new status for the city of Berlin through the negotiations.

This study is, in the first instance, an attempt to construct a reasonably accurate account of all the inter-Allied negotiations on Berlin during and shortly after the Second World War, beginning with the Moscow Foreign Ministers Conference in October, 1943, and ending with the commencement of the Control Council's work and the final decision on the French sector of Berlin in August, 1945.[2] As we shall see, the forum for most of these negotiations was the European Advisory Commission in London, a rather novel type of body for high level multilateral negotiation during wartime.

Impedimenta

As is the case with any such attempt, the effort to reconstruct the story of the particular set of political decisions and agreements concerning Berlin is beset with certain difficulties. In the first place, the negotiations on Berlin constituted only a small segment of the inter-Allied negotiations on Germany in particular and postwar European affairs in general. Any attempt to abstract a specific subject from a set of international negotiations is necessarily artificial to a certain extent. As will be seen, the Berlin negotiations cannot be traced without constant reference to the negotiations on Germany as a whole. However, the attempt to focus on Berlin is both legitimate and worthwhile, since in the negotiations on Germany, Berlin was always treated more or less as a special case. In addition, its significance to the German question, as a sort of microcosm of all the problems associated with postwar Germany, plus the unique status agreed upon for the disposition of the city, would seem to indicate that the Berlin problem should be accorded special treatment apart from the larger German question.

Another difficulty associated with compiling the history of the Berlin negotiations is the fact that available sets of records do not record all the relevant aspects. Negotiations at the military level are recorded in Pentagon files, access to which is not granted except for extraordinary purposes. This difficulty is, however, mitigated considerably by the fact that negotiations at the military level were, for the most part, subsidiary to the primary negotiations conducted within the European Advisory Commission. Fortunately, a full set of records pertaining to the work of the American delegation in the European Advisory Commission was remitted to the State Department at the end of the war. These records contain a treasury of information concerning all major aspects of the Berlin negotiations during 1944–45. Although these files cannot possibly tell the story of the negotiations at all levels, they do contain the major outline, and most of the gaps could be filled in from other published sources.

The results of this inquiry should lead us to some tentative answers to several various sets of political questions. In addition to suggesting outlines of possible answers to the general sets of questions listed above, we might hope that answers to certain more specific questions might also be suggested. We should expect that the study should lead to some conclusions about the overall wisdom of the settlement on Berlin, both in terms of the context of 1945 and the long range of time. Were any important options overlooked by the Western Powers? Was a settlement better suited to the needs of both East and West missed because of the inept diplomacy of one side or the other or both? What conclusions might be drawn about the quality of American diplomacy in 1945 in reference to the Berlin settlement? We might also hope to learn more about the general problems associated with the attempt to negotiate during wartime segments of a radically changed postwar order. More specifically, we should be able to reach some conclusions regarding the efficacy of a quasi-collegial high level forum of negotiation such as the European Advisory Commission.

The Issue of Bias

A word should perhaps be added on the issue of bias. No pretext is made that the study has been written from the vantage point of the totally objective political observer. Apart from the fact that there is probably no such thing as value-free political science or impartial historical-political analysis, it would be sheer folly to claim such impartiality in a study such as this. In reviewing the wartime negotiations between the Western Powers and the Soviet Union, the writer quite naturally draws conclusions from the point of view of one who attempts to improve the quality of and maximize the success of Western, and more specifically American, foreign policy. Perhaps no apology is needed for this bias. As a product of the Western system of political and legal values and of the American educational system oriented towards Anglo-Saxon concepts of democracy and justice in world affairs, the writer would have to betray his own convictions in order to assume a position of complete impartiality in regard to the success or failure of alternative social systems, political ideologies, and foreign policies. In addition, if there is any truth to the inherent suspicion that world affairs would benefit from a wider application of Western values of individual freedom, justice, and the supremacy of law over arbitrary power, then it is indeed the task of the Western scholar to strive both to improve the quality of Western foreign policy and to contribute to its success and effectiveness. The cause of peace is not served merely by concluding from a supposedly objective point of view that a particular dispute could have been avoided if one of the protagonists had bowed to the will of the other at the outset or if one side had adjusted its foreign policy to accommodate the political needs of the other side, regardless of the morality of the issue.

In the case of the Berlin question the writer feels that the issue of morality is particularly important. It would be immoral for a Western scholar to be indifferent to the success of Western political objectives in Germany and Berlin at the end of the Second World War in view of the harshly repressive character of the Stalin regime in Moscow at the time. Hence, taking into consideration both the relevance of morality to the Berlin question and an educational orientation stressing the relevance of Western values in the implementation of foreign policy, the writer disclaims a pretense to impartiality in the analysis to follow. Such a disclaimer should not, however, reduce the value of the present study. If a review of the negotiations which created the postwar status of Berlin can lead to greater depth in our understanding of the entire substance of the Berlin question and hence to greater facility in critical analysis of the problem both present and future, the study will have served its purpose.

TWO

THE ESTABLISHMENT OF THE EUROPEAN ADVISORY COMMISSION

The work of the European Advisory Commission, especially as it concerned the postwar fate of Berlin, represents one of the more interesting chapters in the history of diplomacy during the Second World War. Karl Loewenstein remarks that the EAC was "one of the most influential although least publicized agencies of postwar planning."[1] Ernst Dauerlein quite correctly defines the actual wartime role of the EAC in his assertion that the EAC was "das entscheidende—und auch einzige—Instrument zur Vorbereitung und Festlegung der aliierten Nachkriegspolitik in Deutschland."[2]

The Beginning of the Moscow Conference

The story of the creation of the European Advisory Commission begins with the Tripartite Conference of Foreign Ministers held at Moscow, October 18–November 1, 1943. At this conference, which was held as part of the preparations for the meeting of Roosevelt, Churchill, and Stalin at Tehran in November, a great number of subjects were discussed, among them the creation of a general organization for peace after the war, the postwar treatment of Germany and Austria, postwar economic policies, the problem of German atrocities, and plans for the invasion of northern France in the spring of 1944. One of the major achievements of the conference, however, was the agreement regarding the creation of the European Advisory Commission.

At the beginning of the Moscow Conference it was agreed that the problem of setting up some kind of machinery for consultation on postwar problems should be placed on the conference agenda as item 3. The subject was first discussed at the fourth session of the conference held on October 22, 1943. At this session Foreign Secretary Anthony Eden proposed that the terms of reference for such a "Politico-Military Commission" should include "questions of a wide range of all European problems arising out of the prosecution of the war with the exception of military operations."[3] A broader frame of reference for the proposed body could hardly be imagined. Eden further proposed that the Commission be established in London, since it would be manifestly impossible for it to function properly in Algiers or Italy. He further explained that because of constitutional difficulties the proposed Commission could not have any executive function but would have the widest possible consultative powers. He envisaged that it would function as "some form of clearinghouse . . . with broad consultative powers to deal with general questions arising out of the war."[4]

Immediately following Eden's presentation Secretary of State Cordell Hull read the United States suggestion for the machinery of tripartite consultation. The U.S. proposal, considerably less precise than the British program, suggested merely that the three governments consult on an *ad hoc* basis through their permanent diplomatic representatives in each capital, utilizing when necessary the services of appropriate experts depending upon the subjects under discussion.[5] In response to questions from Eden and Foreign Minister Molotov, Hull admitted quite frankly that the more comprehensive British proposals rendered the U.S. suggestion somewhat less important.

Neither Hull nor Molotov, however, was ready to accept the comprehensive British proposals without substantial modification. At the fifth session of the conference on October 23 Molotov stated that he felt that "if the powers of the Politico-Military Commission in London were made too broad there would be no work left for the Foreign Ministers" and that he personally favored the proposals advanced by Hull the previous day that there be "tripartite meetings utilizing existing diplomatic machinery in the capitals of our three countries under the presidency of the Foreign Minister of the capital selected and with the participation of the Ambassadors of the other two countries."[6] He went on to say that the London mission "might well start with the consideration of the preparation of armistice terms but that perhaps some combination of the British and United States proposals could be worked out on this."[7]

The Divergence of Views

It was apparent immediately that there was a substantial divergence of views between the British on the one hand and the Russians and Americans on the other as to the appropriate terms of reference for the proposed consultative body in London. The British delegation wanted to give the Commission a very broad mandate so that it could recommend not only agreed policies for the treatment of Germany after the war but also policies for dealing with other liberated areas of Europe. In addition the Commission should be given competence to work out the question of future regimes in France, Poland, and Yugoslavia and to settle minority and boundary disputes.[8] Apart from the fact that the British government was so organized as to be well equipped to study such matters and to arrive at concrete policy recommendations, the British view was perhaps motivated by the idea that the wartime military coalition provided a golden opportunity to arrive at a settlement of as many urgent matters as possible during the war, since such a partnership might well not last long after victory had been achieved.[9]

The official view of the United States delegation was that the mandate of the proposed Commission should be limited primarily to working out terms of surrender for the Axis states and to setting up machinery to enforce these terms. The American government did not favor prolonged or extensive commitments to Europe after the war. In addition, since the administration was looking forward to the establishment of a general organization composed of all the United Nations to safeguard the peace after the war, it did not look with favor upon any organization or body which might in any way compromise the goals or jurisdiction of the general United Nations organization.[10] From the beginning, President Franklin Roosevelt was much more confident than Prime Minister Winston Churchill about the possibilities of successful postwar collaboration with the Russians. As far as postwar policy planning was concerned, however, the American president had an instinctive distaste for the entire process, since he felt that the chief executive should make no commitments on matters which were usually worked out in peace negotiations and settled finally in treaties of peace. He also feared that various foreign and ethnic groups in the United States would be alienated or distracted from the war effort if attempts were made to settle boundary disputes and other European problems before the end of the war.[11] George Kennan remarks that the president "would obviously have preferred, in fact, that there be no such commission at all; but the very reasonable desire of the State Department to get on with some sort of preparations for a joint Allied approach to the problems of the German surrender and the immediate post-surrender treatment of Germany, problems which were taking on a new urgency as the time for the invasion of the continent drew nearer, evidently had sufficient force to compel his very reluctant assent to the establishment of the commission."[12]

With both the American and Soviet delegations expressing opposition to the broad frame of reference proposed for the Commission by the British delegation, it became obvious that the competence and jurisdiction of the Commission would have to be narrowed down. Secretary Hull, in accordance with the president's instructions but clearly in accord also with his own ideas,[13] continued to insist on limiting the Commission's mandate to include only the problems of surrender terms, zones of occupation, and machinery for the enforcement of the surrender terms. Eden agreed to accept such limitations on the Commission's work, though he continued to press for as broad a mandate as possible and made it clear that he hoped that additional subjects could be assigned to the Commission by unanimous agreement of the three Allies.

At the eleventh conference session on October 29 Andrey Vyshinsky, Soviet deputy foreign minister, contrasted, somewhat inaccurately, the Soviet position with the British and American positions. He stated that the Soviet government strongly felt that the Commission should deal in the beginning only with the questions involved in the termination of hostilities and the drawing up of armistice terms, whereas the British and American view was that the Commission should have broad consultative powers on all European questions connected with the war.[14] Mr. Eden replied, quite realistically, that "in the last analysis the Commission would deal only with questions which the three Governments considered advisable to submit to it." He continued to point out, however, that in previous conference sessions the Conference itself had already referred to the Commission several questions such as liberated territories, the administration of France, and the Allied attitude toward postwar Germany, which were outside the narrow question of the armistice terms.[15] Molotov responded that he "merely wanted to make sure that the London Commission would have clearly defined functions as otherwise its work would be needlessly complicated, and he felt that the document setting up the commission should express unequivocally its exact purposes."[16] In an effort to dispel Molotov's doubts and meet his objections Eden then proposed to limit the terms of reference of the Commission to "European questions connected with the ending of the war."[17]

A Compromise Is Reached

In the end a substantial meeting of the minds was achieved concerning the purposes, jurisdiction, and work of the European Advisory Commission. Sir William Strang, a member of the British delegation to the Moscow Conference and later the British representative on EAC, recalls that the scheme was not devised without travail: "I remember waking one night in the small hours with a draft for the constitution of the Commission buzzing in my head, and rising and committing it to paper for Mr. Eden's use at the conference next day; and then wrestling with Vyshinsky most of the next night around a green baize table, together with Mr. Bohlen of the United States delegation, trying to reconcile the somewhat varying views expressed by our chiefs at the conference."[18] The conflicting views were finally reconciled, and the record shows no evidence that the negotiations were ever seriously imperiled or conducted with acrimony. Due mainly to Eden's willingness to accept most of the limitations desired by the American and Soviet delegations, the three foreign ministers succeeded in creating a commission which eventually became the chief forum in which the Allies' plans for postwar Germany were reconciled and translated into policy in treaty form.

The Secret Protocol of the Moscow Conference was signed by Hull, Eden, and Molotov on November 1, 1943. The articles setting up the European Advisory Commission are recorded in Annex 2 of that Protocol:

"1. The Governments of the United Kingdom, United States of America and the Soviet Union agree to establish a European Advisory Commission composed of representatives of the three Powers. The Commission will have its seat in London and will meet as soon as possible. The presidency will be held in rotation by the representatives of the three Powers. A joint secretariat will be established. The representatives may be assisted where necessary by technical advisers, civilian and military.

"2. The Commission will study and make joint recommendations to the three Governments upon European questions connected with the termination of hostilities which the three Governments may consider appropriate to refer to it. For this purpose the members of the Commission will be supplied by their Governments with all relevant information on political and military developments affecting their work.

"3. As one of the Commission's first tasks the three Governments desire that it shall as soon as possible make detailed recommendations to them upon the terms of surrender to be imposed upon each of the European states with which any of the three Powers are at war, and upon the machinery required to ensure the fulfillment of those terms. . . .

. . . .

"6. The establishment of the Commission will not preclude other methods of consultation on current or other issues which the three Governments think it desirable to discuss. . . ."[19]

Dr. Philip Mosely, who attended the Moscow Conference as a member of the U.S. delegation, notes that although the U.S. delegation accepted the rather broad wording of Article 2, they placed particular emphasis on the provision that questions could be referred to the EAC only by unanimous consent of the three governments. In addition, the U.S. delegation adhered to a rather strict interpretation of Article 2 as the only real mandate of the new body.[20]

Appointments to the Commission

The agreement regarding the EAC was approved by Roosevelt, Churchill, and Stalin at Tehran the end of November, and the three governments proceeded to appoint their representatives to the EAC during the Tehran Conference. The British government appointed Sir William Strang, later Lord Strang, who was at that time an assistant undersecretary in the British Foreign Office. Strang's appointment was favorably received by the most influential British papers. The Americans were to be represented on the Commission by John G. Winant, a former governor of New Hampshire and successor to Joseph P. Kennedy as American ambassador to the United Kingdom. The Russians also appointed their ambassador to London, Fedor Tarasevich Gusev. The fact that the American and Russian governments appointed their London ambassadors as representatives to the EAC was somewhat of a disappointment to the British, since this action seemed an early indication that the Commission might not function as expeditiously as originally planned.[21] Sir William Strang would be free to direct his entire time and energy to the Commission, while Winant and Gusev would have to tend to their normal ambassadorial duties first and attend the Commission's work with whatever time might be left over. As ambassadors, Winant and Gusev would be fully dependent upon instructions cabled to them from remote capitals, while Strang, as a senior official in his government's foreign office, would be thoroughly conversant with the evolution of his government's policy at every stage. Strang's much more advantageous position in EAC negotiations made it somewhat inevitable that from the outset the British delegation was provided with carefully prepared negotiating positions and had to exercise considerable restraint to avoid becoming impatient with the other two delegations, which characteristically seemed to be awaiting instructions from home.

The Impact of National Decision-Making on International Negotiations

The work of the EAC was, of course, vitally affected by the decision-making processes of the respective governments which transmitted instructions and negotiating positions to the three individual representatives. Since the focus of this analysis is a study of a set of international negotiations, not a study of the decision-making processes of the various governments involved, the discussion of the internal policy-making processes of the various governments must remain rather brief. Nevertheless, some mention of these processes must be made in order to understand fully the constraints under which the work of the EAC had to proceed.

The British wartime decision-making process, at least as far as it concerned the EAC negotiations, functioned smoothly and efficiently and must have appeared to the other delegations as a model of organizational proficiency. In the last instance British policy was approved through the Armistice and Postwar Committee, whose chairman was the deputy prime minister, Mr. Clement Attlee. The most active members of the Committee were the secretary of state for war, Sir James Grigg, and the minister of labour, Mr. Ernest Bevin.[22] Below the Armistice and Postwar Committee was an interdivisional committee known as the Post-Hostilities Planning Committee which prepared detailed and comprehensive plans for submission to the Armistice and Postwar Committee. The system of committees, though elaborate, functioned quite effectively and had the great advantage of being able to coordinate the thinking of civilian and military authorities from the lowest levels clear up to the prime minister.[23] Fortunately for the British delegation to EAC, Sir William Strang was vitally involved in the work of all the relevant committees, and, in addition, enjoyed the close confidence of the prime minister himself. By the time the EAC first began its work the British delegation had properly cleared and comprehensive plans on all of the main subjects relating to Germany which were considered by the Commission.

The situation was quite different for the American delegation to EAC. Winant could in no way join Strang in functioning in this manner. Kennan notes that "the American representative could come up with no thoughts and make no suggestion to his colleagues which had not already come to him as instructions from Washington; and since Washington appeared to have a total absence of thoughts, and only the tardiest and most grudging of suggestions, this obviously limited drastically what the American representative could do."[24] To a great extent Winant's difficulties stemmed from the bifurcated and uncoordinated policy-making process in Washington. From early 1943 on there seemed to be two distinct lines of policy formulation for the postwar period: one running through the State Department, and the other through the Joint Chiefs of Staff and the War Department. The position of President Roosevelt in reference to these alternative policy routes was ambivalent and uncertain throughout 1943 and 1944, though he more often seemed to give attention to the military authorities and the War Department. By late 1942 it seemed that some kind of informal understanding had been reached regarding a proper delineation of responsibilities for winning the war and establishing the peace. The president would work with the Joint Chiefs and military authorities in the task of devising strategies to achieve military victory, while it would be the primary responsibility of the State Department to devise appropriate plans for a just and workable postwar order.[25] This arrangement would seem to have been confirmed at the time of Foreign Secretary Eden's visit to Washington in March, 1943. In his talks with Eden on the subject of the two countries' plans and policies for the postwar period, the president seems to have agreed that the Department of State should be made responsible for working out a plan of postwar procedure in Germany. Harry Hopkins' notes of the meetings record this understanding: "I said I thought it [the postwar order] required some kind of formal agreement and the State Department should work out the plan with the British and the one agreed upon by the two of us should then be discussed with the Russians. The President agreed that this procedure should be followed."[26]

This arrangement is confirmed by Roosevelt's memorandum to Secretary Hull of March 23:

"Apropos of our conversation the other afternoon, I wish you would explore, with the British, the question of what our plan is to be in Germany and Italy during the first few months after Germany's collapse.

"I think you had better confer with Stimson about it too.

"My thought is, if we get a substantial meeting of the minds with the British, that we should then take it up with the Russians."[27]

Proceeding with this mandate, officials in the State Department began immediately to set up the machinery needed to carry out the task. A number of study groups and task forces were created to study various facets of the problem. In addition, an Interdivisional Committee on Germany was set up in an effort to bring together specialists from all divisions of the department and specialists on all aspects of German affairs in the process of planning for postwar Germany. Under the able chairmanship of James Riddleberger, the Committee produced a number of carefully prepared background and policy studies which were forwarded to officials higher in the State Department and other important members of the administration.[28]

Throughout 1943 the Interdivisional Committee reported its studies for review to the Territorial Studies Committee, presided over by Dr. Isaiah Bowman. In January, 1944, the committee hierarchy within the department was thoroughly revamped. Henceforth, the Interdivisional Committee reported to the Postwar Programs Committee, which was charged with the task of reviewing the reports of the original committee, supplementing, and amending them. Papers approved by the Postwar Programs Committee were forwarded to the secretary of state, and, if approved by him, became official State Department policy, though not official administration policy. These committees were set up in response to a widely shared view within the State Department that the department, in line with President Roosevelt's spring mandate, must have available, at all times and on all foreseeable problems, policy recommendations that would reflect the combined knowledge and judgment of all interested divisions of the department.[29]

Following the Moscow Conference in October, 1943, the Interdivisional Committee focused its attention on the primary subjects which, it was expected, would occupy the deliberations of the EAC, and upon which the American representative on EAC would need instructions: an instrument of unconditional surrender, a plan for the occupation of Germany, and the machinery for carrying out a joint Allied administration of the country. Mosely notes that when he returned to Washington from the Moscow Conference he urged the Committee to expedite its work, since he felt that negotiations with the Russians stood much more chance of success if American proposals were submitted in EAC before the Russian proposals. Not only might the American proposals serve as a moderate compromise between Soviet and British proposals, they might well be accepted as a basis for discussion and negotiation, if submitted first.[30] By December the Interdivisional Committee had completed comprehensive studies and made recommendations on all three major topics.

Rivalries in U.S. Policy Coordination

Since John Winant was the American ambassador in London as well as the American representative on EAC, his instructions were telegraphed to him by the secretary of state. From the outset, however, it was recognized that the negotiations within EAC, since they concerned the political, military, social, and economic future of Germany in a rather total way, far transcended the policy competence of the Department of State. Consequently in December, 1943, on the initiative of the State Department, an interdepartmental committee, consisting of officers of the Departments of State, War, and Navy, was created in order to combine the views of all three departments on postwar policy and to provide Ambassador Winant with instructions based on this convergence of views. The body was known by the camouflage name of the Working Security Committee.[31] After the establishment of this committee, the accepted procedure came to be that the secretary of state could transmit instructions or recommendations to Winant only after they had been approved by all the departments represented on WSC. This meant that in practice the representatives of the War or Navy Departments, including the Joint Chiefs of Staff, possessed a veto not only in regard to the approval of policy positions within WSC but also on the transmission of any instructions to Winant. As it turned out, this became a most inefficient and unhappy situation.

From the very beginning the War Department representatives on WSC took an extremely dim view, not only of the deliberations within the Committee, but also of the EAC. From their point of view the EAC, in considering plans for zones of occupation and military administration in Germany, was interfering with military matters which were strictly within the jurisdiction of the military branches of the government and which could be resolved at the appropriate time only at the military level.[32] In addition, the War Department representatives believed that their views, much more than those of the State Department, corresponded to the thinking of the president on such matters. The president, after all, had frequent discussions with the Joint Chiefs which involved highly classified military information entirely outside the purview of the State Department.

The War Department representatives on WSC were provided by the department's Civil Affairs Division. These representatives, in turn, were not well received by the representatives of the Department of State. In the first place, they were of relatively minor rank. The permanent representative of the Army was a lieutenant colonel, who until a few weeks before had been a junior officer in the Department of State; the Navy representative was only a lieutenant. Secondly, the Civil Affairs Division apparently had prepared no studies relating to future policy in Germany, even though the division had been set up in the spring of 1943.[33] The State Department representatives, well-prepared with a number of scholarly and comprehensive papers, found it somewhat difficult to work with the junior and less well prepared Civil Affairs Division representatives, who seemed to possess no views of their own, only a veto over the initiatives of the State Department representatives.[34]

It was clearly the men from the Civil Affairs Division who refused all cooperation and who precipitated, not only a near collapse of the WSC, but a highly embarrassing and nearly untenable situation for Ambassador Winant in London. For over two weeks after the establishment of WSC the Civil Affairs representatives refused to take any part in the proceedings, maintaining that the surrender and occupation of Germany were purely military matters which would be handled by the Joint Chiefs of Staff, not by the European Advisory Commission. The State Department representative attempted to point out in reply that postwar policy in Germany entailed considerations far beyond the bounds of military policy and matters that fell properly within the foreign policy responsibilities of the Department of State. In addition, postwar policy in Germany would necessarily have to be a common concern of all three victor nations. President Roosevelt had entered into a definite international obligation to Britain and the Soviet Union when he agreed to the establishment of the European Advisory Commission at the Moscow Conference, and the United States was now committed to the task of reaching agreed policy recommendations within the framework of EAC.[35]

Finally, on December 21, 1943, the officers of the Civil Affairs Division agreed to take part in the proceedings of WSC. Still, however, they refused either to discuss occupation policy or to concur in any instructions to be sent to Ambassador Winant. Mosely writes that they were apparently given instructions not to agree to anything until clearance was given from higher up in the War Department.[36] As a consequence, the work of WSC remained at a standstill for some time, even though Winant was urgently cabling for instructions. Kennan acidly asserts that the work of EAC met "with a resistance violent almost to the point of insubordination at the hands of the Civil Affairs Division at the United States War Department."[37]

Procedural Tangles in Washington

Another difficulty was the extremely complicated procedure by which the WSC had to operate, a procedure which in itself tended to magnify out of proportion the differences between the State Department and the military and to make compromise impossible. In the first instance it was necessary for the Committee to solicit the views of all the relevant divisions of the State, War, and Navy Departments as well as those of the Joint Postwar Committee of the Joint Chiefs of Staff (JPWC). Any recommendation or policy position which might be agreed to, taking into account all the relevant and sometimes conflicting viewpoints, would have to be referred back for approval either to the JPWC, in cases involving primarily military matters, or to the Civil Affairs Division, in cases involving civil affairs. After either one or both of these agencies had prepared a paper containing the policy recommendations, the paper would have to be sent to the Joint Chiefs of Staff for final approval. Only after such approval could the State Department transmit the paper to Winant as guidance or instructions.[38] Since both the JCS and the Civil Affairs Division held a veto over any instructions to Winant which did not accord with their wishes, the procedure tended to submerge the process of foreign policy formulation in an extreme bureaucratic tangle and to give maximum range to departmental infighting.

The entire process could perhaps have been rationalized to some extent if President Roosevelt had taken the time to delineate clearly the areas of competence and to establish relatively defined policy jurisdictions. This he failed to do for several reasons. His time and energy were more than totally absorbed in the prodigious task of winning the war against the Axis. What little time was left over to thinking about the postwar order was directed to problems relating to the establishment of the general world security organization which would carry the primary responsibility for safeguarding the peace. In addition, the president had an instinctive dislike for the whole process of postwar planning, since he felt that American commitments to Europe after the end of the war, which would be minimal at best, could hardly be defined accurately in advance.

The president's position vis-à-vis the State Department and the EAC remained constantly ambivalent, and at times hostile, during the years 1943–44. Cordell Hull resented the fact that he was often bypassed by the president in important international negotiations and that the State Department often was not given the vital information it needed to formulate intelligent policies on vital questions.[39] Much of the time Roosevelt tended to act as his own secretary of state, behavior which reflected his dominant personality as well as his conception of his office in times of crisis. The president's lines of communication with the Joint Chiefs and the War Department were closer and more personal than his relations with the State Department, a fact which helps to explain why State Department policy often was not in accord with the president's wishes. Roosevelt's close friend and personal adviser, Robert Sherwood, reports that the State Department had fallen from grace with the president. Roosevelt evidently feared that many of the senior career officers were hostile to his administration. He also felt that the overburdened bureaucratic procedures of the department were not well suited for times of crisis.[40] Jean Smith states that Hull at this time had faded from a leading position in the administration and was often kept in the dark by Roosevelt concerning his plans and objectives. Hull was not even permitted to examine the minutes of the Tehran Conference nor was he briefed on it.[41]

It is doubtful that the State Department did all it could have to expedite agreement in WSC or to drum up support for the EAC negotiations from the president and WSC. In mid-December, 1943, Hull telegraphed Winant that George F. Kennan would soon arrive in London to serve as a political adviser and added that, "we plan to have him take with him full documentation supplemented by oral discussions as to our views." Hull then informed Winant that the WSC had been set up "so that there will be no delay at this end in considering the Commission's work. . . . I shall see that you are fully posted with regard to our policies as the work of the Commission proceeds."[42] Mosely reports that at least "at the working level" within the State Department there was support for arriving at viable postwar arrangements for Europe and hence for the work of the EAC.[43] This support, however, was not felt at all junctures within the higher levels of the department, and Hull's promises to Winant far exceeded the performance. George Kennan, shortly

ESTABLISHMENT OF THE EAC

before leaving for London in early 1944, dourly reported that the State Department attitude toward EAC left much to be desired: "So far as I could learn from my superiors in the department, their attitude toward the commission was dominated primarily by a lively concern lest the new body should at some point and by some mischance actually do something, and particularly lest the American delegation, through over-eagerness or inadvertence, contribute to so unfortunate an occurrence."[44]

With the State Department's less than complete enthusiasm for the work of EAC and with the inept procedure in the WSC for transmitting instructions to Winant, it is no wonder that the American ambassador was put in a nearly impossible situation at the negotiating table in London. Nevertheless, the American government had committed itself at the Moscow Conference to the elaboration of joint arrangements for the postwar occupation and control of Germany within the framework of the European Advisory Commission.

The Functions of the European Advisory Commission

The Commission's mandate, as stated in the Secret Protocol of the Moscow Conference, was to "study and make joint recommendations to the three Governments upon European questions connected with the termination of hostilities which the three Governments may consider appropriate to refer to it." (See page 14.) EAC could not "study and make recommendations" on its own initiative. It could not study any matter not specifically referred to it by the three governments. Although, according to the Moscow Protocol, the result of the Commission's deliberations was to be "recommendations" to be forwarded to the three governments, in practice the Commission assumed the power to work out protocols, signed by the representatives on the Commission, which were forwarded to the governments for ratification. The protocols, as we shall see, were in the form of executive agreements with the binding force of international treaties in international law. Thus, "deliberations" became international negotiations, and "recommendations" became protocols ready for ratification. As the practice developed, every individual article of each agreement had to be approved by EAC and transmitted back to the governments for approval as part of a larger protocol. Kennan is correct in asserting that, "little remained, therefore, of the body's advisory function. What did remain was actually a place, rather than a body— a place at which official positions could be filed and registered, it being left to the respective governments to reconcile these positions or not to reconcile them, as the spirit moved them."[45] It is indeed true that the EAC was no longer an "Advisory Commission"; it became a forum of delicate international negotiations involving the most crucial of postwar problems—the fate of Germany—and in the end it proved to be one of the most successful negotiating bodies of recent history. Between the summer of 1944 and the fall of

1945 the Commission concluded no less than twelve international agreements dealing with German, Austrian, and Bulgarian affairs. And as Strang notes, "What is more, the agreements worked out in the Commission, unlike those reached at more august conclaves, were carried out in practice. . . . Our work stood the test of events and our plans went smoothly into operation when the time came to apply them."[46]

The EAC Begins Work

The EAC held an informal organizing meeting on December 15, 1943. At the first meeting it was agreed that the presidency of the Commission should be held in rotation by the chief representatives of the Three Powers, each president serving one calendar month. At Strang's suggestion it was agreed that John Winant should be the first president; he would be succeeded by Gusev, then Strang. It was further agreed that out of necessity all proceedings, minutes, and documents of the Commission must be held in top secrecy, that English and Russian would have equal validity as the official languages of the Commission, and that a secretariat should be set up immediately to keep the minutes, circulate documents, and organize interpretation and translation. It was subsequently agreed at a private meeting that E. P. Donaldson, a British civil servant, should serve as secretary-general.[47]

The first formal meeting of the Commission was held at Lancaster House, adjoining St. James' Palace, on January 14, 1944. After exchanging the necessary greetings and introductions appropriate to diplomatic gatherings, Ambassador Winant spoke briefly about the desirability of informality in the proceedings of the Commission in order to expedite business. Both Strang and Gusev strongly concurred with his comments.[48] The Commission then proceeded to a discussion of priorities on the agenda.

The first two meetings of the EAC were plenary sessions with the full staffs of the respective delegations in attendance. Formal minutes of the meetings were taken by the secretary-general and forwarded to the delegations for subsequent approval. It soon became apparent, however, that this procedure was not conducive to fruitful interchange or to creditable progress. The representatives tended to make set speeches, rather than discuss or negotiate, and there was great delay, quite unnecessary, in negotiating tripartite approval of the official minutes of each meeting. Consequently, after the first few meetings it was agreed that plenary meetings would be held only to register the Commission's formal approval of protocols, agreements, or other understandings. The other meetings would be informal meetings attended only by the heads of delegations with two or three personal advisers each. No formal minutes of the meetings would be kept; each delegation could take its own minutes for its records if it wished. The secretary-general would, however, prepare a brief summary of the meeting which would be made available to the delegations on request. All that would be officially approved tripartitely would be the reports, papers, and protocols embodying the results of the Commission's work.[49] This procedure was found to function smoothly and efficiently. Between January 14, 1944, and August, 1945, the EAC held twenty formal and ninety-seven informal meetings, in addition to frequent private consultations among the delegations.[50] Strang, in his memoirs, poignantly describes the inner workings of the Commission:

> "In our informal meetings we gained each other's confidence; and, though for eighteen months, we relied again and again on unrecorded oral understandings and undertakings, never once, so far as I can recollect, was there ever any serious misunderstandings amongst us or any breach of given word. . . . Step by step we thrashed out our differences, patiently, sometimes, it seemed almost interminably. We worked in private, as diplomatists should work, away from the public eye, apart from the occasional leakage to the press and the consequent rather indignant flurry. We took our time; and although our progress, from week to week and from month to month, appeared to me to be excruciatingly slow, the sum total of our achievement, when looked at as a whole, was impressive."[51]

Relations between heads of the delegations were excellent, since there was a generous measure of respect and esteem on a personal level.* Though the Western delegations were at times impatient with what they thought was unnecessary intransigence on Gusev's part, they never suspected him of devious dealings or mistrusted his word. The progress of the Commission's work was, however, slowed down by Gusev's insistence that only one item could be discussed at a time and one item only could be on the current agenda. Committees were not utilized to as full an extent as they might have been to expedite the work of the Commission, as Gusev characteristically insisted on keeping all matters in his own hands and refused to delegate his duties or responsibilities.[52]

Despite these difficulties, however, the EAC began its work in January of 1944 in an atmosphere of cordiality and with the expectation that the three major Allies would be able to work out common solutions to some of the thorniest problems of the postwar order. Though there were many difficulties and trials along the way, the expectation was indeed realized to a great extent.

---

*As one example, note Strang's comments about Gusev and Winant. Of Gusev, he writes that he was a "grim and rather wooden person with, as a saving grace, a touch of sardonic humour and, as a virtue, a somewhat blunt straightforwardness. His personal word, based upon an accurate and retentive memory, could be relied upon. I remember him with kindly respect." Of Winant, Strang writes that he was "a self-tortured soul, noble and passionate, inarticulate, deceptively simple, the pattern of honor. What he may have lacked in readiness as a negotiator was amply made up by his chief advisers. Of George Kennan and Philip Mosely I would only say that they were the best type of American, than which there is nothing better to be found anywhere in the world." William Lord Strang, *Home and Abroad* (London, 1956), p. 207.

THREE

THE INHERITANCE OF EAC:

PLANNING IN 1943

When the European Advisory Commission first met in formal session in January, 1944, to begin consideration of the substantive issues referred to it, it did not, by any means, begin its deliberations with a clean slate. Throughout 1943 certain ideas for the postwar treatment of Germany had been circulating in various branches of the British and American governments, and by the end of that year some of the ideas had crystallized into concrete plans or policy directions.* Such advance planning was bound to have an impact on the work of EAC, for the heads of the delegations were not left free to develop a wide range of various policy alternatives to present to the governments, but were largely restricted to presenting official proposals worked out, for better or for worse, in the policy-making processes of their respective governments.

The Early Appearance of the Dismemberment Idea

In March, 1943, British Foreign Secretary Anthony Eden visited Washington and had several meetings with President Roosevelt. They reached an apparent agreement that the British Foreign Office should work with the American State Department in developing plans for the postwar treatment of Germany before any approaches to the Russians were made on this subject. The principal topic of discussion, however, was the subject of the possible dismemberment of Germany after the war. Eden stated that, in his opinion, Stalin would probably insist that Germany be partitioned into a number of smaller states.[1] Roosevelt definitely accepted the principle of dismemberment but he also stated an aversion to any forced partition. He evidently felt that strong separatist movements would emerge spontaneously after

---

*The extent of planning within the Soviet government is not known. Since the impact of previous Soviet planning on the work of EAC cannot be evaluated with any precision, this study will of necessity concentrate only upon previous plans put forward within the British and American governments.

the war and that these could be utilized by the Allies to create divisions which would largely correspond with public opinion.[2] Roosevelt's inclination toward dismemberment was shared by Secretary of the Treasury Henry Morgenthau, Jr., and Undersecretary of State Sumner Welles.

The dismemberment issue was responsible to a considerable extent for the failure of the Allies to develop decisive and coherent policies for the postwar treatment of Germany. Within the American administration it was a source of constant confusion and delay in the process of planning for Germany.[3] From the outset the president and certain of his advisers seemed to favor the policy, while the State Department clearly did not, and though the position of the responsible military authorities remained ambivalent, there was always, within the military establishment, a strong segment of opinion favoring dismemberment. Part of the prolonged deadlock within WSC and the resulting delay in the transmission of instructions to Ambassador Winant was caused by the periodic emergence of the dismemberment issue. One trouble was that neither the goals or objectives of dismemberment nor the methods of its application were ever clearly defined. There was never any agreement as to whether dismemberment meant outright partition and separate German states or some sort of loose confederation of states, whether it should be imposed by the Allies or merely encouraged.[4] Furthermore, as the plans evolved within the State Department and WSC for division of Germany into zones of military occupation during 1944, it was never clear how these zones would relate to possible dismemberment or how Berlin, as a zone of joint occupation, could possibly fit into any such scheme. Consequently, from the very beginning the idea of dismemberment confounded thinking and planning for postwar Germany in Washington, and it later caused delay and uncertainty in the proceedings of the EAC, since the American delegation was never quite sure to what extent dismemberment was the official policy of the administration in Washington.

Planning Begins in the Spring of 1943

Following Eden's visit to Washington in March, planning for postwar Germany was undertaken seriously both in the State Department and within the military. By September two major papers on postwar policy in Germany had been produced in the State Department, both of which concluded that dismemberment of Germany after the war would be a very unwise policy.[5] If tendencies toward separation emerged, these should be encouraged; otherwise Germany should be treated as a single state, even though her political and economic structure should be thoroughly decentralized. The second of the two papers, prepared by the Country and Area Committee for Germany, recommended that only "key strategic centers" of Germany should be militarily occupied after the war, since it was unnecessary and undesirable that the entire country be occupied. It also argued against separate, national zones of occupation, recommending instead that the Allied troops occupying the strategic centers be combined contingents. The paper contained no precise or detailed plans for military occupation, since this was clearly a subject which would have to be discussed with the War Department and the Joint Chiefs of Staff. It did recommend, however, that the United States government adopt a program which would eventually bring about the economic recovery of Germany and the "assimilation of Germany, as soon as would be compatible with security considerations, into the projected international order."[6]

This general direction of policy outlined by the State Department contrasted sharply with the lines of policy developed within the military establishment. In April, 1943, a joint Anglo-American military planning group was established in London by the Combined Chiefs of Staff. The group carried the designation COSSAC (Chief of Staff to the Supreme Allied Commander-Designate) and was headed by Lieutenant General Sir Frederick Morgan. The chief task of this planning staff was to develop plans for the projected cross-Channel invasion in 1944, later given the code name OVERLORD. The group was instructed to prepare in addition an alternative plan for a quick descent on the Continent in case German power should suddenly collapse before the Western Allies had even crossed the Channel, a plan later designated by the code name RANKIN.[7] In working out these two plans the COSSAC planning staff necessarily had to consider the question of which troops would be sent to occupy which areas in order to enforce unconditional surrender quickly and effectively. It was eventually decided that during the Channel crossing and the subsequent push through occupied territory into the German heartland American forces would remain on the right flank of the British contingents. This troop deployment, in turn, would determine the arrangement and placement of troops for military occupation.

In July, 1943, General Morgan was directed to prepare his plans for presentation to the Combined Chiefs of Staff at the forthcoming meeting of Roosevelt, Churchill, and the Combined Chiefs at Quebec in August, code-named QUADRANT. As presented to the Combined Chiefs at Quebec, the OVERLORD and RANKIN plans called for the Allied troops to enter northwest Germany through the Rhineland in order to establish effective control and enforce unconditional surrender. American forces were to assume primary responsibility for France, Belgium, and the Rhine valley from Switzerland to Düsseldorf, drawing their supplies through Antwerp and the French ports. British forces would have primary control over the Netherlands, Denmark, Norway, and northwestern Germany from the Ruhr to Lübeck, with Rotterdam and Hamburg as their main ports of supply.[8] The COSSAC plans were predicated on the assumption that, in order to enforce unconditional surrender, it would not be necessary for

Allied forces to occupy all of Germany; an occupation of the most strategic areas, including the Rhineland and the Ruhr as far north as the Kiel Canal, would be sufficient to accomplish Allied objectives in Germany. Since it was assumed that Soviet forces would overrun Germany from the east, the RANKIN plan made no mention of eastern Germany or Berlin.

Early Divergencies at Many Levels

In the process of developing their plans, the COSSAC planning staff, like the planning groups in the State Department, gave consideration to the question of a joint occupation without national zones. The idea, while accepted by the State Department, was rejected by COSSAC. The reason is that presumably the planners in COSSAC were dealing with military information not available to the planning staffs in the State Department. COSSAC was aware that the plans called for the British forces to drive into northern Germany while American forces would drive via northern France into southern Germany. This troop deployment would necessarily give rise to separate spheres of immediate military responsibility, even though civil affairs would be the responsibility of the combined SHAEF command. Any subsequent zones of military occupation would of necessity have to conform more or less to the original troop deployment. Logistical complications dictated against the advisability of attempting to switch areas of responsibility or interlard the occupation forces after the initial conquest.[9] Consequently, even at this early stage there was significant divergence between the State Department and COSSAC plans.

The RANKIN plan was accepted in principle by the Combined Chiefs of Staff at the First Quebec Conference on August 23. Although Roosevelt did not attend this meeting, he is reported to have said, after reading the final report of the Combined Chiefs, that he wanted "United Nations troops to be ready to get to Berlin as soon as did the Russians."[10] Apparently, however, the president's desire was never reported to General Morgan or the COSSAC planners. There were also several private conferences between Secretary Hull and Foreign Secretary Eden at the Quebec Conference, and the two men found that they were in fundamental agreement that Germany should not be dismembered, if any other feasible plans could be found.[11] Here again is evidence of a lack of coordinated planning between the State Department, the military staffs, and the president. Although the CCS plan did not recommend dismemberment, there was considerable difference between the State Department plans and the COSSAC plans, and there is evidence that neither of these accurately reflected President Roosevelt's thinking on the matter. Hull did not attend the meetings of the Combined Chiefs of Staff, where the plans for Germany's occupation were discussed in some detail.

CHAPTER THREE

Just before leaving for the Moscow Conference of Foreign Ministers in October, 1943, Hull was informed by President Roosevelt that he favored the partition of Germany into three or more states, joined only by economic arrangements, though he had not yet made any decision about the final dismemberment of Germany.[12] At the conference itself, however, the discussions did not center on the question of dismemberment, but on two policy papers submitted by the U.S. delegation, which reflected primarily the thinking of the State Department's Country and Area Committee for Germany.[13] The basic document, entitled "U.S. Proposal With Regard to the Treatment of Germany," was drafted at Moscow by Philip E. Mosely with some assistance by Henry P. Leverich. It was essentially a redrafting and abbreviation of the papers prepared by the Country and Area Committee for Germany. The document was well received by both Eden and Molotov and was subsequently accepted as a basis for the conference discussion.[14] The paper proposed that during the armistice period Germany should be placed under strict military, political, and economic control. Such control would "be exercised through an inter-Allied Control Commission charged with the carrying out of the terms of surrender and the policies agreed upon by Great Britain, the U.S.S.R. and the United States." With regard to the occupation of Germany the paper recommended only "that the occupation of Germany be effected by contingents of British, Soviet and American forces," and that the occupation should be "For the purpose of securing the execution of surrender terms and assuring the creation of conditions for a permanent system of security."[15] The proposals on occupation were brief and exceedingly general. No zonal boundaries were proposed and no mention was made of Berlin. It is clear, however, that the American proposals were based on the assumption of joint Allied occupation of and responsibility for Germany, and that they did not look forward to dismemberment. William Franklin notes that since the State Department planners "did not want to encourage Roosevelt's inclination toward dismemberment, they were hesitant about carving the country into zones of occupation lest any such boundaries be taken as lines of permanent cleavage or spheres of influence."[16] Actually the American proposal represented the official policy only of the State Department, not of the administration. It was presented to the Conference for study purposes, not as a proposal to be negotiated. The Russian delegation did not realize that the proposal was not official U.S. government policy, though the British certainly understood this because they were continuously negotiating with the various parts of the U.S. government. At any rate the Conference decided to refer the proposal to the European Advisory Commission for consideration. Indeed the very decision to set up the EAC at the Moscow Conference was to a great extent the result of an intention not to reach any firm conclusions at the Conference as to what the Allies should do with Germany after winning the war.

At the Moscow Conference the Foreign Ministers were concerned with a substantial number of pressing problems and were able to give only an initial cursory review to German problems.

Planning in Britain

Following Eden's visit to Washington in March, 1943, planning for Germany was undertaken seriously also within the more integrated structure of the British government. On May 25 Eden presented to the War Cabinet a memorandum proposing that Germany be divided into three zones after the war and subjected to a total military occupation. Since the War Cabinet was unable to reach any conclusion on the proposal, mainly due to disagreement over the advisability of a total occupation, it was referred to the Armistice and Postwar Committee chaired by Clement Attlee, the deputy prime minister.[17]

The Attlee Committee continued to study the proposal throughout the spring and summer of 1943. Various alternative suggestions were also given consideration, including the proposal for a joint occupation with interlarded forces. The Committee concluded, however, that in order for the Allies effectively to enforce terms of unconditional surrender, Germany should be divided into three separate zones of occupation, excepting the Berlin area, which should be placed under a separate regime.[18] The Committee's final report proceeded to set forth the three zones of occupation. The eastern or Soviet zone, excluding East Prussia, which it was assumed would be given to Poland, extended to a point less than one hundred kilometers east of the Rhine, near the city of Eisenach. It included the provinces of Mecklenburg, Pomerania, Brandenburg, Saxony-Anhalt, and Thuringia. The British zone in the northwest included the province of Brunswick, Hesse-Nassau, Hannover, Westphalia, and the Rhine Province. The southern zone, allocated to the United States, included Bavaria, Württemberg, Baden, Hesse-Darmstadt, and the Westmark (Saar and Palatinate). Since the American zone was the smallest, the plan suggested that the United States also take over the occupation of Austria. The city of Berlin was to be subject to a special regime of joint occupation and was not to form part of the Soviet zone. No provision was made for any transit rights to Berlin from the western zones.

The British plan seemed coherent and logical for a number of reasons. It placed Germany's major productive and commercial resources under British control and Britain, because of geographical proximity to the Continent, was the logical Western Power to assume this role. The zonal boundaries followed the borders of the German Länder, except in the case of Prussia, but even here the boundaries followed traditional provincial divisions. Though the Soviet zone was the largest in area, the British zone was largest in population. This division seemed equitable, since the Soviet Union could lay claim to a larger zone than the other Powers because of the relatively greater damage it had suffered in the war. It was estimated that the Soviet zone would contain 40 percent of Germany's pre-1937 land area, 36 percent of the population, and 33 percent of the productive resources.[19] The British plan also took account of the lines of communication and supply for the respective national forces by allotting appropriate "spheres of influence." France would be an American sphere of influence, while Belgium, Holland, Luxembourg, and Denmark would be a British sphere of influence, reflecting Britain's traditional interest in the Low Countries and the North Sea.[20] The plan also envisaged a special occupational arrangement for the great capital city of Germany, Berlin.

Circulation of the British Proposal

The Attlee Committee proposal was submitted to Churchill and Eden in the late summer of 1943 and approved by them in essential outline. It was then forwarded by the British government to General Morgan and the COSSAC staff as a British proposal for modification of the RANKIN plan, which had just been approved at Quebec by the Combined Chiefs of Staff. The timing of this proposal to COSSAC was awkward, and so likewise was the channel of communication, for it appears that although the plan was submitted to COSSAC, it was not communicated at this time either to President Roosevelt or Secretary Hull.[21]

General Morgan immediately recognized that the American Joint Chiefs of Staff would have to be consulted before COSSAC could proceed to modify the already approved RANKIN plan along the lines of the British proposal. During his visit to Washington in October he presented a copy of the British plan to General George C. Marshall, Army Chief of Staff, who in turn forwarded it to the Joint Chiefs of Staff. If finally reached President Roosevelt via a memorandum from Admiral William D. Leahy, the president's personal chief of staff.[22] The plan, however, never reached Secretary Hull or the planning staffs in the Department of State, who by this time had developed plans based upon entirely different premises. The British proposal had no relation to the proposal presented to the Moscow Conference by Secretary Hull in October, which had already been referred to the European Advisory Commission.[23]

On November 13, 1943, President Roosevelt, together with his military advisers, embarked for the Cairo and Tehran Conferences aboard the battleship *USS Iowa*. On November 19, in a meeting with the Joint Chiefs of Staff, the president discussed the proposed British directive to COSSAC. With no hesitation the president stated that he "did not like that arrangement."[24] After observing that the British wanted the northwestern part of

Germany and wished the United States to be responsible for France and Germany south of the Moselle River, the president stated that, "We do not want to be concerned with reconstituting France. France is a British 'baby.' United States is not popular in France at the present time." He felt that the United States should be in control of northwest Germany, while the British should be responsible for Bavaria, Baden, Württemberg, Luxembourg, Belgium, and France.[25]

The president's discussion of occupation zones was manifestly related to the issue of dismemberment, "an idea to which he was obviously attached despite the lukewarm reaction of Secretary Hull and the Department's postwar planners."[26] After noting that the Soviet government would offer no objection to breaking up Germany after the war, Roosevelt said that "practically speaking there should be three German states after the war, possibly five." The zones of occupation should correspond to the possible lines of dismemberment.[27]

The president's discussion, interestingly enough, included several observations about Berlin. In describing what he thought should be the U.S. zone of occupation, Roosevelt said that it should extend "up to and including Berlin to form a second state." He continued that "The Soviets could then take the territory to the east thereof," but "the United States should have Berlin."[28]

Both General Marshall and Admiral Ernest J. King, chief of naval operations, sought to point out to the president the various reasons why the British proposal had placed the British occupation forces in northwest Germany, especially the fact that American armies would be on the southern flank of the Allied forces invading Germany. Admiral King stated he felt "that the military plans for OVERLORD were so far developed that it would not be practicable to accept any change in OVERLORD deployment." The argument seemed unconvincing, and Roosevelt was not about to change his mind. He felt that the occupation forces need not be the same as those assigned to OVERLORD, and at any rate, the forces of occupation should not be dependent upon supply lines running through France. He was convinced that "we should get out of France and Italy as soon as possible, letting the British and French handle their own problem together. There would definitely be a race for Berlin. We may have to put the United States divisions into Berlin as soon as possible." Harry Hopkins agreed with the president that "we be ready to put an airborne division into Berlin two hours after the collapse of Germany."[29]

At the close of the discussion Roosevelt took a National Geographic Society map and sketched in the zones of occupation according to his own ideas on the matter.[30] An enormous northwest zone, allotted to the United States, included all of Germany west of a line running from Stettin on the Baltic to the Czech border. The British zone was in the south, while the eastern

Soviet zone appeared rather small, long, and narrow. The position of Berlin in this sketch is not clear. Franklin states that the American zone included both Berlin and Leipzig,[31] while Smith says that Berlin was located on the frontier *between* the American and Russian zones.[32] A careful examination of the map itself leads to inconclusive results. Even though the heavy black line appears to go around the city of Berlin to the left, it can hardly be thought that Roosevelt meant the city to be inside the Soviet zone, given his strong comments a few minutes earlier. At best, it is unclear exactly what Berlin's disposition was to be in the president's primitive sketch.

The Tehran Conference of The Big Three

Following the president's trip on the *USS Iowa*, the first meeting of the Big Three was held at Tehran, November 28 to December 1, 1943. Whether the Attlee Committee proposals were discussed at this Conference is not clear; at any rate they were not approved.[33] The three heads of government were, however, agreed that Germany should be divided up in some way, although there were differences as to the form such partition should take. There was general agreement that the first step should be to divide Germany into three zones for purposes of military occupation and that Berlin should be jointly controlled by all three. Roosevelt suggested that Germany eventually be partitioned in five autonomous states and two additional areas under the international control of the United Nations.[34] Churchill, on the other hand, favored a partition which would take into account historical and ethnic factors and insisted that any new states must be capable of an independent political and economic integrity. He suggested that Prussia be diminished and isolated and that Germany be divided into two states, a north German state and a south German state including Bavaria and Austria. Stalin avoided committing himself to either plan of partition, though he said that he was somewhat more inclined towards Roosevelt's suggestion, since he favored weakening Germany to the fullest possible extent.[35] Since the Big Three failed to reach any agreement on the issue, it was decided to refer it to the European Advisory Commission for further study and recommendations. "In referring the question of postwar Germany to it [the EAC], the Big Three were getting rid of a hot potato."[36]

The Planning Process Jolted at Cairo

From Tehran the president proceeded to Cairo where he continued consultations with Churchill and the Combined Chiefs of Staff. In preparation for the Cairo discussions, the United States Chiefs of Staff, according to the president's instructions, prepared a new paper on RANKIN (CCS 320/4) which was presented to the British Chiefs at Cairo on December 4.[37] The paper was in the form of a proposal to COSSAC and was, in fact, a counterproposal to the Attlee Committee proposals, which had been submitted to COSSAC in late summer. The JCS plan proposed that COSSAC planning proceed on the assumption that the northern sphere of occupation, including the Netherlands and Scandinavia, would be the responsibility of the United States, while Britain's responsibility would be for the southern sphere, including Austria. It stated that "The United States Chiefs of Staff . . . propose that COSSAC be directed to examine and report on the implications of revising his planning on the basis of the new allocation of spheres of occupation."[38]

The most interesting point about this new proposal is that the boundaries of the U.S. sphere specifically excluded Berlin. In view of Roosevelt's insistence aboard the *Iowa* that the U.S. "must have Berlin," this modification in the JCS proposal is difficult to explain. The most plausible answer is perhaps provided by William Franklin's suggestion that Roosevelt had "discussed the problem at Cairo with Churchill on December 3, and it is possible that the Prime Minister had convinced him that Berlin should be a special area of tripartite responsibility, no matter how the rest of the zonal lines were drawn."[39]

The British Chiefs of Staff replied to the American plan by noting that "the proposals would entail a crossing of the lines of communication," and that "this did not appear acceptable from a military point of view."[40] Nevertheless, they agreed that CCS 320/4 should be submitted to COSSAC for review and a possible revision of the basis of planning in that organization. The directive was sent to General Morgan shortly after the Cairo Conference adjourned on December 7.

General Morgan at first thought he was the victim of some kind of practical joke, but after receiving assurance that the American president was quite adamant on the subject of zones of occupation, he set his planning staff to work. The staff reported, after much serious consideration, that the military complications involved in switching the American and British zones of occupation would be nearly insurmountable. General Morgan reported this to the respective governments and records that "No more was ever heard, by us at any rate, of this particular proposition."[41] The proposition was, however, as we shall see in the next chapter, far from dead. It provided a dreadful shock to the European Advisory Commission the following year.

State Department Planning in Late 1943

During the month of December, as preparations were being made in London for beginning the work of the EAC, various committees in the State Department worked diligently to complete policy studies for submission to the newly created Working Security Committee and possible transmission to Ambassador Winant as instructions. By mid-December the Country and Area Committee for Germany had formulated a tentative proposal on zones of occupation in Germany which included maps and demographic and economic studies of the suggested zones.*

Interestingly enough, this study designated Berlin as the seat of a joint Allied authority, even though Berlin was located within the eastern or Soviet zone of occupation. If there were a central German administration still functioning in Berlin at the end of the war, the Allies would work through the administration while keeping it under rigid control. If no such central German administration existed, the Allies would create their own governmental machinery. This would still be located in Berlin because of Berlin's status as former capital and central city of the Reich and because of the location of German staffs and records in the city.

This CAC proposal is interesting, since it shows the similarity in thinking between planning staffs in the American State Department and the British Foreign Office. The State Department, like the British Foreign Office, planned that the Soviet Union should occupy an eastern zone of Germany which would extend considerably to the west of Berlin and that some sort of special regime be established for the city of Berlin itself. The similarity in the evolution of British and American plans is striking, since neither Secretary Hull nor the State Department had any official knowledge whatever of the proposals which had been formulated in the Attlee Committee and later forwarded to COSSAC and President Roosevelt. Neither did the State Department know that the president had already expressed a strong distaste for the Attlee proposals on his way to Tehran.

An alternate suggestion from within the State Department was a proposal by Philip Mosely that a corridor "be established connecting the prospective western areas of occupation with Berlin." Such a corridor would be formed by "joining certain intervening districts of Saxony-Anhalt and Brandenburg to the western zones."[42] Such a plan would have two distinct advantages: it would create direct access for the Western Powers to the seat of joint Allied authority in occupied Germany; and it would accomplish the breakup of Prussia, which was a primary objective of both the Americans and the British. The plan ran counter to the opinion that in forming zones of occupation the traditional German provincial boundaries should be followed. The ill effects of such disruption would, however, be mitigated if

---

*The following paragraphs are based principally on the account given by Philip Mosely in "The Occupation of Germany: New Light on How the Zones Were Drawn," 28 *Foreign Affairs* (1950), pp. 586–589. At this time Dr. Mosely was chief of the Division of Territorial Studies in the Department of State. He served as a member of the Country and Area Committee for Germany continuously from October, 1943, until June, 1944. He also served on the Working Security Committee, occasionally as acting chairman, from December, 1943, until June, 1944. In June, 1944, he traveled to London for consultations on a temporary basis. At Winant's request he remained in London as political adviser, replacing George F. Kennan, who had returned to Washington in April.

the Committee's basic assumption about the postwar order in Germany were realized—that Germany, though divided into occupation zones, would be treated as one economic and political entity by the Allies. Concerning the proposal Mosely observes, "I realized that such a proposal by the United States would probably meet with Soviet objections, but I believed that if it could be presented first, with impressive firmness, it might be taken into account by the Soviet Government in framing its own proposals. I believed that the dignity and security of the American authorities to be installed eventually in Berlin required that provision be made in advance for free and direct territorial access to Berlin from the West."[43]

Logjam in the Working Security Committee

When the CAC plan was presented to the Working Security Committee, it met with immediate, almost savage criticism from the representatives of the Civil Affairs Division of the War Department. From the outset of the WSC deliberations the Civil Affairs representatives insisted that the EAC did not possess the competence to make any recommendations concerning zones of occupation in Germany. The division of the country into zones of occupation was a strictly military matter which would have to be dealt with at the military level when the appropriate time came, since such zones would obviously depend primarily upon the deployment of the various national forces at the time of German surrender. The State Department representatives in WSC attempted to point out, in reply, that the subject of zones of occupation was a matter that far transcended the narrow confines of military strategy, that it was an issue which concerned the entire fabric of postwar policy in Germany as well as the vital interests of the State Department in planning for the postwar order. In addition, it would be sheer folly to neglect to reach advance agreement with the Russians on occupation zones after Germany's defeat, since the expectation was that a sizeable area of Germany would be overrun by the Red Army. The State Department representatives emphasized that at the Moscow Conference the United States had entered into a definite international commitment to work with the Russians and the British in EAC in attempting to formulate agreed solutions to "European questions connected with the termination of hostilities," and that the subject of zones of occupation in Germany was certainly one of these questions.

Despite their cogency the arguments of the State Department representatives failed to budge the representatives of the Civil Affairs Division, who continued to refuse any discussion on the subject of zones of occupation. In January, 1944, the Civil Affairs Division exercised its right to veto, and WSC was prevented from providing Mr. Winant with any American proposals on zones, thus leaving him completely without guidance in the delicate task of negotiating with the Russians and the British on the subject.

CHAPTER THREE

An Alternative Proposal Briefly Considered

In December of 1943 one other proposal for the postwar disposition of Germany was considered briefly by planning staffs in the State Department. The proposal was evidently put forward as an informal suggestion by a British Foreign Office representative during a reconnaissance visit to Washington. The proposal obviated the need for zones of occupation, since it suggested that Allied forces after the German surrender be deployed in a dispersed or interlarded fashion throughout Germany. The idea was not new, since in September the Country and Area Committee for Germany had issued a paper recommending that the key strategic centers of Germany be occupied by combined contingents of forces. (See pages 25–26.) Although the Committee later abandoned the idea in favor of separate, national zones of occupation, the British representative's suggestion in December briefly became the focus of renewed interest. When, however, the idea was presented to the Civil Affairs Division of the War Department, it met with immediate and resolute rejection. The Civil Affairs Division seemed certain that the Soviet Union would insist on a separate zone of occupation for Soviet forces. In addition, the Civil Affairs representatives felt that problems of supply, communication, and command in the case of interlarded forces would be nearly insurmountable. In the face of nearly unanimous rejection of the proposal in military circles, the State Department decided not to support it, but to return instead to the idea of separate, national zones of occupation. Unfortunately, however, the State Department still had no inkling of the proposals drawn up by the Attlee Committee, of the president's feelings toward these proposals, or of the planning that had been going on in the COSSAC staff. In addition, the department was prevented by WSC from getting any of its own proposals cleared for transmission to Ambassador Winant in London. Consequently, by the end of 1943, planning in Washington for postwar Germany seemed to be going off in several different directions at once.

FOUR

THE FIRST ROUND: EAC NEGOTIATIONS IN 1944

The uncoordinated and tangled efforts at policy formulation during 1943, efforts which often worked at cross-purposes, formed the confused background against which the EAC began its formal deliberations. The mandate of the Commission was far from crystal clear, its task was ill-defined, and the beginnings of its work were clouded by lack of information concerning the conflicting lines of policy which had emerged in Washington and London during 1943. The first formal session of the Commission was held on January 14, 1944, at Lancaster House in London. The Commission officially had before it only four proposals: the two American memoranda submitted by the Moscow Conference, and the Roosevelt and Churchill suggestions on eventual partition submitted by the Tehran Conference. The EAC had no official information about the Attlee Committee proposals or the Roosevelt directive (CCS 320/4), since both of these plans had traveled through military channels to the Combined Chiefs and were never referred to EAC. The EAC also had no knowledge of the military plans which had been discussed in the COSSAC planning staff.

Winant Senses Difficulty

In the early days of January Ambassador Winant seemed to sense that he was being put on a short leash as far as his freedom of thought and action in EAC was concerned. On January 9 he was informed by Secretary Hull that when the Joint Chiefs of Staff learned of the Commission's establishment, "they were apprehensive at once," and were now insisting that any studies or recommendations given to the Commission by the American representative "directly or indirectly involving military matters should be referred to and approved by the Joint Chiefs of Staff."[1] A few days later Winant drafted an answer in which he pointed out that the restrictions outlined by the department amounted to "advance approval by all the interested organs of our Government for any steps which I may take in the

Commission," and that this would "make it difficult for me to participate in free discussions with my colleagues in the Commission and will tend to confine my action largely to the tabling of documents advanced by our Government and the solicitation of instructions on proposals advanced by the others."[2]

It is perhaps worth noting that even the composition of the U.S. Delegation to EAC demonstrated the interdepartmental basis of American policy making. Ambassador Winant's staff included a political adviser and two political officers from the State Department, a military adviser with staff, a naval adviser with staff, and later an air adviser with staff. The ambassador's political adviser was initially Mr. George F. Kennan, who was replaced by Dr. Philip E. Mosely in June, 1944; the military adviser was Brigadier General Cornelius W. Wickersham, replaced by Brigadier General Vincent Meyer in June, 1944; the naval adviser was Admiral Harold Stark; the air adviser was Brigadier General C. P. Cabell, replaced by Colonel Charles G. Williamson in July, 1944. The service advisers communicated through military channels with their superiors in Washington, while Winant and his political adviser communicated with the Department of State.[3] In view of the many obstacles and difficulties facing Mr. Winant, it is indeed fortunate that he possessed a substantial reserve of patience for the difficult months ahead.

Britain Preempts the Proceedings

At the first formal meeting on January 14th the EAC invited the delegations to circulate any papers they had prepared "bearing on the question of the terms of surrender for Germany and of the machinery required to ensure their fulfillment."[4] The British were more than prompt. The following day Sir William Strang submitted three memoranda for the Commission's consideration: one on "Terms of Surrender for Germany," a second on "Military Occupation of Germany," and a third on "Allied Control Machinery in Germany During the Period of Occupation."[5]

The memorandum on military occupation was essentially the same document drawn up by the Attlee Committee that had been discussed by Roosevelt and the JCS aboard the *USS Iowa*. The boundaries of the proposed zones of occupation had not been changed, though all references to spheres of influence in Western and Northern Europe, and to COSSAC or the CCS had been omitted. Franklin notes that "the memorandum was new to Winant and Gusev, but it was 'old stuff' to Roosevelt, Churchill, COSSAC, and the Combined Chiefs of Staff."[6] Although Winant had attended the Cairo Conference, he had not been invited to attend the CCS discussions on zones of occupation, nor had he received any information on the Attlee proposals or on President Roosevelt's strong objections to them. What attitude was he now expected to take?

On January 15, the same day as the presentation of the British proposals, Secretary Hull cabled Winant that the Joint Chiefs of Staff had not yet given approval to several of the papers submitted to them, and that "in view of our inability to obtain clearance on these papers, you have no alternative but to proceed on the basis of such documents as the British or Russian representatives may submit."[7]

The British proposal on military occupation divided Germany into three main zones of occupation with the Russians in the east, the British in the northwest, and the Americans in the south. One assumption of the proposal was that at the end of the war some kind of German central administration, although not necessarily a central government, would still exist in Berlin with which the Allies could deal. Accordingly, the plan suggested that: ". . . the Berlin area should be a separate Combined Zone occupied by selected troops representing, in due proportions, all the Allied forces of occupation. The principal role of this mixed force would be to support the authority of any Allied Military Government, the Control Commission and other Allied bodies and also to ensure the maintenance of order in the Capital."[8]

Several relevant features of the proposal should be noted. Berlin is referred to as the "Capital" of defeated Germany and as the seat of any Allied Military Government or Control Commission which might be set up. The Berlin area is called a "separate Combined Zone," the word "separate" meaning evidently that the Berlin area would *not* form a part of the surrounding Soviet zone. This conclusion is supported by an examination of the map accompanying the proposal. The Berlin area is surrounded by a heavy red line, the same red line which marks the boundaries between the other zones of occupation, and presumably sets Berlin apart from the Soviet zone.

Lacking instructions, Winant was unable to make any relevant reply to the British proposals. As yet, however, Gusev also seemed to lack any instructions from Moscow. On January 27 Winant placed before the Commission a very brief and vague memorandum relating to terms of surrender. With the lengthy and comprehensive British proposals already before the Commission, it seems somewhat strange that Winant should present such an indefinite, innocuous document. Probably, however, he felt that he should present at least something, and this was about as much as the American delegation could offer at the time. The memorandum merely stated that the Three Powers should assume all the rights of occupying Powers in Germany, that they should have the right to occupy any and all parts of Germany, and that "For political purposes Berlin and other principal cities to be designated should be occupied, at least temporarily."[9]

Such suggestions seem almost unnecessary. It is incomprehensible that a victor nation would conquer and occupy an enemy country without occupying the capital city. The British evidently felt the same way. Winant reported to Hull on February 5 that the British proposal provided for outright military government as one of the implicit rights belonging to an occupying Power and that the British felt that the provision in the American draft for occupation of Berlin and principal cities was quite unnecessary.[10]

The Soviets Reply

On February 15 Ambassador Gusev circulated in the Commission the Soviet draft of surrender terms for Germany. Article 15 of this document contained the Soviet proposal on zones of occupation, and, surprisingly enough, the Soviet plan proposed zones identical to those sketched on the British map, meaning, of course, that the Soviets were actually accepting the zone proposed for them by the British. The Soviet document also accepted a "special system of occupation" for Berlin, and provided that: "There shall be established around Berlin a 10/15 kilometer zone which shall be occupied jointly by the armed forces of the Union of Soviet Socialist Republics, the United Kingdom and the United States of America."[11]

The Soviet document included all of East Prussia as part of the Soviet zone and, in contrast to the British proposal, suggested that Austria, like Berlin, be jointly occupied by forces of all Three Powers. Mosely notes that, "The Soviet acceptance, without bargaining, of a zone of slightly more than one-third of Germany, appeared a sign of a moderate and conciliatory approach to the problem of how to deal with postwar Germany."[12] Even more, Soviet acceptance of a special system of occupation for Berlin within the Soviet zone represented a major victory for the Western Powers.

At the February 18 meeting Strang forcefully pointed out that it would be undesirable to delineate the boundaries of occupation zones in the surrender instrument, since this might seem to give the Germans rights in this respect vis-à-vis the Three Powers, which might then have difficulty in making any necessary changes or adjustments.[13] Gusev seemed to agree to this point readily, and it was consequently decided that a document on zones of occupation, completely separate from the surrender instrument, should be drawn up. As soon as Strang was able to agree to East Prussia as part of the Soviet zone, the British and Soviet proposals on zones of occupation became identical, and the United States delegation was confronted with an agreement on zones already accepted by the other two delegations.

President Roosevelt Reacts

All during this time it would seem that President Roosevelt had been paying very little attention to the activities of EAC. He had meanwhile exchanged a series of telegrams with Churchill discussing American vs. British occupation of a northwest zone in Germany. When news of the

British-Soviet accord reached him on February 18, he fired off a memorandum to Acting Secretary of State Edward R. Stettinius, Jr., inquiring, "What are the zones in the British and Russian drafts and what is the zone we are proposing? I must know this in order that it conform with what I decided on months ago."[14]

The State Department, of course, had no idea about what Roosevelt had decided on months ago. Stettinius' reply, sent the following day, informed the president that no American proposal at all had been put forward so far, and that "we are not sure as to what understanding will have to be reached on this subject until we know what your thinking on the subject has been."[15] The reply briefly outlined the identical British-Soviet proposals on zones, and pleaded that Roosevelt send an outline of his own views on the matter as soon as possible.

Roosevelt's memorandum to Stettinius of February 21 made no mention of zonal boundaries or of joint occupation of Berlin. It expressed primarily the president's preoccupation with American occupation of a northwestern zone in Germany, placing the British in the south and giving them the responsibility of policing France and Italy if necessary. No mention was made of any previous discussion of zones of occupation by Roosevelt, Churchill, COSSAC, or the Combined Chiefs of Staff. On the issue of American occupation of a northwest zone the president seemed absolutely determined: "If anything further is needed to justify this disagreement with the British lines of demarcation, I can only add that political considerations in the United States make my decision conclusive."[16] Stettinius duly relayed the president's comments to Winant on February 26 without attaching any commentary or interpretation, thus leaving the ambassador as much in the dark as ever.[17]

Meanwhile, the Working Security Committee had been unable to make any progress in working out instructions or guidance for Ambassador Winant. The representatives of the Civil Affairs Division refused either to accept or amend the British-Soviet proposals on zones. They continued to insist that the matter of occupation zones was outside the competence of EAC, indeed even the WSC, and would have to be decided by the military commanders at the appropriate time.

One might well ask why such confusion and lack of coordination was allowed to persist. In the last instance it can be traced to the very highest levels of government—the president and the prime minister. The two leaders had been exchanging a series of telegrams concerning the occupation of the northwest zone ever since the Cairo Conference. Churchill, however, assumed that the EAC should settle the matter of zones of occupation, and accordingly, he submitted the Attlee Committee proposals to that body. Roosevelt, on the other hand, was unenthusiastic about the EAC from the beginning and assumed that, at any rate, the occupation zones were a military matter under the jurisdiction of the Combined Chiefs of Staff. Consequently, the subject was treated as classified information and never discussed with the State Department. The lines of authority and jurisdiction were now completely confused.[18]

Roosevelt's attitude toward postwar planning in general and the EAC in particular is indicated in a telegram he sent to Churchill on February 29: "Dear Winston: I have been worrying a good deal of late on account of the tendency of all of us to prepare for future events in such detail that we may be letting ourselves in for trouble when the time arrives.... I am trying as hard as I can to simplify things—and sometimes I shudder at the thought of appointing as many new Committees and Commissions in the future as we have in the past."[19]

At the end of February the Civil Affairs Division reversed its position and decided to submit a proposal on occupation zones to WSC. This about-face is perhaps best explained by the fact that the Soviet government had already accepted the British proposal on zones, and now even President Roosevelt was inquiring as to what was happening in the EAC deliberations. In submitting the proposal to WSC the Civil Affairs Division emphasized that it represented directly the wishes of President Roosevelt; indeed the division demanded that it immediately be dispatched to Ambassador Winant for presentation in EAC.

There is some question as to exactly what proposal or proposals were submitted by the Civil Affairs Division to WSC. Franklin says that the plan was a copy of CCS 320/4 which had been approved by the Combined Chiefs of Staff at Cairo and sent by Roosevelt as a directive to COSSAC.[20] Both Mosely and Smith, on the other hand, write that the plan provided for a meeting of all three occupation zones at Berlin and that the zonal boundaries radiated north, west, and south from the city like the spokes of a wheel.[21] The CCS 320/4 plan did place Berlin on the boundary between the Soviet and American zones, the American zone being in the northwest; zonal boundaries, however, did not converge at Berlin.

Before transmitting the plan to Winant, the State Department representatives on WSC asked the Civil Affairs Division for background information on the development and meaning of the proposal. The Civil Affairs representatives declined to produce any information, stating merely that the proposal had been approved by President Roosevelt. After several days of fruitless discussion, the State Department finally transmitted the proposal to Winant on March 6. What Winant actually received was a verbatim copy of CCS 320/4, worded in the form of a directive to COSSAC.[22]

Winant was, quite naturally, taken aback. The plan proposed an enormous northwestern zone for the United States, comprising 51 percent of the population and 46 percent of the territory of Germany, excluding Berlin and East Prussia. It made no mention of Berlin, which had already been accepted as a zone of joint occupation in the British and Russian proposals, although the boundary of the American zone specifically excluded Berlin.

It failed to state where the boundary should run between the Soviet and British zones, and since the American zone did not extend to the Czech border, there was no way of telling where the British zone was supposed to end and the Soviet zone begin. The crude straight lines on the map cut across all German provincial boundaries indiscriminately, so that the zones bore no relationship whatever to the established administrative divisions of Germany. And, since the proposal was worded as a memorandum from the Joint Chiefs to the Combined Chiefs, it was impossible to see how it could be presented as a document for negotiation in EAC without extensive revision.[23]

Kennan's Journey to Washington

Since the document put him in a highly embarrassing position, Winant declined to present it to the EAC. He cabled the State Department on March 23 that his recommendations on the subject would be personally presented to the secretary of state and the president very shortly by George F. Kennan, counselor to the American delegation.[24] Kennan recalls that he became highly dubious of the document when he was told by one of the military officers who had accompanied Roosevelt to the Cairo Conference that the instructions most probably represented "an attempt to reduce to words something President Roosevelt had once casually drawn on a chance scrap of paper while en route to Cairo."[25]

At the end of March Kennan traveled to Washington with General Cornelius W. Wickersham, Winant's military adviser, with instructions to do everything possible to straighten out the confusion. On April 3, with State Department approval, Kennan met with President Roosevelt. Kennan reports that although he was graciously received by the president, he experienced a great deal of difficulty in communicating to the president what the crux of the confusion actually was. Finally, however, the president was brought to realize that the major problem in EAC was the boundary of the Soviet zone, not the argument with the British over the northwest zone. When Mr. Kennan explained to him the confusion which had arisen over the new American proposal and showed him a copy of it, the president "laughed gaily and said, just as I had expected him to say: 'Why, that's just something I once drew on the back of an envelope.'"[26] The president then agreed that the American proposal was unsuitable for presentation to the EAC. At the conclusion of the conversation Roosevelt agreed to accept all the zonal boundaries as proposed in the British-Soviet plan, but on the condition that the American delegation insist upon American occupation of the northwest zone. Thus, the net result of Mr. Kennan's patient and persistent diplomacy was a virtual overruling of the position taken by the Civil Affairs Division of the War Department, a position asserted by CAD to be the decision of the president.

After sufficient clearance with WSC and the Joint Chiefs of Staff, new instructions were cabled to Winant by Secretary Hull on May 1. He could accept all the boundaries in the British-Soviet proposal, but must insist that American forces occupy the northwest zone.[27] The acceptance was communicated orally to EAC in early May, but not officially in writing. Again Winant felt that he must delay action on his instructions, this time for two basic reasons: first, before definitely accepting the Soviet boundary, Winant felt that some provisions for Western access routes to Berlin should be agreed upon; secondly, he felt that the Anglo-American dispute over occupation of the two western zones should be settled before he could accept definitely the southern boundary between those two zones.[28]

The Ambassador Goes to Washington

Mr. Winant's ideas and his delay in acting in EAC were obviously matters which required consultations at the highest level. Since Kennan had begun an extended leave from active service for medical reasons in April, Winant himself traveled to Washington on May 13. In his discussions with Roosevelt Mr. Winant learned that the president was absolutely adamant that American forces should occupy the northwest zone of Germany but that he was still far from reaching an accord with Churchill on the matter. Roosevelt instructed Winant that in the EAC negotiations he must, at all costs, insist upon American occupation of the northwest zone.

Winant's discussions at the War Department are the subject of a considerable controversy. They concerned principally the matter of whether or not specific provisions for access to Berlin should be negotiated before the United States accepted finally the western boundary of the Soviet zone. Until this time there had been no discussion of Western access to Berlin. It was not mentioned in the British-Soviet proposals, which placed Berlin as an enclave within the Soviet zone, nor was it mentioned in the instructions sent to Winant on May 1. Professor Smith, basing his statements on an account given by Major General John H. Hilldring, chief of the Civil Affairs Division of the War Department, states that there was an agreement between Winant and representatives of the Civil Affairs Division that Winant should attempt to negotiate routes of access to Berlin before approving the boundary of the Soviet zone. Smith asserts that, despite this agreement, Winant made no effort to raise the matter of access in the EAC. The clear implication is that the absence of provision for access to Berlin in the EAC agreements is a failure which can be attributed substantially to Mr. Winant's ineptitude.[29] General Clay would seem to agree with the substance of Smith's account.[30]

Philip Mosely, on the other hand, states that it was only after Winant's death in October, 1947, that a strong effort was made to pin the lack of ar-

NEGOTIATIONS IN 1944

rangements on access to Berlin on Winant personally.[31] Mosely records that Winant expressed a strong opinion to the Civil Affairs Division that concomitant with American acceptance of the Soviet zonal boundary, the U.S. delegation should place on the negotiating table a set of fairly explicit terms providing for Western access across the Soviet zone to Berlin. Mosely states that Winant believed it might not be too difficult to reach agreement on such provisions with the Russians, since Gusev had stated several times that Western co-occupation of Berlin naturally carried with it all the necessary rights of access. Indeed, Winant felt it would be highly unwise to fail to reach agreement on terms and routes of access together with agreement on zones, since Berlin lay so far within the Soviet zone. The reaction of the Civil Affairs Division to Winant's suggestions was, however, immediately and decidedly negative. Again the Civil Affairs representatives felt that the matter of access was a strictly military matter which could only be dealt with by the proper military authorities at the appropriate time. They were convinced that it would be impossible to provide in advance for specific routes of access, since there was no way of knowing whether these would be in usable condition at the end of the war. If specific routes had been previously allocated by agreement, it might be impossible to change these, and the hands of the Western Powers would be tied. The Civil Affairs Division also felt that the EAC was encroaching once again upon territory clearly belonging to the War Department. The War Department had already acquiesced to EAC jurisdiction in the matter of occupation zones; now it was being asked to give up jurisdiction in reference to terms of access to Berlin also. This it refused to do, insisting that access routes were purely a military matter and that Winant should not broach the subject with the Russians in EAC.[32]

Mr. Winant returned to London on May 30. Dr. Mosely recalled two separate occasions in late June and July when Winant discussed with him the opposition he had encountered by the Civil Affairs Division to discussing terms of access in EAC. The ambassador also asked Mosely if the latter thought that he would be condemned later for not having secured guarantees of access even over the opposition of the War Department. Being faced with such strong resistance, however, Winant declined to pursue the matter further. At a meeting on May 31 Winant informed the Commission that he agreed to the following four points: three zones of occupation, one for the forces of each of the Three Powers; the north-south boundary of the Soviet zone as proposed by the British and Soviet delegations; all the territory east of that line to be part of the Soviet zone; tripartite occupation of the Berlin area.[33] Winant did not, however, state American agreement to any East-West boundary line, owing to the deep disagreement still persisting between Washington and London concerning occupation of the northwest zone.

CHAPTER FOUR

The British Draft on Zonal Occupation

During the month of June the Commission finally got down to the task of considering various drafts of a protocol to establish the zonal occupation of Germany. In drawing up and discussing the various drafts, the delegations had to give particular attention to the special status to be given Berlin, in order that this status might be cogently and accurately defined by the provisions of a written document. The British delegation, with characteristic promptness, submitted the first workable draft of a protocol of military occupation on June 12. (Document reproduced in Annex 1. From Department of State lot file 52 M 64, Section 144–I.) Article 1 of this draft provided that "Upon unconditional surrender Germany, with the exception of the Berlin area and Austria, will be divided for purposes of occupation into three zones." Article 2 set down approximate descriptions of the three zones. Article 3 provided that "The Eastern Zone, with the exception of the Berlin area, will be occupied by forces of the Union of Soviet Socialist Republics." Finally, Article 5 provided that "The Berlin area, consisting of the City of Berlin and surrounding territory, will be occupied jointly by the three countries."

It is important to note that twice a specific exception is made for the Berlin area to the general scheme of zonal occupation. From this draft it is entirely clear that Berlin does not in any way belong to any of the zones of occupation. It is also evident that Article 5 lacks any clear definition of what territory should comprise the special "Berlin area."

The following day, June 13, the British delegation submitted a complete and revised text of Article 2. (Document reproduced in Annex 2. From Dept. of State lot file 52 M 64, Section 144–I.) The new Article 2 provided descriptions of the three zones of occupation in subparagraphs (a), (b), and (c). Subparagraph (a) provided that the eastern zone would be occupied by Soviet forces "with the exception of the Berlin area, for which a special system of occupation is provided in sub-paragraph (d) below." Subparagraph (d) read, "The Gau Berlin (Greater Berlin) will be under joint occupation by the armed forces of the U.K., the U.S.A., and the U.S.S.R." The comprehensive new Article 2, by simply providing blank spaces for naming the Powers to occupy the northwest and southern zones and by including reference to Berlin as the special area of joint occupation, obviated the need for Articles 3, 4, and 5 of the previous draft. It also made it clear that the British delegation had decided upon the existing Nazi military district or Gau Berlin as the appropriate area for joint occupation.

An American Redraft

At the informal meeting of June 19 the American delegation submitted a redraft of the British draft. (Document reproduced in Annex 3. From Dept. of State lot file 52 M 64, Section 144–I.) Though this was a rather second-hand contribution, it had the virtue of at least getting the American representative in on the discussion, as the American redraft was used as the basis of discussion that day. Interestingly the new redraft mentioned Berlin in the first article of the proposed protocol by providing that Germany would "be divided into three zones . . . and a special Berlin area." Years later the tiny word "and" became the subject of controversy among international lawyers. Perhaps it would have been better, for purposes of Western legal argumentation, to leave the original British wording that "Germany, with the exception of the Berlin area," would be divided into three zones. Such wording detaches Berlin from the scheme of division into three zones more unequivocally than the American redraft. It is perhaps possible that the American redraft of Article 1 of June 19, subsequently incorporated in the final version, represented a negative contribution to the Commission's work from the standpoint of the Western Powers' ability to make legal claims later against the Soviet Union.

Meanwhile, on June 17, Winant received a memorandum from his military advisers suggesting that the Gau Berlin, as proposed by the British, might not be large enough for the needs of all three occupying forces.[34] It would be advantageous to use the Berlin Autobahn Ring as the boundary of the Berlin area, since this would take in the military grounds and barracks to the west of Spandau. It would also include Potsdam, which had many public buildings and palaces which could be employed as office space by the joint administration in case many of the government buildings in Berlin were destroyed. The memorandum suggested that in the Commission Winant press for acceptance of the Autobahn Ring or at least certain portions of it containing military installations as the boundary of the Berlin area. This Winant proceeded to do at informal meetings on June 19 and 21. His suggestions met with strong objections from Gusev, who insisted that Gau Berlin or Gross-Berlin was quite adequate. Since Winant apparently received no support from the British in advancing his suggestions, he withdrew them at the June 21st meeting.*

---

*At the end of June Brigadier General Vincent Meyer replaced Brigadier General C. W. Wickersham as military adviser to Ambassador Winant. Beginning June 21 General Meyer made extensive notes of the discussions at all the informal and formal meetings of the EAC. Until this time no systematic notes had been kept by the American delegation. Beginning June 21 systematic notes were kept until the end of the Commission's work in August, 1945. Philip Mosely arrived in London in late June as consultant, then political adviser, to Ambassador Winant. The notes of each meeting taken by General Meyer were given to Dr. Mosely, who edited them the following morning for Winant and other members of the American delegation. Three copies of each set of minutes were sent by courier to the State Department usually twice a week with a covering dispatch from the U.S. delegation to EAC. In September, 1945, three sets of the complete minutes were escorted via ship to Washington by Captain Leona Herman. They are now contained in State Dept. lot file 52 M 64, the files of the United States Political Adviser to the American delegation to the European Advisory Commission.

The final days of June saw two events which became of crucial importance to the further discussion of the Berlin problem in EAC. On June 28 Winant was notified by Brigadier General C. P. Cabell, his military air adviser, that the U.S. Air Transport Command had prepared a detailed estimate of anticipated requirements for airport facilities in the Berlin area following the surrender of Germany. The report concluded that there was only one airport in the vicinity of Berlin which could meet the heavy demands placed upon U.S. air transport during the occupation and which could accommodate the C-54 and other heavy aircraft of the Air Transport Command. That was the Staaken airport, located on the western outskirts of the metropolitan area between Staaken and Doeberitz. It was absolutely essential that Winant get an interpretation of the Greater Berlin line which would include the entire Staaken airport, so that the U.S. could use the airport by right and would not be dependent upon the sufferance of the Soviet Union.[35] The Staaken airport issue became, unfortunately, a major bone of contention in EAC negotiations during July.

The Soviet Berlin Proposal

The following day, June 29, Ambassador Gusev presented to the Commission a Soviet proposal for the division of the Berlin area into three zones of occupation plus a Soviet proposal for the administration of the city. It is perhaps noteworthy that the Soviet delegation was the first to put forward a proposal on the actual division of the city into zones or sectors. The proposal on Berlin zones was incorporated into Article 2 of the previous British-American drafts, while the proposal on administration appeared as a new Article 4. (Document reproduced in Annex 4. From Dept. of State lot file 52 M 64, Section 144-I.) Several important aspects of the new Soviet proposals should be noted. The Soviets proposed, first of all, that "Greater Berlin" should mean the twenty administrative districts or boroughs which comprised the city as of 1920. This city boundary was eventually accepted and appears in the final protocol. Secondly, the Soviets proposed that the Verwaltungsbezirke (boroughs) of Pankow, Prenzlauerberg, Mitte, Weissensee, Friedrichshafen, Lichtenberg, Treptow, and Koepenick should be occupied by Soviet armed forces. For better or for worse, these are precisely the eight boroughs which became the Soviet Berlin sector in July, 1945, and have comprised the Soviet dominated city of East Berlin until the present day. The name of the borough of Pankow subsequently gained notoriety as the location of the governmental headquarters of the East German regime.

Perhaps in anticipation of a heated dispute over airport facilities, the Soviet plan proposed that Tempelhof airport, located in the southern part of the city to be occupied by a Western Power, be used by all Three Powers on equal terms. The detailed Soviet proposal for the administration of the city—the establishment of the Komendatura and its subsidiary agencies—was later accepted almost in its entirety by the Western Powers.

NEGOTIATIONS IN 1944

It is quite evident that the comprehensive Soviet proposals on Berlin caught both the American and British delegations by surprise. In his cable of July 1 to the State Department reporting the Soviet proposals, Winant stated that he believed that "our delegation is in much the same indefinite position of error as the British find themselves at this stage with respect to the Russian proposals regarding Berlin."[36] Although the British had been the first to present comprehensive, concrete proposals on both zones of occupation in Germany and control machinery for the occupation period, they had evidently neglected to prepare such detailed proposals for the joint occupation of Berlin. This is perhaps unfortunate, since by this time it was quite clear to everyone in EAC that the delegation which presented carefully documented proposals first automatically gained a considerable psychological and procedural advantage in the subsequent proceedings. The British proposals on zones and control machinery were not only accepted as the initial basis of discussion in EAC but were, in large measure, determinative of the final product. The Soviet delegation perhaps counted on a similar outcome when they presented their Berlin proposals on June 29. They were not to be disappointed.

At the informal EAC meeting of June 30 both Winant and Strang agreed that the Soviet idea of dividing Berlin into three zones was a good one, but they naturally attempted to avoid any discussion of the zonal boundaries proposed by the Russians or the allocation of zones between Britain and the United States, until receiving instructions from their governments.[37] Strang expressed doubt that it would be advisable to introduce into the zones protocol the plan for the administration of Berlin, since that subject really concerned the control machinery for Germany which had not yet been discussed by the Commission. He suggested that it might be better to put Article 4 of the Soviet proposal into a separate protocol and consider it at the time that the Commission took up the subject of control machinery. Both Winant and Gusev felt, however, that it would be logical to state at some point in the zones protocol that a tripartite control authority would be located in Berlin.

The June 30 meeting settled the matter of nomenclature for the Berlin area in the official protocols. Strang invited attention to the fact that the draft copy of the protocol submitted by the Russians referred to the "city of Berlin" at one point. He suggested that for the sake of uniformity the term "Greater Berlin" should always be used. His suggestion was accepted by Winant and Gusev.

In line with the communication he had received from his air adviser on June 28 Winant proposed an additional paragraph which read: "The Staaken aerodrome, which for purposes of administration will be included in the Greater Berlin area, will be used by blank." In his July 1 cable to the State Department Winant stated that the Russians had indicated that a paragraph to this effect might be acceptable.

CHAPTER FOUR

Fateful Decisions in July

It was during the month of July, 1944, that the most crucial decisions were reached in EAC concerning Berlin's future status after the war. During July Berlin was the major topic of discussion at most of the EAC meetings, and it was at this time that the major problems concerning Berlin were examined, debated, negotiated, and for the most part settled. Early in the month the American delegation began a detailed examination of the new Russian proposals. A study was made of the Prussian Gesetzsammlung for 1920 which contained descriptions of the boroughs in Berlin. It was found that in some cases the Russian proposal used more recent designations of the boroughs than those given in the Prussian law of April 27, 1920. Kreuzberg in the Russian proposal seemed to correspond to the former Hallesches Tor district and Prenzlauerberg to the former Prenzlauer Tor. In the case of Friedrichshain (improperly cited as Friedrichshagen in the Russian proposal), however, the Russians apparently reverted to the older name in order to avoid the more recent designation of Horst Wessel.[38]

At the informal meeting of EAC held on July 5 the British delegation submitted a revised draft of that section of Article 2 of the Russian proposal dealing with Berlin. (Document reproduced in Annex 5. From Dept. of State lot file 52 M 64, Section 301.2–I. General Meyer's EAC minutes, Enclosure to Meeting of July 5, 1944.) Unfortunately, Gusev seemed anything but enthused about the British revisions. The British also produced a large scale map showing the Berlin zones as proposed in the Russian plan. During the discussion, Sir William Strang repeatedly emphasized two points: the delimitation of the Greater Berlin area should not be absolutely fixed and final; and it should be clearly understood that all necessary facilities in Greater Berlin would be available to all Three Powers. After considerable discussion a tentative decision on the wording of the first part of the Berlin section of Article 2 was reached as follows: "The Berlin Area (by which expression is understood the Territory of 'Greater Berlin' as defined by the law of 27th April, 1920) will be *jointly* occupied by armed forces of the U.S.S.R., U.K., and U.S.A. *designated by the respective* Commanders-in-Chief. For this purpose the territory of 'Greater Berlin' will be divided into three ~~zones~~ *parts:-*

"North-Eastern part of the city Greater Berlin . . . "

[The italicized words were added to the Soviet proposal of June 29. The word "zones" was replaced by the word "parts."]

No changes were made in the paragraphs delineating the three zones. The delegates were unable to come to any agreement as to whether or not the statement concerning Tempelhof Aerodrome in the original Soviet draft should be retained. They also could not decide whether the last two paragraphs of the British revision concerning adjustment of zones and equal use of facilities should be included. Mr. Winant was unable to offer any constructive suggestions on either issue, since he had not yet received any reply from Washington concerning the Soviet Berlin proposals.

When the discussion turned to Article 5,* Strang stated that he felt the entire subject of the Komendatura** really belonged more properly to the discussion of control machinery for Germany. He explained that Article 5 set forth the principles of government for Greater Berlin before such principles had been established for the zones and for Germany as a whole. This was unsound as a matter of draftsmanship. He believed that Article 5 should be removed if the protocol on zones were completed and forwarded to the governments; or, if Article 5 were left as is, the protocol should not be completed until the question of control machinery for all of Germany had been settled.[39]

Mr. Winant's instructions came one day too late to be of any help to him at the July 5 meeting. On July 6 he received a lengthy telegram from Secretary Hull informing him of the ideas of WSC and the State Department in reference to the Soviet proposals. The department could agree to divide Berlin into three zones "on the assumptions that the actual administration of the city is a combined function and that the zones are for billeting and police purposes only." Within WSC the proposal to divide Berlin into zones was now meeting with the same stubborn resistance on the part of the Civil Affairs Division that the earlier proposals to divide Germany into zones had met with. This is clearly reflected in the next sentences of the telegram to Winant: "Under such assumptions the disposition of troops would appear to be largely a matter of detailed planning for final decision on a military level rather than a matter for immediate consideration by EAC. An agreement on specific delimitation of the zones at this time seems premature, since due to destruction, facilities in zones delimited now may be inadequate at the time of occupation."[40]

With respect to the proposals concerning the administration of Berlin and the Komendatura, the department felt that such provisions should not be included in the protocol on zones but should form an integral part of the plan for control machinery. In the zones protocol there should be only a general statement to the effect that the administration of Greater Berlin would be under the control of a combined administrative authority. The department also believed that rather than make any references to airdromes

---

*At the meeting of June 30 the representatives had agreed that for purposes of logical order, Articles 4 and 5 of the Russian draft should be switched around. Thus Article 4 dealing with the Komendatura became Article 5 of the proposal under consideration.

**The term "Komendatura" is the approximate Russian word for "inter-Allied governing authority," and appears in parentheses after "inter-Allied governing authority" in all the draft proposals and in the final protocols on Germany. The American version, "Kommandatura," did not gain currency until the body was actually set up in July, 1945. Discussions in the EAC referred either to "inter-Allied governing authority," or "Komendatura." In this treatment the term "Kommandatura" will not be used until referring to events after July, 1945.

or other specific facilities, it would be desirable to state that all facilities in the combined area would be accessible to all Three Powers under the overall control of the tripartite authority.[41]

The American ambassador dutifully reported his government's views to the Commission at the meeting of July 10. Surprisingly, Gusev seemed in an unusually conciliatory mood on the matter of not including the Russian provisions for the administration of Berlin in the zones protocol. He readily agreed that all the provisions dealing with the administration of Berlin could be deleted from Article 5 of the zones protocol and transferred to the discussion on control machinery. It would be sufficient to have a short, general article in the zones protocol stating the principle of the Soviet Article 5. Gusev's concession was not offered with no strings attached, however. He also felt strongly that no restrictions or qualifications should be added to the division of Berlin into three zones. It would not be necessary to include an article stating that the division of the city into zones might be subject to later adjustments by the inter-Allied governing authority. In other words, he wanted the zonal divisions to be set, final, and not subject to change.

In support of Winant's earlier proposal, Strang suggested that the Staaken Airdrome be considered as within the area of "Greater Berlin," since only half of the airfield actually lay beyond the city boundary. Gusev did not agree, but suggested alternatively that instead of making any alteration in the city boundary, it would be better simply to reach some agreement on the joint use of the airfield. He felt that if the boundary were altered at one place, it might have to be changed at a dozen other places later. A long discussion then followed on the question of the joint use of various facilities by all three occupying Powers. Gusev strongly opposed including any articles in the zones protocol relating to the joint use of facilities, his argument being that the question of facilities more properly belonged to the discussion on control machinery. Strang, in answering Gusev, attempted to toss in his own *quid pro quo:* he might be willing to defer the discussion of facilities until control machinery was discussed, but only if some provision could be made somewhere in the protocol for possible adjustment of the Berlin zonal boundaries in the light of the conditions found when the Allies entered the city. To Strang's suggestion Gusev reacted like a cake of ice. It would, he felt, be quite impossible to arrange matters in this fashion.[42]

Winant Hears From the War Department

The day after the July 10th meeting Mr. Winant received an urgent memorandum from his military adviser, Brigadier General Vincent Meyer. Meyer, utilizing his own military channels of communication with his superiors in Washington, naturally felt it was his duty to bring to Winant's clear attention the views of the responsible military authorities in the War Department. The memorandum urged that Winant attempt to avoid any designation of districts in the three parts of Berlin and get instead a simple statement that Greater Berlin would be divided into three parts. In the covering letter transmitting the protocol to the governments the Commission could state that the three parts of Berlin were tentatively composed of the districts as indicated in the original draft proposal. The covering letter should state further that the proposal to divide Berlin into three parts was acceptable in principle but that an agreement on specific delimitation seemed premature and was considered by the Commission as a matter of detailed planning for a final decision by the three Allied military commanders. The memorandum further urged that the first two sentences of the 6th paragraph of Article 2, giving the reasons for zonal division and providing for later adjustments, be omitted. However, a comprehensive statement on joint use of facilities should be retained.[43]

The July 12 Decisions

Mr. Winant did not actively negotiate on the basis of the premises set forth in Meyer's memorandum when he attended an informal meeting of the Commission the following day, July 12. He was quite aware of the fact that the proposed drafts and negotiating positions meanwhile had overtaken the requests in the military memorandum. It would look foolish for him to suggest at this point that the Berlin zones actually should not be defined at all.

As it happened, much was accomplished at the July 12 meeting, and several important decisions were made which were to have deep consequence for the future status of Berlin.[44] Mr. Winant, rather than attempting to avoid any delineation of Berlin districts at all, pressed hard for some provision providing for necessary adjustment of the zonal boundaries according to the needs of individual commanders in chief. He said that his government felt very strongly on the matter. It would be eminently unwise to fix the lines of division in Berlin inflexibly, without making some provision for the possibility that one zone might be so damaged that it would be difficult if not impossible to billet troops there after they arrived.

Mr. Gusev, in reply, stated that inadequate billeting facilities would be a common problem in all three zones in Greater Berlin and that all three commanders would have no alternative but to occupy ordinary houses for billeting. If one zone were much more damaged than the others, the only possible solution would be for the commander of that zone to make more demands on the Germans living there, perhaps even move some of them out of Berlin. Winant observed at this point that it would of course be a simple matter for the Russians to spill out of Berlin into their own zone in Germany; the United States, on the other hand, would be obliged to accommodate its troops in a restricted Berlin area without being able to spill out into a surrounding zone. Gusev failed to answer this point, his only comment being that "it will be necessary to take buildings from the Germans and move these Germans out somewhere else. I do not see any other way."

Strang strongly supported Winant's contentions. He stated that even though he agreed in principle that the boundaries proposed in the Russian draft were reasonable, the commanders should not be bound to rigid lines, but should have some element of elasticity in case of need. The effect of leaving out any provision for boundary readjustment would be to make the document excessively rigid. The three commanders, using the protocol as a guide, would not be empowered to make any alterations; in fact, they would be bound not to. This could well put them in an impossible situation.

Mr. Gusev was not about to be moved. He said he felt that the provisions sought by his colleagues would only lead to chaos. The real problem was to find adequate accommodations for the occupation troops. Adding a provision for boundary readjustment would do nothing to increase the number of buildings or houses for accommodations; it would only deprive the three commanders of the necessarily strict guide as to precisely what they might count on and where. "In all three zones the troops of the Allies will live in huts—not in barracks," Gusev observed tersely.

Faced with Gusev's iron intransigence, Winant and Strang now attempted to find some other solution to the problem. Winant suggested that the matter of boundary adjustment could be dropped for now, if Gusev would agree to consider the subject later as part of the protocol on control machinery. Alternatively, Strang suggested that reference to adjustment be deleted from the protocol itself but added to the report of the Commission which officially transmitted the protocol to the three governments for consideration. Gusev was unable to accept either suggestion. He noted that previously all the delegations had agreed to the division of the Berlin area into three parts; now, however, all the restrictions proposed by the British and Americans would act to nullify that principle. He felt there was really not much left of the original Soviet proposal on Berlin.

The discussion then turned to the subject of the airdromes in the Berlin area. Winant tried first to get Gusev to agree that all three Allies should share all of the airfields in Berlin. Failing in this attempt, he concentrated his remarks on Tempelhof and Staaken. Strang, supporting him, declared that some provision about Staaken Airdrome would have to be put in the protocol; even though Staaken was not entirely within the "Greater Berlin" area, it would have to be used by all Three Powers. Gusev countered that the Western delegates should bear in mind that the Soviet zone completely surrounded Berlin, the communications and transportation center of Germany. Since Soviet authorities would be obliged to transport much of the material needed to supply the Soviet zone through Berlin, the Soviet Union would require more transportation facilities than the other Powers.

Following this exchange the delegates turned their attention to new drafts of the zones protocol submitted by the British and American delegations. Mr. Winant submitted a new draft of Article 2 which was considered paragraph by paragraph. (Document reproduced in Annex 6-A. From Dept. of State lot file 52 M 64. General Meyer's EAC minutes, Enclosure to Meeting of July 12, 1944.) As finally agreed to tentatively, it omitted all reference to Staaken Airdrome, since Gusev finally agreed to discuss some provision for joint use of this airport later in connection with final drafting of Article 5(b). On the basis of a British draft the commissioners agreed to a tentative wording of Article 5(a), stating that Berlin would be administered by an Inter-Allied Governing Authority or Komendatura. (Document reproduced in Annex 6-B, *loc. cit.*) Agreement was also reached on a possible tentative wording for Article 5(b), the article which, if included, would provide for joint use of facilities. (Document reproduced in Annex 6-C, *loc. cit.*) Finally, a tentative wording emerged for a paragraph which might be included in the Covering Report transmitting the protocol, stating that the boundaries of the three parts of the city might be subject to readjustment. (Document reproduced in Annex 6-D, *loc. cit.*) It should be noted that agreement on the tentative wording of these various provisions relating to Berlin did not imply a final agreement on whether or not some of the provisions would appear at all in the final version of the protocol. Gusev was very careful to reserve his position on that. Nevertheless, it was evident by now that in agreeing to a tentative wording of several key articles paragraph by paragraph, the Commission was making slow but steady progress in formulating the outlines of those provisions which would eventually regulate the postwar status of the German metropolis.

The War Department, taking note of the evolving agreements, was naturally concerned that military interests be fully safeguarded in any articles agreed to by Ambassador Winant. It was beginning to look as if the zonal division of Berlin originally proposed by the Soviet delegation on June 29 would ultimately be accepted. This division had been repeated without change in British and American redrafts of Article 2, and so far, neither the British nor the American delegation had seriously challenged the proposal or tabled an alternative proposal suggesting a different division. Furthermore, Gusev seemed adamantly opposed to including in the protocol any provision which would allow readjustment of the boundary lines. The War Department thereupon decided that military opinion at the operational level would have to be consulted before any rigid division of Berlin into zones or parts could be finally accepted. On July 13 Vincent Meyer, acting apparently under War Department instructions, dispatched a memorandum to the assistant chiefs of staff of all the major divisions of SHAEF (Supreme Headquarters Allied Expeditionary Force) asking for their views regarding an inflexible delimitation of boundaries in Berlin.[45] If the Soviet ambassador remained adamant and refused to consider any provision for adjustment of the boundaries of the three parts into which Berlin would be divided, could the military authorities function from an operational viewpoint? Was a provision for boundary readjustment absolutely essential?

The various replies received by Meyer seemed to agree on the point that U.S. military authorities could function properly and feasibly from an operational viewpoint in the areas proposed. Although provision for boundary readjustment would be highly desirable, it was not considered absolutely necessary from a military standpoint. The various replies stated that certain conditions should, if possible, be met if an inflexible delimitation of the zonal boundaries in the city were accepted. The most important of these conditions were that transportation, communication, and public utilities facilities be used in common and that the Russians accept the movement of both Germans and foreigners from the northwest and southwest areas into the Russian zone if necessary in order to obtain adequate accommodations for American and British forces. The views of the military authorities were sent to Winant immediately in a memorandum from Brigadier General Meyer.

No progress was made at the meeting of July 14 in resolving any of the outstanding issues relating to Berlin. Gusev continued to insist that provisions for either boundary adjustment or joint use of facilities in Berlin were quite unnecessary. The reason that such provisions were unnecessary, he said, was that all such questions were settled by the principle set forth in Article 5(a) that the administration of Berlin would be carried out "jointly" by the Three Powers.

July 17: Soviet Successes

The deadlock on both of these outstanding issues was ended at the meet- of July 17.[46] Strang admitted that Gusev's argument about Article 5(a) was logical. He continued that although he felt it would be wise to provide for boundary adjustments, he was prepared not to insist on the point at this time. Winant stated that he had spoken with Secretary Stimson the previous day in an effort to help clear the protocol on zones and that he could now agree to the fixing of the zonal boundaries in Greater Berlin without provision for future adjustment. Strang concluded the discussion by remarking that he assumed that the members of the governing authority would be reasonable men and that if something had to be done about the boundaries they would do it. With Strang and Winant both conceding, it was now settled that there need be no provision in the zones protocol for adjustment of the zonal boundaries in Berlin.

Winant, acting as chairman of the meeting, directed the discussion to the matter of joint facilities. Ambassador Gusev, in reply to a question from Winant, stated that he was still convinced that it was not necessary to include in the protocol Article 5(b) providing for joint use by all Three Powers of the transportation, communication, public utilities, and airport facilities in the

Greater Berlin area. His objection was that such an article was operational in scope and intention, while the protocol at hand should contain only the general principles governing the postwar administration of Germany. Winant then observed that Article 5(a), by clearly stating that the administration of Berlin would be "joint," already determined certain questions in respect of public facilities. He seemed to be accepting Gusev's previous argument in stating this premise. Winant then asked Strang if he felt that the needs of the three governments would be adequately covered without any provision in the protocol concerning joint use of facilities. When Strang answered in the affirmative, Winant stated that he would be prepared to agree to delete Article 5(b) from the zones protocol, if Gusev could assure him that the Article would be discussed later when the Commission discussed control machinery. Gusev promptly gave his assurance, and the issue was settled that no provision for joint use of facilities would be included in the protocol on zones. In less than one hour on July 17 both of the outstanding matters at hand relating to the Berlin articles of the protocol on zones were settled—in favor of the Russians. Whether there was ever a realistic chance that they could have been settled any other way is a very difficult question, one that will be considered later.

During the remainder of the meeting, the delegates were unable to make any headway on the matter of airdromes. Even though airdromes would seem to be facilities for joint use within the purview of the now deleted Article 5(b), they nevertheless had been treated as a separate issue in the Commission from the outset. Gusev now attempted to catch his Western colleagues off guard by saying that he thought the Commission had already agreed on joint use of Tempelhof, which was the city's central airdrome. Both Strang and Winant immediately rejected his statement. Strang pointed out that no one dissented from the proposition that Tempelhof should be available for all Three Powers, but that it would be improper to treat Tempelhof as a single exception in the zones protocol. The question of the use of Tempelhof, Staaken, and all the other airdromes in the area should be taken up when the Commission considered control machinery, since it had already been agreed to eliminate Article 5(b) from the protocol on zones and to discuss the article under control machinery.

On July 19 Winant received a memorandum (Dept. of State lot file 52 M 64, Section 144–I) on air matters from his military air adviser, Colonel Charles G. Williamson, who had recently replaced Brigadier General Cabell. The memorandum pointed out that Staaken Airdrome was not wholly either in or out of the Greater Berlin area, since it lay on the prescribed boundary line. Problems of administration, operation, and police would be confused unless there were specific clarification of the status of this facility. It definitely should be available for American use, since no other airdrome in the vicinity of Berlin was known to be suitable for operations of the heaviest American bomber and transport aircraft. It would, of course, be preferable for the

United States to have exclusive control over Staaken Airdrome in the interest of efficiency, military security, and flying safety. However, the situation did not, by any means, preclude a compromise involving joint control by two or more nations. Actually, the conclusions of the memorandum, as was often the case with military memoranda, lagged behind developments at the EAC negotiating table. It was already evident that Winant would have considerable trouble getting any kind of joint use of Staaken Airdrome from the Soviet delegation. It would most probably be nonsense to entertain any expectations at all about getting exclusive American control of the airdrome.

By this time the EAC had completed work on the instrument of German surrender and on the Report which would transmit the instrument to the three governments. Winant and Strang wished to forward these documents to the governments as soon as possible. Gusev, however, refused, on the grounds that there had been a previous agreement within EAC to forward the instrument of surrender together with the protocol on zones of occupation in Germany. The latter protocol remained unfinished because of the continuing disagreement between Britain and the United States over occupation of the northwest zone and certain other matters not related to Berlin.[47]

On July 20 Germany was plunged into crisis by the attempt made to assassinate Hitler at his headquarters in East Prussia. Mr. Winant, in an attempt to take advantage of the German crisis in order to speed up the work of EAC, asked both Gusev and Strang to meet him at his apartment the evening of July 21. Impressed by the swiftness of events and by the change in Allied military fortunes since the Normandy invasion, all three commissioners agreed at the meeting that the business of EAC simply had to be expedited. As a result of the meeting the Russian delegation decided to free the surrender instrument for immediate forwarding to the governments, together with a Covering Report, and to release a letter which the EAC had prepared for transmission to interested European nations informing them in broad outline of the surrender terms.[48] The surrender instrument was consequently approved officially by the EAC at the seventh formal meeting held on July 25.[49]

Difficulties with Boundaries

At the meeting of July 27 the three representatives found that there were major complications involved in trying to describe accurately the three zones into which Germany was to be divided and the three parts into which Greater Berlin was to be divided.[50] These difficulties resulted from numerous changes of German boundary laws between 1938 and 1944. Winant's suggestion that the Commission appoint a subcommittee to iron out the boundary difficulties was readily agreed to.[51] The Soviet delegation also insisted that the time had come for the United States and the United

Kingdom to settle their dispute over occupation of the northwest zone. Gusev said that since he had agreed to forward the instrument of surrender, the protocol on zones of occupation should be completed as soon as possible. He felt that sufficient time had elapsed to permit a decision on the question, and he did not want to forward a paper containing blanks. After the meeting Winant cabled the State Department that "unless a decision is made we will be deadlocked on this issue in the German protocol. . . . Further progress is at a standstill until the decision on the zones of occupation is reached by the United States and United Kingdom Governments. This matter is beyond the power of adjudication by the three representatives of the European Advisory Commission."[52]

During the final days of July a great deal of useful work was accomplished by the Committee on Boundaries. Dr. Mosely, as chairman of the committee, rendered a lengthy report to the EAC at the meeting of July 31, first concerning the internal and external boundaries of Germany as a whole, secondly concerning the boundaries of Berlin.[53] Mosely stated that the committee had found no changes in the exterior boundaries of Greater Berlin since the law of 1920. Therefore, the committee recommended retention of the wording of the initial Berlin section of Article 2 as originally proposed by the Soviet delegation on June 29 and modified in subsequent drafts: "The Berlin area (by which expression is understood the territory of 'Greater Berlin' as defined by the law of 27 April 1920) will be jointly occupied by armed forces of the USSR, UK, and USA. . . ." The committee found further that the decree promulgated on March 27, 1938, which took effect on April 1, 1938, had made no changes in the city's external boundaries but had made several changes in the internal boundaries. The result of the changes was to smooth out anomalies and make more rational the district lines within Greater Berlin. The two major changes of the 1938 law were the transfer of the Potsdam railway station (Potsdamerbahnhof) from Kreuzberg to Mitte and the division of the Gruenewald, which had formerly lain within Wilmersdorf, equally between Wilmersdorf and Zehlendorf. For purposes of precision the committee recommended the following paragraph for insertion in the protocol following the paragraph on the division of the districts of Greater Berlin: "The boundaries of districts within 'Greater Berlin' referred to in the foregoing descriptions, are those which existed after the coming into effect of the decree published on 27th March, 1938 (Amtsblatt der Reichshauptstadt Berlin No. 13 of 27th March, 1938, page 215)." Mosely continued that Major Filmer's office had agreed to prepare three maps for the Commission. Map A would accompany the protocol on zones and would show the international frontiers as of December 31, 1937, and the internal boundaries after the coming into force of the law of the 3rd of July, 1941. Map B would show the external boundaries of Greater Berlin as of April 27, 1920, and the internal boundaries of the city as of April 1, 1938. Map C would be a map of Austria to accompany the draft protocol on Austria. The Commission formally approved the work of the committee at the meeting of August 2 and proceeded to amend the zones protocol exactly as proposed by the committee's report.

Diplomatic Wheels Bog Down

Unfortunately, August was for the most part a lost month for the EAC. While the Allied armies advanced steadily through France and Belgium, the wheels of diplomacy were grinding to a halt in EAC. Gusev repeatedly indicated that he was unwilling to discuss any further questions in the EAC until the dispute between the British and Americans over their respective zones of occupation had been settled. President Roosevelt sent an impatient memorandum to the secretary of state on August 4 expressing dismay over the deadlock in the Commission and requesting the secretary to get the wheels moving again.[54] Hull cabled Ambassador Harriman in Moscow and also requested the British Foreign Office to cable British Ambassador Sir Archibald Clark Kerr in Moscow to put pressure on the Kremlin to permit the continuation of discussions in EAC pending settlement of the zones question. All such efforts were in vain; the Russians would not be moved. Some discussion took place on the subject of armistice terms for Bulgaria; otherwise the work of the Commission stood still.

It would be easy to place all the blame on the Russians for holding up the work of EAC during this period. It must be remembered, however, that the Russian attitude was rooted in dismay and disgust over the long-extended and quite unnecessary squabble between Roosevelt and Churchill over occupation of the northwest zone. During the summer months the president progressively lost support for his belligerent attitude toward the British on this issue. After a briefing by Harry Hopkins, Secretary of War Stimson, who had not intervened until this time, became quite concerned. In his diary he notes that Roosevelt was "hell-bent" on occupying the northwest zone and that Undersecretary of State Stettinius and Assistant Secretary of War John J. McCloy agreed that this was a mistake.[55] Stettinius cabled Roosevelt in the Pacific in early August urging him to accept the southern zone and listing a half-dozen reasons why he should do so.[56] Admiral King indicated his willingness to accept the southern zone, and General Eisenhower cabled that he would continue to advance with American forces maintaining responsibility for the southern flank, and British forces maintaining responsibility for the northern flank, unless instructed to do otherwise.[57] Stimson notes that the president's obstinacy on the issue was related to his obsession with the possibility of civil war in France after the war. At a White House luncheon on August 25 Stimson made an earnest effort to convince the president that he might be mistaken on this point.[58]

As things happened, General de Gaulle was able to establish a fairly effective control over France more rapidly and more adequately than many officials in Washington and London had imagined. As August wore on top officials in Washington as well as the EAC delegates could only hope that a solution to the issue would emerge from the Second Quebec Conference, scheduled for September.

The Soviets Propose Control Machinery

On August 25 the Russian ambassador softened his position somewhat and circulated in the EAC a memorandum setting forth the proposals of the Russian delegation concerning control machinery for Germany. (Document reproduced in Annex 8. Complete text printed in *F. R. U. S., 1944–I*, pp. 299–301.) His action evidently reflected a modified attitude on the part of the Russian government that it would not be wise to immobilize EAC's proceedings too long for the simple reason that the three governments needed to have agreements on control machinery ready to use at the same time that the agreement on occupation zones would go into effect.

Gusev's substantial contribution put the Russian delegation, as had been the case with various zone proposals, one vital step ahead of the other two delegations. In addition to proposing various bodies to compose the central Allied governing machinery, the Russian proposal also included detailed special provisions concerning the tripartite administration of Greater Berlin. Neither the previous British nor American papers had included any special provisions for Berlin at all. Dr. Mosely, Ambassador Winant's political adviser, decided that the American delegation's inadequate instructions on control machinery required a special plea to the State Department. On September 5 he cabled the chief of the Division of Central European Affairs that: "Unless we can get some papers through the JCS our situation here is going to be desperate. . . . One of these days we shall have to agree on a lot of policies with regard to Germany and unless we can have some papers approved by the JCS we shall be in a position of merely commenting on the carefully prepared British papers or of charging with a feather duster at the carefully prepared but less elaborate Russian statements of policy."[59]

Russian strategy in EAC, with characteristic careful timing, was carried one step further on September 11, when Gusev announced that the Russian delegation had decided to approve the protocol on zones of occupation with the blanks and to leave it up to the U.S. and U.K. governments to decide later the allocation of the zones.[60] This of course meant that the Russian ambassador would now proceed to discuss the other urgent issues pending in EAC, especially control machinery. At first glance it might appear that this Russian move was a major concession to the work of EAC. The timing makes it appear so. However, the Russians, after holding up progress in EAC for several weeks, could now well afford to appear conciliatory. On the same day that Gusev made his announcement in EAC, Roosevelt and Churchill held the first of their meetings at the Second Quebec Conference. It was widely assumed on all sides that at this late date they would finally, out of sheer necessity, have to reach accommodation on the thorny issue of the western occupation zones.

Quebec: Settlement of the British-American Quarrel Over Zones

Such an assumption, as it turned out, was well-founded. At the Quebec Conference Roosevelt finally gave in and agreed to American occupation of the southern zone, giving the British the northwest zone. For this concession he demanded of Churchill an extraordinary price. Churchill notes in his memoirs his surprise at Roosevelt's choice as chief adviser at Quebec: "I had been surprised when I arrived at Quebec that the President was accompanied by Mr. Morgenthau, the Secretary of the United States Treasury, though neither the Secretary of State nor Harry Hopkins was present."[61] In return for accepting the southern zone for American occupation, Roosevelt urged that Churchill accept the ill-fated Morgenthau Plan, the plan which called for the destruction of German industry and the transformation of Germany into a "pastoral" agricultural country after the war. Underlying the plan was the assumption that Germany would ultimately be dismembered into several independent states. Though Churchill was not kindly disposed toward the plan, he ostensibly accepted it. In addition he acceded to Roosevelt's demands that the port cities of Bremen and Bremerhaven, both located in the British northwest zone, be placed under American jurisdiction and that ironclad agreements be drawn up providing for American access through the British zone. Finally, the two leaders agreed upon certain changes in the boundary between the two western zones.[62]

On September 12, the second day of the Quebec Conference and the day following Gusev's concession, the EAC at its ninth formal meeting officially approved and signed the text of the Protocol on Zones of Occupation in Germany and the Administration of Greater Berlin. Mr. Winant immediately took the protocol to Quebec for approval at the highest level by the two Western chiefs of state. Roosevelt and Churchill approved the protocol as expected, but directed the EAC to fill in the blanks and to incorporate in the protocol the additional provisions they had agreed upon.[63]

Although the decisions of the Quebec Conference formally ratified the work of the EAC, they also had the practical effect of placing a new can of worms at the Commission's door. Though the decisions may have been clear to Roosevelt and Churchill, they were not to the negotiators at Lancaster House. During the next few weeks, the British and American representatives became entangled in a dreadful wrangle as to precisely what terms should be drawn up to provide for American "control" of the northern ports and American "access" across the British zone. These negotiations were carried on directly between the American and British delegations rather than at EAC. The American delegation, however, was handicapped by the same familiar problem: dependence upon instructions from the Joint

Chiefs of Staff in Washington which were often not forthcoming or were unclear when received.

Even more serious was the effect of the Quebec decisions in placing the entire work of the EAC under suspicion. From the outset the EAC deliberations had been based upon two implicit assumptions: first, that Germany would not be dismembered, and second, that an agreed network of economic, social, and political policies would be worked out by all three Allies to provide uniform administration in Germany after the war. These assumptions were clearly reflected in the September 12 protocol on zones of occupation. The Quebec decisions represented, however, a virtual overturning of these assumptions. Though no final decision on dismemberment of Germany was made at Quebec, the idea was certainly one of the bases of the Morgenthau Plan. Acceptance of the Morgenthau Plan meant that, beyond provision for zones of occupation and machinery of control, no firm Allied policies for the disposition and treatment of Germany could be developed. There was clearly an inbuilt contradiction between the dismemberment idea of the Morgenthau Plan and the September 12 protocol which envisioned the development of unified policies for treatment of a nonpartitioned Germany.[64] Also, the new dispute over American access across the British zone and control of the northern ports seemed to imply, at least in spirit, that the zones of occupation would be independent, nationally administered entities.

These contradictions were reflected in Washington in the conflict between the State Department on the one hand and the president and several of his close advisers on the other, a conflict which had been brewing for months but which now threatened to explode into the open. At the end of September Secretary Hull informed the president that he had received the memorandum of the Quebec Conference embodying the Morgenthau Plan but had found it "decidedly at variance with the views developed in the State Department. This memorandum seems to reflect largely the opinions of the Secretary of the Treasury in the treatment to be accorded Germany. I feel that I should therefore submit to you the line of thought that has been developing in the State Department on this matter." Hull strongly urged the president not to make any final decision on the question of the possible partition of Germany and informed him that, "In the meantime, the European Advisory Commission is going ahead on plans for a tripartite control machinery and military government for Germany during the occupation period."[65] The president, after a three-week period of virtual silence, finally stifled the protests of the State Department in late October.

New Shockwave from Washington

Meanwhile in London Mr. Winant had to endure another communications breakdown with the State Department. Ever since the Quebec Conference he had been patiently negotiating with the British delegation in drawing up the amendments to the zones protocol which would embody the Quebec decisions. Only when these articles were agreed to could the blanks in the protocol be filled in naming the Powers which would occupy the northwest and southern zones. On September 29 Winant sent the State Department a progress report on the drafting of the various provisions. The report noted that "the names of the United Kingdom and the United States would be inserted at the conclusion of the descriptions of the northwestern and southern parts of Berlin respectively."[66]

It should be noted that the decisions of the Quebec Conference as transmitted to Mr. Winant made no mention whatever of Berlin, even though they were explicit on the allocation of the northwest zone of Germany to Britain and the southern zone to the United States. It is interesting to speculate whether the Commission, being thus left in the dark, was merely to assume logically that the same allocation would hold for Berlin: northwest part to Britain, southern part to the United States. At any rate, it would seem that this was the assumption upon which the Commission based its work from the outset.[67] The matter was actually never even discussed at the meetings, though Mosely kept Gusev informed in very general terms of the U.S.-U.K. discussions. Consequently Winant's report to the department on the allocation of Berlin zones would seem perfectly logical and routine.

Quite naturally Winant was taken aback when he received a telegram from the State Department dated October 3 informing him, among other things, that: ". . . it is our opinion that no provision should be made in this protocol for the division of Berlin into zones of occupation. The condition in which Berlin will be found at the time of Germany's defeat cannot now be determined and it would be unduly restrictive upon the several military commanders to divide Berlin into zones of occupation at this time."[68] The telegram directed that all facilities in the city should be subject to the unified control of all Three Powers and that if it were necessary to divide Berlin into zones, such division should be for billeting and police purposes only. It emphasized that the department's view was that the question of dividing Berlin into zones should not be handled in the EAC at this time but should be left for decision by the three military commanders on the spot at the time of occupation. Winant was instructed to have his military adviser consult General Eisenhower on the subject in order to obtain his views.

Mr. Winant was understandably aroused by this unusual communication. In view of the fact that negotiations on Berlin had been completed some two months ago and the zonal divisions of the city written into the zones protocol, how could the State Department now demand that these provisions be abolished? Each draft and redraft of the provisions had been reported day by day meticulously to the department and the WSC. President Roosevelt had approved the protocol at Quebec, which meant that the

NEGOTIATIONS IN 1944

Commission's task was now to fill in the blanks naming the Powers which would occupy the respective zones. Quite obviously, the State Department's telegram reflected the wishes of the Civil Affairs Division of the War Department, which still held a veto in the Working Security Committee. It repeated verbatim the arguments transmitted to Winant in an old telegram of July 6, when the Berlin negotiations were just getting under way in EAC.

Mr. Winant drafted a reply to the State Department on October 9.[69] In it he pointed out that the language of the protocol did not establish "zones" in Berlin but merely referred to "parts" of Berlin. He stated that the department had apprised him of all the arguments against dividing Berlin into parts the previous July. He had presented these in the Commission repeatedly and emphatically. However, in order to achieve any agreement at all on the protocol, certain compromises were made in the course of the negotiations. He emphasized that all the delegates to EAC fully agreed with the department's view that the divisions of Berlin were for billeting and police purposes only. He said that it was also agreed informally that, if great disparities of facilities were found upon actual occupation of Berlin, they would be adjusted by the three commanders in chief on the spot. He went on to point out that if he were to give effect to the instructions in the October 3 telegram, "the result may be to jeopardize all our efforts to arrive at a tripartite agreement prior to surrender. I doubt very much whether the logically and technically justifiable preference for leaving the assignment of the parts of Berlin to the Commanders on the spot should be allowed to outweigh the larger interest in having a firm agreement with our Allies on the occupation of Germany." Winant then stated that, pending consideration of his comments, he would refrain from presenting in EAC the proposals in the October 3 telegram since he had concluded that, "Their potential impact on our policy of securing pre-surrender agreement in respect to the treatment of Germany and on our relations with our two major Allies goes far beyond the technical issues raised and may open up issues of the highest political significance."[70]

In an effort to justify his action and clear up some of the confusion Ambassador Winant sent his military adviser, Brigadier General Vincent Meyer, over to SHAEF for consultation on October 17.[71] General Bedell Smith, speaking for Eisenhower, stated definitely that SHAEF could accept both the zonal division of Germany and the division of Greater Berlin into three parts. The attitude of SHAEF saved the day for Mr. Winant and confirmed the work of the Commission in the protocol on zones. Winant notified the department of SHAEF's views the following day, and this apparently settled the matter. Mr. Winant received no more communications questioning the tripartite division of Berlin, and the Commission proceeded to fill in the blanks of the protocol on zones naming Great Britain as the occupant of the northwestern part of Berlin and the United States as the occupant of the southern part.

CHAPTER FOUR

Winant Commits His Prestige

The State Department's confusing telegram of October 3 concerning the disposition of Berlin was the clincher which prompted Ambassador Winant to take an unusual action. For months he had been putting up with intolerable delays in instructions, inadequate guidance papers, and crisscrossing lines of policy emanating from departmental rivalries in Washington. Now, at last, he felt he must make his position crystal clear to the State Department. On October 7 he placed his prestige as ambassador on the line and dispatched a sharply worded telegram to the authorities in Washington. He emphasized that the Russian delegation never formally introduced a paper in EAC or stated a policy which had not been fully cleared by the Soviet government and could be therefore considered authoritative. He reminded the State Department that no less than twenty-one draft directives on policy toward Germany had been prepared by the U.S. delegation to EAC and forwarded to Washington for approval. Though he needed clearance in order to present these papers to EAC, Washington had remained silent. Winant continued:

> I have found in negotiating that advancing papers which have not had full clearance by our Government and on which I am not, therefore, able to take a definite position simply confuses our relationship with the other two delegations, and particularly with the Russian delegation, and retards business rather than expediting it.
>
> I feel it my duty to call your attention most urgently to the tremendous lag in clearing our documentation on Germany. . . .
>
> If . . . these delays have occurred because of the present cumbersome machinery for inter-departmental clearance in Washington, I must urge that the Department examine most seriously means for expediting the consideration of these questions and for providing me with the materials which I have been promised for several months if negotiations are to be carried on successfully in the EAC. . . .
>
> In recent years I have tried to study the negotiations which have shaped the relationships among the great powers. I would like to say that I do not think that any conference or commission created by governments for a serious purpose has had less support from the governments creating it than the European Advisory Commission. At least I do not know of any like example in recorded history.
>
> Please show this telegram to the President, to the Secretary of State, and to the Secretary of War.[72]

Winant's telegram received a prompt and conciliatory reply from the secretary of state. Hull congratulated Winant on the statesmanlike job he had done in such adverse circumstances and promised that the State Department would spare no effort to clear the red tape in supporting his further efforts. The telegram explained that the procedure within WSC had turned out to be much more cumbersome than had been expected, since the War and Navy representatives lacked authorization to make decisions and insisted that each individual paper be cleared through the various branches of the War and Navy Departments before remittance to the Joint Chiefs of Staff for approval and ultimate dispatch to London. In addition the lines of policy developed by both the State and War Departments had been placed in question, if not reversed, by the president's acceptance of the Morgenthau Plan. Hull promised to do everything possible to break the logjam and expedite the transmission of fully cleared instructions.[73]

The President Calls a Halt

Ten days later, however, on October 20, President Roosevelt intervened. In a memorandum to the secretary of state he stated:

> I dislike making detailed plans for a country which we do not yet occupy.
> ... we must emphasize the fact that the European Advisory Commission is 'Advisory' and that you and I are not bound by this advice. This is something which is sometimes overlooked and if we do not remember that word 'advisory' they may go ahead and execute some of the advice, which, when the time comes, we may not like at all.
> In view of the fact that we have not occupied Germany, I cannot agree at this moment as to what kind of Germany we want in every detail.
> Much of this . . . is dependent on what we and the Allies find when we get into Germany—and we are not there yet.[74]

Roosevelt's action represented a very definite negative answer to Winant's pleas for strong administration support for the work of EAC, and it effectively quashed Hull's efforts to rationalize the process of policy formulation for transmission to London. By a further memorandum to the Civil Affairs Division on October 25 the president in effect halted all postwar planning for Germany and even placed in doubt the directives which had already been cleared in WSC and sent to Winant. The EAC was now estopped from taking any further action beyond its current projects. It still possessed a clear mandate to amend and complete the protocol on zones of occupation and to finish work on the protocol on control machinery. Beyond these projects, however, EAC was effectively barred from acting. The result was that for several months the responsibility for planning occupation policies in Germany was returned to the military. Planning was not resumed in EAC until April, 1945.[75]

There is some opinion, perhaps best expressed by Professor Smith, that Roosevelt acted wisely and should have taken matters out of the hands of EAC even sooner. Smith writes: "One may well speculate what might have happened had this decision been taken six months earlier. Probably the occupation boundaries in Germany would have been negotiated by the military authorities and a zonal arrangement much closer to that which President Roosevelt initially proposed would have resulted. . . . By this time, however, the damage had been done and the boundary of the Soviet zone as it exists today had been agreed to."[76]

It is perhaps true that had the EAC not negotiated the protocol on zones of occupation the matter would have been settled at the military level. In this case, however, the United States could have been accused of violating the international obligations assumed at the Moscow Conference by all Three Powers. From the very first meeting of EAC in January, the Commission had assumed that one of its primary tasks was to reach agreement on zones of occupation in Germany. Had the U.S. pulled the rug out from under the EAC during these delicate negotiations, the results would have been highly unpredictable, volatile, and fraught with unforeseeable risks. Furthermore, there is little reason to assume that an agreement negotiated by the military authorities would have produced either a more rational division of Germany or a settlement closer to Roosevelt's wishes. Roosevelt's initial idea on zones, as penciled on the National Geographic Society map, represented an extremely unrealistic and irrational division of the country, giving the United States fully half of Germany and offering the Soviet Union only about one quarter. The unwillingness of the American delegation even to present a similar JCS proposal to EAC in March is good evidence that such a proposal never had even a slight chance of being accepted by the Soviet Union. To have presented it and insisted on its adoption could only have led to stalemate and breakdown, and this is true whether the proposal were presented at the diplomatic or the military level for negotiation, since both levels are political in the Soviet view. One may conclude then with considerable justification that the quiet, unharried forum of EAC was the most reasonable place to seek agreement on the delicate matters of zones and control machinery and that the EAC did an admirable job in extremely adverse circumstances in drawing up rational, practicable agreements for the postwar disposition of Germany.

Despite Roosevelt's arrest of EAC's further activity, the Commission continued to bring to completion its work on the two primary projects on which it was at the time engaged: amendment of the protocol on zones of occupation and signature of the protocol on control machinery. There was also some discussion of the various directives and proclamations which the three commanders would issue to the German people at the end of the war. In a telegram of October 19 Hull inquired of Winant whether the policies stated in these directives would be applicable to Berlin, in view of the fact that most of them contained no specific provision for application to the Berlin area. In his reply of October 21 Winant replied that: "This question has been canvassed informally in the European Advisory Commission and the three delegations are in agreement that the general orders, proclamations, and directives will apply to the Berlin zone *which should be considered as a fourth zone having a tripartite governing authority (komendatura) instead of a single national commander.*"[77] The statement is extremely important in that it shows that the conception of the American delegation at this time clearly was that Berlin in no way formed a part of the Soviet zone of occupation. On the contrary, it was to be considered a "fourth zone." There is good reason to believe that this conception was shared by the other two delegations.

Ambassador Winant made a trip to Washington for consultation on October 26 and did not return to London until November 18, four days after EAC had formally signed the two protocols. His visit to Washington did nothing to expedite the flow of guidance or instructions to London or to modify the administration's coolness toward EAC. He was, in fact, probably never even informed of the president's decision to halt virtually all policy planning in EAC.[78] Consequently, the Commission, in his absence, continued negotiations on the Quebec amendments to the zones protocol and on control machinery.

British-American Deadlock Over Access

The British and American delegates remained for weeks on end deeply enmeshed in various disputes as to how precisely to define American jurisdiction over the port cities of Bremen and Bremerhaven and how to provide for American access rights across the British zone. The dispute was annoying to the Soviet delegation, and several times Gusev strongly urged his colleagues to get the matter settled in order that the amendments to the protocol on zones could be completed at long last. The dispute is beyond the purview of this study. What is important for our purposes, however, is to take note of the fact that as far as the subject of access was concerned, the entire dispute was one between the two Western delegations concerning access through the British zone to the American zone. There was never any dispute between the two Western delegations and the Soviet delegation over access to Berlin through the Soviet zone. Such a paradoxical situation will perhaps never be fully explained, as it relates to so many conflicting factors at once: the departmental rivalries in Washington resulting in the Civil Affairs Division's veto on action by Winant in EAC; the shortsighted military view that access to Berlin could be provided for only at the military level at the appropriate time; the feeling on the part of officials in both the American and British governments that the very fact of Western presence in Berlin carried with it all the necessary and sufficient rights of access and that specific provisions for access to the city should not be written into the protocol.

Whatever the reasons, there was a total absence of discussion concerning access to Berlin at this time in EAC. There is, however, an interesting anecdote concerning a statement made by the Soviet representative at a meeting in early November. On November 6 Gusev was particularly outspoken in urging the British and American delegations to conclude their argument about access through the British zone and at least agree upon some general provision. That evening Dr. Mosely, in Winant's absence, cabled Washington that Gusev had "stressed the cogent point that similar arrangements for transit facilities will be made, providing United States and United Kingdom forces and control personnel full access to the Berlin zone across Soviet-occupied territory."[79] The significance of the Soviet representative's statement was overlooked at the time. The British and American delegations were unfortunately too involved in their own dispute to demand that Gusev make good on his promise immediately. Consequently, perhaps the last opportunity to negotiate terms of access through the Soviet zone to Berlin as an integral part of the zones protocol passed without notice.

Invitation to France

During the final week of October and the first two weeks of November, the Commission continued work on the two protocols with unusual eagerness. A new development in mid-October worked to produce a new sense of earnestness. During the visit of Churchill and Eden to Moscow, it was decided that the new French Provisional Government should be invited to take part in the deliberations of EAC, despite the fact that Roosevelt and Stalin initially had been opposed to giving the French either a zone of occupation or a share in the control machinery. The invitation to the French was to be extended on November 11, Armistice Day of the First World War. It was evident to all three delegations that French accession to EAC would create many new problems, especially since it could be logically assumed that, once in EAC, the French would inevitably demand a share in the occupation and control of their age-old enemy, Germany. They might even insist on scrapping all the tripartite agreements which had been reached by the Three Powers, thus making it necessary for the Commission to start over again from scratch. Even French participation in the deliberations would in itself put a new strain on the work of EAC, since the Commission functioned on the basis of consensus and unanimity.

While Ambassador Winant was consulting in Washington, negotiations for the American delegation were handled by Dr. Mosely, his political adviser. Mosely was strongly convinced that the two protocols on zones of occupation and control machinery must be completed and signed before the French joined EAC if major trouble were to be avoided. If the French entered EAC before the protocols were completed, they would have much greater leverage to hold up the deliberations until some of their own demands had been met. Possibly the entire structure of the protocols would have to be altered, meaning that months of slow progress would be lost and all the completed work would have to be begun anew. On the other hand, if both protocols were already signed when the French joined EAC, the French delegation would have little room to maneuver and little basis for voicing new demands. If the French succeeded in getting a share of the German

NEGOTIATIONS IN 1944

pie, the French government would have to adhere to the signed protocols largely as they stood, thus preserving intact most of the work laboriously accomplished by the EAC.[80] Privately, Mosely assumed that the French would eventually be given a zone of occupation in Germany. Since, however, the U.S. government had not issued any instructions to proceed in the negotiations on this assumption, he felt that it was imperative to complete the Three-Power agreements as quickly as possible in order to avoid giving the French a veto over all the agreements.[81]

Russian Pressure on Britain and the United States

One problem, however, threatened to defeat all efforts to complete agreement on the protocols quickly. Gusev constantly avoided setting a definite time for signing the protocol on control machinery, even though all outstanding points of disagreement had been settled. Evidently he had instructions not to sign that protocol until agreement on the protocol on zones of occupation had also been reached. The Russians were thus holding up the control machinery protocol in an effort to put pressure on the British and American governments to settle their differences concerning control of Bremen and Bremerhaven and access to the American zone. On November 11 Mosely cabled the State Department that the Russians

> ... have applied this pressure in a most tactful and indirect way. ... The Russian stand is a logical one. The two protocols stand or fall together. If the occupation is shifted from a tripartite to a four party basis as a result of French membership in the EAC, it will obviously be necessary to change the control machinery to a four power basis too. In view of this logic, the Russians may possibly suspect that the British and we are stalling on a relatively minor point in the Protocol on Zones in order to bring in the French as full partners in both occupation and control, since this would actually be the effect of failing to complete both protocols before the French join the European Advisory Commission.[82]

During the first two weeks of November, Mosely made every possible effort to harmonize the views of the British and American military authorities. Both the American and Soviet governments were opposed to giving the French any share in the occupation and control of Germany. If, however, this could not be avoided, it was essential to have the two major protocols signed before the French joined EAC. As the days ticked away, Mosely strongly urged that the Anglo-American dispute be postponed for the time being and that some general provision be drawn up to express the area of maximum agreement, leaving the details until later. Mosely records that on many occasions he served as a go-between in sharp exchanges between British and American military authorities.[83] In his cable of November 11, he dourly warned that, "if we do not complete the Protocol on Zones now, we must be prepared to assume that the Russians will believe that we did so deliberately in order to change the whole basis of the control of Germany to a four power basis and that they may draw far-reaching conclusions from that with regard to American support for a British led west European bloc."[84]

The Protocols Are Signed at Last

Mosely's tireless efforts led to productive results. The War Department finally agreed to accept a British draft of the disputed provisions with the understanding that the American Joint Chiefs of Staff would have further opportunity to define those provisions at the military level after the amended protocol on zones had been signed.[85] At two formal meetings on November 14 the EAC formally approved first the Agreement on Control Machinery in Germany and second the Amending Agreement to the Protocol on Zones of Occupation in Germany and the Administration of "Greater Berlin." With the signature of these agreements, the EAC had completed the enormous project of securing tripartite agreement on the general outline of the postwar disposition of Germany. It is perhaps no exaggeration to say that only a body which possessed the informality, flexibility, and the good will of EAC could have succeeded in this delicate task. (See Annex 9 for text of the relevant provisions of the Agreement on Control Machinery in Germany dealing with the administration of Greater Berlin. Text printed in Department of State, *Treaties and Other International Agreements*, volume 5, part 2 (Washington, 1956), p. 2062.)

The agreements on Germany were signed none too soon. On November 27 Monsieur René Massigli, the French ambassador to the United Kingdom, took his seat as the French representative on the European Advisory Commission. At the meeting of December 7 Mr. Massigli stated that the French delegation would soon present to EAC a paper which would request a zone for French occupation in Germany and French participation in the control machinery for Germany.[86]

Due to the timing of events it was, of course, no secret to the French Provisional Government that there had been pressure within EAC to get the protocols on Germany signed before the French were admitted to the deliberations of that body. On several occasions in late November and December Dr. Mosely spoke informally with Mr. Massigli in order to apprise him of the manifold difficulties faced by EAC in its work. Though he was at first somewhat indignant, Mr. Massigli seemed to be sympathetic to the problems and to have an awareness of the urgent need for agreed policies on Germany which had prompted EAC to speed up its work. Mosely has stated that Massigli used his considerable talents to the fullest in explaining this difficult situation to the French government. Massigli's astute diplomacy played no small part in mollifying de Gaulle and creating an attitude of friendly cooperation with EAC on the part of the French government.[87]

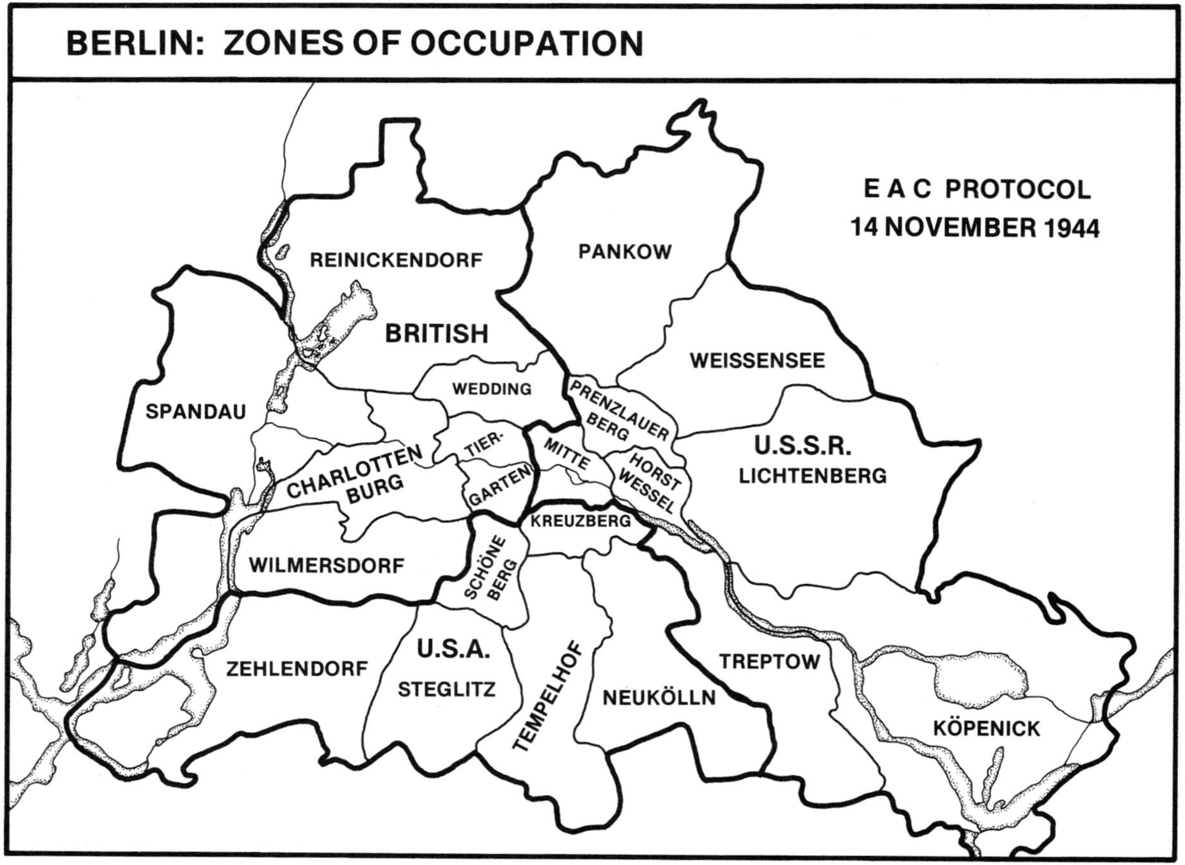
BERLIN: ZONES OF OCCUPATION
E A C PROTOCOL
14 NOVEMBER 1944
REINICKENDORF
BRITISH
PANKOW
WEISSENSEE
SPANDAU
WEDDING
PRENZLAUER BERG
U.S.S.R.
LICHTENBERG
TIER-
GARTEN
CHARLOTTEN BURG
MITTE
HORST WESSEL
KREUZBERG
WILMERSDORF
SCHÖNE BERG
U.S.A.
STEGLITZ
ZEHLENDORF
TEMPELHOF
NEUKÖLLN
TREPTOW
KÖPENICK

Winning Approval

The British government approved the Protocol on Zones as amended on December 5. Soviet approval could not realistically be expected until both the British and American governments had registered their approval. The approval of the United States, however, was not immediately forthcoming. The American military authorities predictably would not approve the agreement until the terms of American jurisdiction over Bremen and Bremerhaven and transit rights across the British zone had been precisely defined. This was, they insisted, the understanding at the time the amended protocol was signed. A series of complicated negotiations ensued involving the Joint Chiefs of Staff, the Department of State, the British Embassy, and the British Staff Mission at Washington, which eventually produced agreements satisfactory to both British and American military authorities in late January, 1945.[88]

Meanwhile Ambassador Winant, who was greatly concerned about the consequences of further delay in American approval, was sending a series of telegrams to the State Department urging prompt ratification. Both Winant and McCloy were convinced that undue delay of American approval might not only destroy the hard-won work of the Commission but might ultimately leave the Allies with no tripartitely agreed plan when Germany collapsed. In addition, the deployment of troops in Germany made it highly desirable that the Western Allies get Russian ratification of the zones of occupation protocol as soon as possible, since Russian troops in January, 1945, had advanced to within forty-five miles of Berlin, while Western troops were still held up on the Rhine.[89] When Harry Hopkins passed through London in January on his way to the Yalta Conference, Winant warned him that if the protocol remained unapproved, "the Russians might reach the border of their zone and then keep on going."[90] On February 1 Stettinius, now the secretary of state, conferred with Eden at Malta, urging him to do his utmost to win the agreement of the military authorities since it looked like the Russians would soon be in a position to take over Berlin.[91] These efforts were successful. Winant was informed by Stettinius from Malta on February 1 that he could register the approval of the United States to the zones protocol in EAC. Russian approval was received on February 6, thus giving the Protocol on Zones of Occupation in Germany and the Administration of "Greater Berlin" the status of a tripartite executive agreement, with corresponding privileges and responsibilities under international law.

No further business was transacted in the European Advisory Commission during the year 1944 following the signature of the two protocols on Germany on November 14. The Commission remained largely immobilized for three main reasons: first, the spell cast over its work by the negative attitude of President Roosevelt and the departmental rivalries in Washington; second, the lack of any new instructions to Gusev from Moscow; and third, the uncertainty as to what new business the Commission could attend to until French demands vis-à-vis Germany were made known to the Commission.

Year-End Immobilism

Meanwhile the implicit contradiction between the assumptions of the Morgenthau Plan and the assumptions underlying the two signed protocols on Germany continued. The policies of the responsible governmental authorities in Washington still seemed to be moving in two different directions at once. Toward the end of the year, however, one could observe a slight but noticeable shift of influence from the Treasury and War Departments to the Department of State. The president by this time may have begun to have second thoughts about the wisdom of certain aspects of the Morgenthau Plan. There were, at any rate, definite signs that the treasury people were prepared to abandon or modify a number of points in their original plan if this could lead to agreement with the State Department.[92]

Toward the end of the year a memorandum was drawn up in the State Department which, inadvertently, pronounced a kind of benediction upon the work of the American delegation to EAC for the year 1944. It said: ". . . a word of commendation to our delegation in London is in order. Mr. Winant has now had his procedure reversed several times. He has received a minimum amount of guidance from this Government. Recriminations as to why this is the case will serve no useful purpose, but I feel we should once more urge upon the War Department the necessity of rapid replies to his urgent and repeated requests for guidance. . . ."[93]

As 1944 drew to a close the three delegations to EAC could only hope that the logjams and snarls of the past few months could be removed and that EAC could recover the momentum and vitality it had possessed in midyear. Still, however, the representatives, in looking back over the year, could take considerable pride in the fact that the Commission had successfully completed the prodigious task of designing a tripartite blueprint for the disposition of Germany at the end of the war. There were those who had contended all along that a body such as the European Advisory Commission could never accomplish such a work. The Commission had, however, by the end of 1944 admirably proved that it could.

FIVE

THE SECOND ROUND:

EAC NEGOTIATIONS

IN 1945

The first meeting of the European Advisory Commission for the year 1945 was held on the 2nd of January. Although the meeting was short, it provided a miniature preview of the new year's business in that the representatives discussed briefly the two major items which later became the Commission's major problems for the year: the French zone in Germany and Berlin and the occupation of Austria and Vienna.

France Makes Demands

Sir William Strang, the Commission's chairman at this time, noted that a memorandum had been circulated by the French delegation which presented certain French proposals in respect to the occupation and control of Germany.[1] Point 4 of the French memorandum read: "Following the French Committee of National Liberation, the Provisional Government of the French Republic has already on several occasions emphasized the importance, both from the political and moral standpoints, of France being associated from the outset with an event which will be vitally important to her, as it will decide for the near future the relations between France and Germany which have for centuries weighed so heavily on the fate of Europe."[2] Point 6 contained the major French demands vis-à-vis the Allied plans for Germany:

> (c) A zone of occupation, the boundaries of which will be fixed later, shall be assigned to the French army which shall also take part in the occupation of Greater Berlin; the Protocol of 12th September, 14th November to be amended accordingly;
> (d) Similarly, the Agreement of 14th November, 1944, on Control Machinery in Germany shall be amended so as to substitute quadripartite for the tripartite agencies at present provided for;[3]

Mr. Massigli presented the Commission with two alternative suggestions for forming a French zone. One would be to assign a small zone initially, with provision for increasing the size later; the other would be to agree upon a definitive zone, presumably equal approximately to the other three from the outset.[4] The French ambassador further implied strongly that if the three governments would agree in principle to modify the agreements on Germany so as to include France as an equal partner, the French government would not then plan to present amendments of substance to these basic documents.[5] This implication could not but be of major encouragement to the other three delegations.

In his telegram to the State Department reporting the meeting Winant strongly urged the department to give very careful consideration to the French request. In his opinion, "As soon as the three Governments decided to admit France without reservation to full membership in the European Advisory Commission, ultimate French participation in German affairs on a footing of equality with the other three powers, it must be supposed, became only a question of time."[6] Winant's political adviser, Philip Mosely, recalled that he also felt personally that the only wise course was for the EAC to meet the French request in a just and rational manner, since it had to be assumed that France, as it recovered its strength, would eventually become one of the pillars of the postwar European order.[7]

The Beginning of Prolonged Paralysis

No more progress was made on the matter of the French requests during January. The EAC held only two more informal meetings before the end of the month, both of which were devoted to a discussion of zones of occupation in Austria and Vienna.[8] This was the beginning of a protracted period of stalemate and immobilization in EAC, since the Commission was not to meet again until April 4. The fact that no meetings were held did not mean that diplomatic activity ceased. Mosely reports that he met several times each week with members of various delegations in an attempt to clarify demands and harmonize views.[9] There were, however, three major issues that paralyzed the EAC and made further agreement impossible: new confusion over the dismemberment issue arising from the Yalta Conference, a deadlock over the boundaries of Vienna, and an inability of the three Western delegations to agree upon the boundaries of the French zone of occupation in Germany. If it were not for the excellent personal relationships between heads of delegations and between various members of the delegations, the EAC might have folded up entirely. Patience, a large reserve of goodwill, plus unceasing attempts to clarify, modify, and compromise kept the EAC not only alive but ready and willing to go back to work at the first possible moment that sufficient agreement among the four governments permitted it to do so.

The work of the American delegation to EAC was hampered at this time by the less than cordial relationship between Ambassador Winant and Edward R. Stettinius, who had succeeded Cordell Hull as secretary of state shortly after Roosevelt's reelection in November, 1944. In Winant's opinion Stettinius was an amiable man but woefully unqualified for the heavy responsibilities of the secretary of state.[10] Winant felt that Roosevelt had selected Stettinius largely upon the advice of Harry Hopkins, who wanted a weak secretary of state so that his own authority in matters of foreign policy decision making would not be seriously challenged. It is, of course, possible, though no concrete evidence exists to support the conclusion, that Winant felt Stettinius was occupying the office that he himself should have moved into after Hull's retirement. After all, Winant had returned to Washington in October, 1944, and traveled extensively throughout the country making speeches in support of Roosevelt's bid for a fourth term. He was the only U.S. ambassador to take such action, and there were many in Washington who felt Mr. Winant would be the logical choice to succeed Hull as secretary of state. At any rate, Stettinius was not a dominant secretary of state and his inability to articulate the department's interests and policies to President Roosevelt did not endear him to Winant.[11] There was, however, never any acrimony between the two men, and the distant quality of their relationship was certainly not the major cause of the paralysis in EAC.

The Gaps Left by Yalta

The discussion of a French zone in Germany was influenced by Roosevelt's offhand comment, in the midst of the Yalta negotiations, that the United States would probably withdraw most of its forces from Europe within two years of the war's end. This ominous intimation naturally alarmed Churchill greatly and increased his insistence upon getting full French participation in the postwar Allied regime in Germany. The French request for participation in the occupation and control of Germany was not given an affirmative answer at the highest level by the Three Powers until the Yalta Conference. The subject of zones of occupation in Germany was not taken up until late in the conference proceedings, when the energies of the Big Three had been drained considerably by more pressing issues. After much urging by Churchill, Roosevelt finally agreed to admit the French to full participation and to use his influence to secure Stalin's agreement on the matter. Stalin finally agreed, but only on the condition that the French zone of occupation would be formed from the British and American zones, leaving the Soviet zone unchanged.[12] The final protocol of the proceedings of the conference reads: "It was agreed that a zone in Germany, to be occupied by the French Forces, should be allocated to France. This zone would be formed out of the British and American zones and its extent would be settled by the British and Americans in consultation with the French Provisional Government.

It was also agreed that the French Provisional Government should be invited to become a member of the Allied Control Council for Germany."[13]

For our purposes the most curious aspect about the Yalta agreements is that they make no mention whatever of Berlin. They state that the French zone of occupation must be carved out of the two western zones; what is left unclear is whether or not the French are to be given a sector of occupation in Berlin and, if so, from what areas the new sector would be carved out. (The word "sector" in relation to the assigned areas of occupation in Berlin gradually came into use during 1945. Later the word "zones" denoted the areas of occupation in Germany as a whole, as opposed to the word "sectors," which denoted the areas of occupation in Berlin.) Since the French government was admitted to full membership in the Control Council, located in Berlin, it was perhaps only logical to assume that French forces would also have to be given a sector of occupation in Berlin. The Yalta agreements, however, left the matter in complete obscurity, an omission which later gave rise to extended argumentation at the negotiating table at Lancaster House. The reasons for such a glaring omission are difficult to explain. It is possible that the Big Three failed to reach any final agreement on the question of a French military presence in Berlin and remitted the whole unpleasant question to the EAC as another "hot potato." Mosely stated, on the other hand, that the Big Three never got to a discussion of the Berlin problem simply because they were too busy and too pressed for time. They did not feel that Berlin was that important a question anyway, and they felt that they had decided all that was necessary in relation to Germany at the time.[14]

It is probable that had Ambassador Winant been at Yalta, he would have asked for some guidance on the Berlin question. Winant was somewhat upset that he was not summoned to the conference by Roosevelt. Stettinius notes that the president at Yalta made it clear that he was not altogether happy with the work of the EAC, even though the Big Three had just given official approval to the two protocols on Germany already prepared by the Commission.[15]

The Yalta Conference contributed to paralysis in EAC in two ways: first, by providing no guidelines for the formation of a French zone in Germany, beyond the fact that it be taken from the two western zones, and by making no mention whatever of the disposition of Berlin; and second, by tossing the corpse of dismemberment right into the room with the EAC negotiators. At Yalta the Big Three decided that the instrument of surrender should be modified to provide for the possible dismemberment of Germany if the Allied Powers found it necessary for future peace and security. The secret formal protocol stipulated that:

> It was agreed that Article 12(a) of the Surrender Terms for Germany should be amended to read as follows:
> 'The United Kingdom, the United States of America, and the Union of Soviet Socialist Republics shall possess supreme authority with respect to

Germany. In the exercise of such authority they will take such steps, including the complete disarmament, demilitarisation and the dismemberment of Germany as they deem requisite for future peace and security.'

The study of the procedure for the dismemberment of Germany was referred to a committee, consisting of Mr. Eden (Chairman), Mr. Winant and Mr. Gousev. This body should consider the desirability of associating with it a French representative.[16]

There was no agreement at Yalta as to whether the French should have a seat on the Dismemberment Committee; this was left for the committee itself to consider and report to the three governments accordingly. At least initially, however, the French would not be represented. This arrangement created a confusing situation for EAC. While the French were to have an equal share in the occupation and control of Germany and full membership in the EAC, they were not to be represented in the Committee on Dismemberment, the body which would presumably decide the ultimate fate of Germany.[17]

The task given the Committee on Dismemberment also placed a shadow of doubt on all the work so far completed by EAC and on the value of its future deliberations. The new committee was not directed to make any study of the feasibility or desirability of dismembering Germany. It was directed instead to study "the procedure for the dismemberment of Germany," the clear implication being that the Big Three had already decided that Germany should be partitioned. Since no such momentous decision had actually been reached, the newly created committee was left with no clear mandate whatever and even, as it turned out, with no instructions or proposals. Up to now the EAC had proceeded and had based all its work on the assumption that Germany would not be dismembered, but that after a period of military occupation and strict control on the basis of tripartitely agreed policies, Germany would be restored as a peaceful member of the international community. Now there were to be two commissions sitting in London working with somewhat contradictory mandates. The European Advisory Commission was to amend the surrender instrument to provide for dismemberment and to carve a French zone of occupation out of the two western zones. The Committee on Dismemberment was to recommend a "procedure for the dismemberment of Germany," with no provision for French participation in making such decisions. Both the British and the American delegations were extremely dismayed by the Yalta decision to take seriously the matter of dismemberment.

As noted earlier the Yalta protocol was silent on the disposition of Berlin, even while admitting the French to an equal role in Germany. Mosely immediately wrote a private letter to the State Department asking for instructions on Berlin. He asked specifically if an analogy existed in that the EAC negotiators should assume that the French sector of Berlin should be drawn from the two western sectors of the city. Unfortunately, but characteristically, the State Department was at the time in no position to give any answers or guidance.[18]

The French Proposals

The French delegation was prompt in submitting proposals to EAC for the formation of a French zone in Germany and a French sector in Berlin. On February 7, before final approval of French participation at the Yalta Conference, Mr. Massigli verbally presented French proposals to Mosely, Winant, and Strang, and on February 8 to Arkadii Sobolev, the Soviet chargé in London. For the sake of greater flexibility in negotiation, Ambassador Massigli did not formally present them to the EAC at this time. In reference to Berlin, Massigli proposed that Greater Berlin be enlarged by addition of the district of Potsdam in order to make a new division of the area easier.[19] The French proposals were formally submitted to the Commission in writing on February 15. At this early stage neither the proposal for a French zone in Germany nor a French sector in Berlin included any delimitation of boundaries.[20] Clearly, the French were waiting to see what might first be offered by Britain and the United States.

The formal invitation to France to accept full participation in German affairs, including a zone of occupation, was extended to de Gaulle on February 12. The American ambassador in Paris reported that the atmosphere at the meeting with de Gaulle was chilly; after reading the telegrams de Gaulle's only comment was, "I am taking due note."[21] De Gaulle, of course, never made any secret of the fact that he was sorely displeased that he had been bypassed in London during planning for the invasion of France and that, even after France's liberation, planning for Germany had proceeded without his advice and consent.[22]

Britain Replies First

Following the usual pattern, it was the British government which first circulated a concrete proposal for a new division of Berlin into four sectors in order to provide for French participation in the occupation of the capital. The British proposal was circulated informally to the other three delegations on February 28. The EAC was not holding any meetings at this time. According to the British proposal the new division of the city would be as follows:[23]

SOVIET FORCES: districts of Mitte, Friedrichshain, Weissensee, Lichtenberg, Neukölln, Treptow, Köpenick.
FRENCH FORCES: districts of Prenzlauerberg, Pankow, Reinickendorf.
BRITISH FORCES: districts of Wedding, Tiergarten, Charlottenburg, Wilmersdorf, Spandau.

BERLIN: ZONES OF OCCUPATION

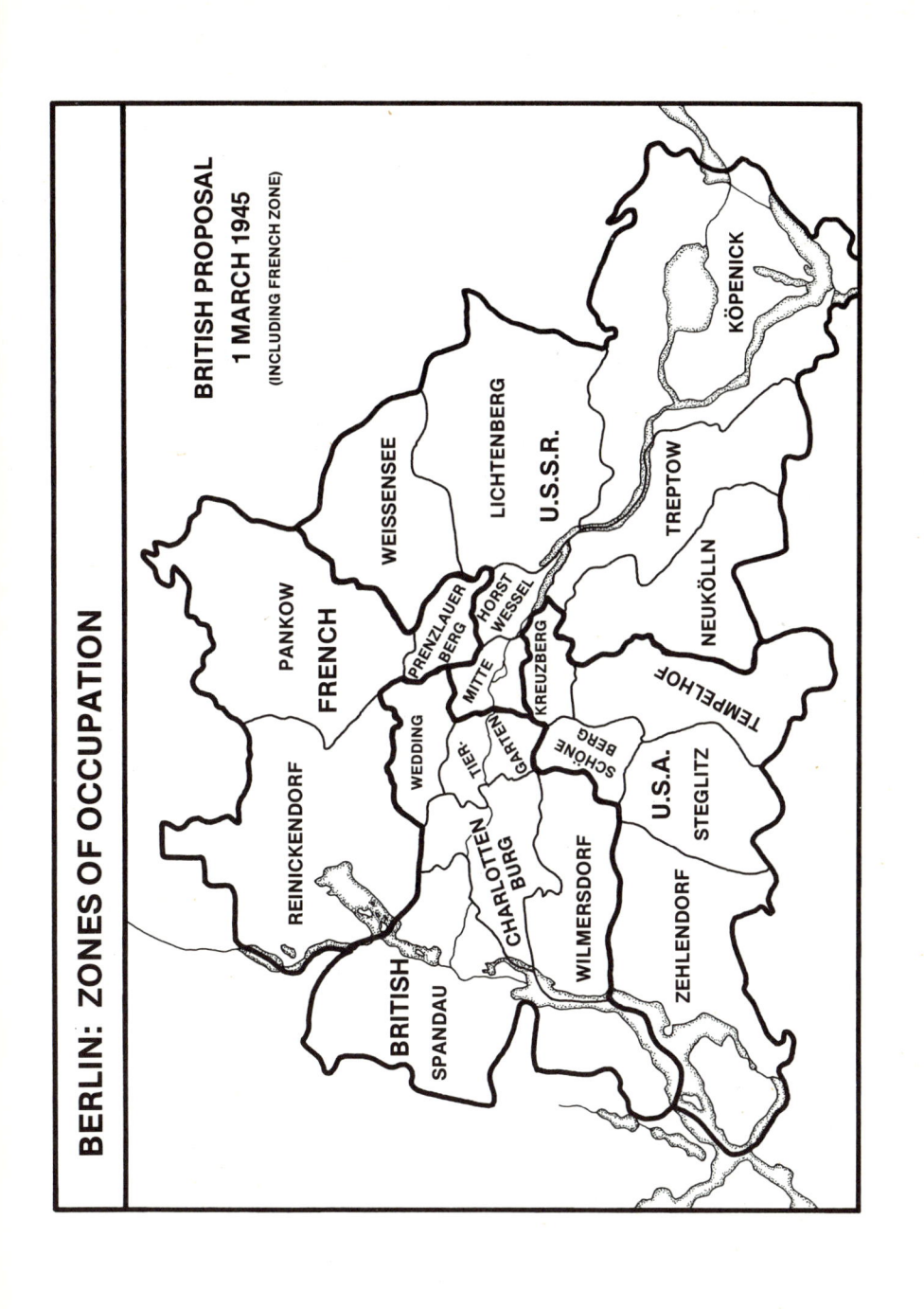

**BRITISH PROPOSAL
1 MARCH 1945**
(INCLUDING FRENCH ZONE)

AMERICAN FORCES: districts of Kreuzberg, Schöneberg, Tempelhof, Steglitz, Zehlendorf.

The month following saw no action and very little discussion of the British Berlin proposal. This was the height of the period of paralysis in EAC following Roosevelt's virtual work stoppage of October, 1944, and the additional confusion added by the decisions of the Yalta Conference. Since no meetings were being held, business had to be conducted by means of informal conversations at delegation offices.

The French Redivision Plan

The next delegation to come forward with a Berlin proposal was the French delegation. On the evening of March 22 Comte Pierre Marie de Leusse, Massigli's assistant on the EAC, presented the ideas of the French delegation to Dr. Mosely informally, not as an official proposal. Naturally, Mr. Winant immediately cabled the French "ideas" to Washington. The informal French proposal envisioned the following division of Berlin:[24]

FRENCH AREA: Tiergarten, Charlottenburg, Wilmersdorf, Zehlendorf.
UNITED STATES AREA: Kreuzberg, Schöneberg, Steglitz, Neukölln, Tempelhof, Treptow.
SOVIET AREA: Weissensee, Prenzlauerberg, Mitte, Friedrichshain, Lichtenberg, Köpenick.
UNITED KINGDOM AREA: Wedding, Pankow, Reinickendorf, Spandau.

Winant's cable to Washington, transmitting the informal French proposal, pointed out that the French obviously were not satisfied with the area proposed by the British and were seeking some adjustment which would give them better railroad and hotel facilities. When Comte de Leusse discussed the new proposal with Viscount Samuel Hood, a member of the British delegation, Hood's reaction was that the British area in the French plan was not adequate in terms of facilities and probably would not be acceptable to the British government. De Leusse suggested in reply that it might be possible to transfer Charlottenburg from the French to the British area.[25]

The EAC Gets Moving Again

On April 4 the EAC representatives finally came together again for an informal meeting. The problems which had kept the Commission immobilized for over two months seemed once again to be at least manageable. Mr. Gusev apparently had received instructions from Moscow to resume participation in the work of the Commission. The waning influence of the Morgenthau Plan in high government circles in Washington plus the president's absence from Washington with illness made the value of the London Commission more apparent to U.S. government officials. In addition, there seemed to be a new willingness in the State-War-Navy Coordinating Committee, successor to WSC, to find agreement on policy guidelines for Germany and to transmit agreed instructions to Winant.

The Working Security Committee was replaced in December, 1944, by the State-War-Navy Coordinating Committee (SWNCC) as the interdepartmental body concerned with the preparation and clearance of papers for the EAC. The new body was created chiefly because the volume and range of problems had increased to such an extent that officials in all three of the departments realized that a more effective body than the WSC was essential. The SWNCC had a broader mandate and functioned at a higher level than WSC. Whereas WSC usually met at the level of divisional chiefs, SWNCC met at the level of assistant secretaries with a regular agenda. Mosely reported in an interview on April 26, 1969, that John J. McCloy gave the Committee great vigor by his ability to cut through petty jurisdictional and other obstacles to action. Though not free of conflicts and logjams, the SWNCC was a vast improvement over the WSC.

The impending surrender or collapse of Germany and the urgent need to have an agreed master plan to put into immediate effect undoubtedly put pressure on the respective governments to get the EAC moving again. After all, several vital tasks which were clearly within the province of EAC remained to be finished. The surrender instrument for Germany had to be amended according to the Yalta formula, the two protocols on Germany had to be amended to provide for French accession, and the protocols for zonal occupation and control of Austria had yet to be completed and approved. In addition, the Commission still had to complete the document containing the basic principles of joint policy for the administration of Germany after the war. Much remained to be done, while the clock fast seemed to be running out.

The April meetings were devoted almost exclusively to work on the Austrian protocols.[26] On May 1 two formal meetings were held, the first to sign the document admitting the French Republic as the fourth participating Power in the Instrument of Unconditional Surrender, the second to approve the document providing for French participation in the control machinery for Germany. The protocol on zones of occupation in Germany still required agreement on a French zone and French Berlin sector before it could be formally amended and approved, this regardless of the fact that Germany might collapse any day.

Washington Instructs Winant

On April 23 Winant at long last received instructions from Washington concerning Berlin. Certainly he had waited long enough. The British proposals had been presented February 28; the French plan had been circulated March 22. Now, a full month later, it was high time that the State Department finally have something to report. The telegram to Winant did not contain any American proposal for delimiting sectors in Berlin. It merely reported the views of the Joint Chiefs of Staff, concurred in by SWNCC, on the British and French proposals. The JCS memorandum noted first the changes the British proposal would make in the original division of the September 12th protocol. It would transfer two Soviet districts to France (Pankow and Prenzlauerberg) and one British district to France (Reinickendorf). It would then transfer one American district (Neukölln) to the U.S.S.R., in order to equalize matters by having each of the Three Powers lose one district. The Joint Chiefs felt that the elimination of Neukölln from the American sector would not reduce either space or facilities below the requirements necessary for the support of U.S. forces.

The JCS found, on the other hand, several things wrong with the informal French proposal. It would amend the original division first by transferring Zehlendorf from the U.S. to the French sector. Such a change would be undesirable, since the U.S. would thereby lose desirable residential areas. Secondly, the French proposal would add the district of Treptow to the U.S. sector at the expense of the Soviet Union. This would also be undesirable, since the rail and storage facilities in Treptow were believed to be essential to the Soviet forces, while they would not be needed by U.S. forces. Taking all these factors into consideration the Joint Chiefs were of the opinion that the British proposal for a new quadripartite division of Berlin was definitely preferable to the French proposal and should be accepted from the U.S. point of view.[27] It is quite likely that the Joint Chiefs were influenced subtly by the British who, with their excellent system of governmental coordination and communication, had probably been able to present their views directly to the Civil Affairs Division of the War Department.[28]

During the month of May, informal EAC meetings were held almost daily. Although all manner of subjects were discussed at these meetings,* there were no negotiations at all concerning either the French zone in Germany or the French sector in Berlin.[29] The proposals and suggestions on these issues which were discussed were exchanged during informal conversations outside the meetings. Various arguments circulated concerning the proposals for a French zone in Germany, but very little was said or done in reference to Berlin. Practically speaking, Berlin had receded into the

---

*The principal subjects discussed at the May meetings were: communication of EAC agreements to other United Nations governments; final agreement on the Declaration of Unconditional Surrender to replace the original instrument; the General Order to be issued to the German people by the commanders in chief; occupation zones and control machinery in Austria.

background as far as priorities were concerned. Many of the other subjects before the EAC, especially the preparation of a Declaration of Unconditional Surrender to replace the original instrument, seemed much more pressing. There was also the feeling that, should it prove necessary, the commanders in Berlin could somehow arrange room for French occupation forces.

A New Reversal of Instructions

At the end of May Ambassador Winant received another reversal of instructions from the Department of State. On May 26 the Joint Chiefs of Staff sent a memorandum to the secretary of state stating that they had reconsidered the British proposal for a reallocation of districts in Berlin.[30] Previously, on April 21, the JCS had notified the secretary that there were no military objections to transferring Neukölln from the American sector to the Soviet sector as proposed in the British plan. Now, however, the JCS had new information based on reports provided by Dr. Mosely and transmitted by Army Signals to the Army Air Staff in Washington by Colonel Williamson, Winant's military air adviser. The reports pointed out that the maps the Joint Chiefs had used in their original evaluation had erroneously placed Tempelhof airfield completely within the district of Tempelhof. In reality the airfield actually was located on the boundary between Tempelhof and Neukölln, with the landing field in Tempelhof and the shops and other facilities in Neukölln. The JCS stated that present plans called for extension of the runway, and such extension would be feasible only to the east and northeast into Neukölln. They concluded therefore that it was essential for United States forces to retain Neukölln, or at least a sufficient portion of Neukölln, in order to permit uninhibited use of the Tempelhof Airdrome and a possible extension of the runways.[31] The text of the JCS memorandum was transmitted to Winant by the acting secretary of state, Joseph C. Grew, on May 31.[32] The new instructions obviously placed Winant in an awkward position vis-à-vis both the British and French proposals. The Joint Chiefs not only found the French proposals unacceptable for a number of reasons but now also found a fatal flaw in the British plan. They had, however, no plan of their own to advance. Fortunately for Mr. Winant, this reversal of instructions did not represent a major setback in his negotiating position for the simple reason that Berlin had not been an active subject of negotiation in EAC during May. The subject of Berlin, in fact, remained in almost total eclipse until the end of June.

Negotiations on the French Occupation Zone

Meanwhile the EAC continued its attempts to find some solution to the thorny problem of carving a French zone of occupation out of the British and American zones. Following the discussions on Austria at the April meetings, the EAC once again turned part of its attention to the problem of a French zone. As noted earlier, however, these negotiations were not carried on at the EAC meetings but were largely bilateral, either Franco-American or Franco-British, since they did not concern the Soviet delegation.[33]

These negotiations go beyond our interests in this book. For our purposes it is important only to note that this set of negotiations was in many ways a repetition of the earlier Anglo-American squabble over occupation of the northwest zone. Once again the American military authorities were almost paranoid in their insistence that adequate guarantees for rights of passage through the French zone to the American zone be negotiated in ironclad agreements with the French government.[34] Again we witness the peculiar paradox of excessive military concern with access rights through Western Allied territory while nothing was being said or done about access rights through Soviet territory to Berlin.

The negotiations on formation of the French zone were not confined to the European Advisory Commission. The United States embassy in Paris and the United States political adviser for Germany, Robert Murphy, attached to SHAEF Headquarters at Versailles, were also vitally involved at various stages. The Americans found their French counterparts at times exasperating. At a dinner on May 14 Gaston Palewski, the director of General de Gaulle's Cabinet, told Murphy that the French government might be willing to make some "concessions" to the Americans concerning the use of Karlsruhe and Mannheim. The suggestion obviously irritated Murphy. The following day he cabled the State Department: "I suggested very tactfully that he shouldn't look at it in that light, because the whole matter consisted of a concession on our part of part of a zone won by the hard fighting of American troops as part of the huge war effort of the United States."[35]

The American and French negotiators tended to view the problem from quite different perspectives. The American desiderata, reflecting the heavy influence of military authorities, were based primarily on logistical considerations, while the attitude of the French government was based fundamentally on political considerations.[36] The major proposal put forward by the American delegation during the negotiations was opposed by Winant, Mosely, and Murphy because it disregarded the major administrative and traditional divisions in Germany.[37] The War Department, however, insisted that the proposal must be agreed to, and the French had little choice but to accept the proposal, with minor revisions. As a result, the states of Baden and Württemberg, both with strong traditions of liberal democracy, were broken up,[38] but at least the French government seemed satisfied with the zone accorded to it.[39]

By July 4 the EAC was able to approve in substance the draft agreement on the French zone of occupation in Germany, subject to checking by a subcommittee of experts. On July 6 the Commission approved the agreement and the report transmitting the agreement to the three governments, with the exception of the last paragraph of the report.[40] The disputed last paragraph contained a statement to the effect that the EAC had not been able to agree on the delimitation of a French sector in Berlin. The amended protocol on zones of occupation in Germany could not be officially approved and signed until some settlement on the Berlin issue had been reached.

Disposal of the Dismemberment Plan

The negotiations on Berlin were actively resumed in late June. Before considering these, however, two other matters should be mentioned: the disposal of the dismemberment issue and the dispute over withdrawal of troops into their respective zones of occupation. It will be recalled that the EAC had been to a large extent immobilized for several weeks after the Yalta Conference because of the confusion created by the decisions to amend the surrender instrument to provide for dismemberment and to create a Committee on Dismemberment (COD) parallel to EAC to study the "procedure for the dismemberment of Germany." The COD never really fulfilled the task given it. From the time of its first meeting on March 7 it subordinated the study of a procedure of dismemberment to a study of the desirability and feasibility of dismemberment as a viable policy alternative, and no concrete studies or proposals were ever submitted to the committee by any of the delegations. The committee was, of course, much influenced by the general assumptions under which EAC had been working since January, 1944, namely, that Germany would be subjected to military occupation on a zonal basis and treated in accordance with unified, tripartitely agreed policies in preparation for ultimate restoration as a peaceful member of the international community.[41]

On March 29 Winant cabled the State Department that Gusev had submitted to the COD a letter which "makes it plain that at this stage his Government is not committed in principle to a policy of dismemberment."[42] Both Winant and the State Department were opposed to dismemberment, but the problem was to convince President Roosevelt of the irrationality of implementing such a policy. Slowly but surely the president seemed to change his mind. On April 10, two days before the president's death, Stettinius cabled Winant that, after considering Winant's March 29 report on the work of the COD, Roosevelt had stated, "I think our attitude should be one of study and postponement of final decision."[43] It now looked as if the State Department might win the day on the issue.

The Committee on Dismemberment held only two formal meetings, in addition to a number of informal conversations. No substantive proposals on the issue of dismemberment were ever discussed. The committee could act only on instructions from the respective governments, and no concrete instructions were ever received. By April Allied armies were marching into Germany and the Nazi regime was in process of collapsing. The Allied heads of state were overburdened in coping with immediate problems on a day-to-day basis. "Dismemberment, which had seemed so attractive a goal at Yalta, remained among the topics which had least urgency."[44]

The absence of a French representative on the COD also contributed to a lack of vigor within the committee. The representatives could only wonder what real value their deliberations might have as long as the French government, with full membership in EAC, had no voice in deciding such an important issue as the dismemberment of the enemy state. Both Winant and Eden worked to bring about agreement on including a French representative, but Gusev stated over and over that the Soviet government could not concur. All during March and the first part of April the French government was unaware of the existence of the committee. On the 11th of April the French government learned informally, apparently through the American embassy in Paris, of the existence of the secret committee. Quite understandably de Gaulle was deeply angered over what he considered was a callous disregard of the vital interests of France. Again the patient, tactful diplomacy of Mr. Massigli, after he had discussed the problems at length with Mosely, helped to assuage de Gaulle's aroused feelings and keep French policy from any abnormal deviations in the course of Allied planning.[45]

In the course of its work the Committee on Dismemberment had prepared, in fulfillment of the Yalta mandate, a revised version of the instrument of surrender which included "dismemberment" as one of the choices open to the victor Powers in the disposition of Germany. Thus in early May, on the eve of Germany's collapse, there existed two versions of the surrender instrument: the one originally approved by EAC in July, 1944, and the one prepared by the COD containing the word "dismemberment." On May 1 the EAC approved a protocol providing for French signature to the original instrument. The Soviet government had not yet, however, authorized Gusev to inform the French of the existence of the alternate instrument, even though the French government knew of it. Consequently, there was no provision for a French signature on the alternate surrender instrument. Faced with the incredibly rapid disintegration of Germany, all four of the representatives on EAC were urgently asking their governments for instructions.

As it turned out, neither of the instruments so painstakingly prepared in London was used. When German forces finally surrendered to the Allies on May 7 and 8, the German generals were required to sign a purely military surrender instrument prepared by SHAEF.[46] An analysis of this confused set of circumstances goes beyond the bounds of this study. Quite naturally, however, the representatives on EAC were highly dismayed, and the Soviet government protested vehemently to London and Washington, demanding to know why the agreed Instrument of Unconditional Surrender had been thrown into the discard. Obviously, the Kremlin suspected some complex and sinister motives in this sudden switch rather than a chain of misunderstandings and mishaps.

Following this scenario the EAC set to work preparing a Declaration Regarding the Defeat of Germany and the Assumption of Supreme Authority with Respect to Germany. The new instrument was to be issued later by the commanders in chief in order to lay down a more adequate legal basis for the military occupation and control of Germany. The document was approved by the EAC on May 12, although work on it had begun even before the defeat of Germany in preparation for the contingency that no German government competent to sign a surrender document would be in existence at the conclusion of hostilities. The new document, simply a redrafting of the agreed Instrument of Unconditional Surrender approved by the EAC on July 12, 1944, contained no reference to the Yalta inserted provision for dismemberment.

Actually, the Soviet government was largely responsible for dumping the last grounds of the dismemberment idea down the drain. In his victory speech to the Soviet people on May 8, Marshal Stalin declared that: "The Soviet Union is celebrating victory, although it does not intend either to dismember or to destroy Germany."[47] On May 10 Winant telegraphed the State Department that the Soviet and British governments, as well as the American delegation to EAC were now in agreement that the word "dismemberment" should not appear in the new declaration. Aside from a few cables by Harry Hopkins from Moscow on the subject, this was the last that was heard about the dismemberment of Germany. That policy alternative was now apparently dead. As things turned out, however, the actual dismemberment of Germany, without formal agreement, began on the day the Allied forces entered German territory without an agreed basis on which to coordinate their policies.

Pursuit of the dismemberment idea had been a costly venture. It had introduced a great deal of confusion and delay into the proceedings of the European Advisory Commission. Mosely states that the "mirage of dismemberment" contributed substantially to the failure of the Allies to work out a consistent and fully agreed plan for the postwar disposition and treatment of Germany, with all the dire results that thereby ensued.[48]

Churchill and Truman: The Great Debate

Dismemberment was not the only matter which slowed down the work of EAC. Another factor which heavily influenced both the tone and content of negotiations and delayed agreement on the French zone and French sector of Berlin was the great debate between Churchill and Truman concerning withdrawal of forces into the previously agreed zones of occupation. The debate began in late April and ended finally in mid-June. It concerned subjects of interest not only to the EAC, namely, whether the agreement on occupation zones would be honored, but other matters that were also to affect profoundly the future history of Europe.

Churchill, evidently basing his thinking on an analysis of post-Yalta Soviet behavior in Eastern Europe and his appraisal of Russian motives and intentions, concluded that at the end of hostilities the Allied armies, which had penetrated deep into what was supposed to be the Soviet zone of occupation, should not withdraw westward to the previously agreed zones of occupation, but should stand firm on the *de facto* line of the ceasefire until such time as agreement had been reached with the Soviet Union on several other outstanding issues. He was convinced that the Russians, as occupants of the chief food producing areas of Germany, should agree to an equitable distribution of available food resources among all four zones. He also felt that occupation of the eastern areas could be used for bargaining purposes with the Soviet Union to ensure that the Yalta agreements were carried out and that Soviet policy in Germany remained in harmony with that of the Western Allies.[49] Churchill saw the continued occupation of East Germany by Western forces as a golden opportunity to exert pressure on the Soviet Union to refrain from sovietizing all of Eastern Europe.

Churchill's idea naturally placed in jeopardy the work of the European Advisory Commission by casting doubt upon whether the agreement on zones of occupation would be honored by the Western Powers. In his telegram of April 18 to President Truman, Churchill stated, somewhat inaccurately, "These occupational zones were outlined rather hastily at Quebec in September 1944 when it was not foreseen that General Eisenhower's armies would make such a mighty inroad into Germany."[50] If, however, Churchill's suggestion to remain in the eastern areas were adopted, there was a definite possibility that it would set in motion a process of bargaining and counterbargaining which might ultimately upset completely the agreement on zones of occupation. More seriously, however, the postwar world would begin with an act of bad faith by the Western Allies, which might even cause the general public in the Western nations to lose faith in their leaders. The Soviet government would be justified in disregarding the tenuous promises to which the Western Powers were trying to hold it. The United Nations might be torpedoed before the Charter was even signed, and the Soviet government would be free to take whatever actions it wished in Asia at the same time that the American military leaders were stressing the necessity of bringing Russia into the war against Japan.

The issue was vital also to the fate of Berlin. The Red Army finally conquered Berlin in ferocious fighting in the early days of May. If the Western Powers refused to withdraw from the eastern areas allotted to the Soviet Union in the zones agreement, the Soviet Union would most assuredly refuse the Western Powers any presence in Berlin. With Berlin completely under the control of the Soviet army, how was the quadripartite control of

Germany to be carried out? The entire complex of control machinery, according to the agreements, was to be located in Berlin, while the city itself was to be under Four Power occupation. Indeed, the very fact of continued Soviet control of the capital would have far-reaching psychological consequences for Germany and all Europe.

Upon receipt of Churchill's telegram, President Truman immediately asked the State Department for a statement of its views. Stettinius' reply of April 21 left no doubt as to where the State Department stood on the matter:

> Certain implications in the message are disturbing. The zones of occupation for Germany were the subject of long and careful study and negotiation. They were definitely and formally agreed upon by the American, British and Soviet Governments just prior to the Yalta Conference. ... The fact that the Russian zone contained the greater portion of German food producing areas, and that the zone the British sought and obtained was a deficit area was well known throughout the negotiations. The formal acceptance by the three Governments of their zones of occupation was in no way made contingent upon the conclusion of satisfactory arrangements for an equitable distribution of available German food resources. A position taken by this Government (or the British Government) of refusal to withdraw to the agreed boundaries of its own zone pending either (a) some modification of agreed zone boundaries or (b) an agreement on more equitable food distribution would, in the Department's opinion, have serious consequences. The Russians would certainly consider such a bargaining position as a repudiation of our formal agreement and the resultant Soviet course of action would be difficult to foresee. ... The Department of State believes that every effort should be made through the Allied Control Commission to obtain a fair interzonal distribution of food produced in Germany but does not believe that the matter of retirement to our zone frontiers should be used for such bargaining purposes.[51]

Both Winant and Mosely concurred in the views expressed by the State Department and maintained a vigorous opposition to Churchill's proposal. Winant sent several urgent telegrams to the president during May imploring him to reject the proposal. Both Winant and Mosely were convinced that Churchill's proposed course of action would destroy the basis of Allied confidence as well as the fabric of all the agreements which had been so painstakingly negotiated.[52]

Even though Truman's telegrams to Churchill in late April and early May represented a definite negative response to Churchill's proposal, the prime minister continued to press his recommendations and to spell out the deeper reasons for his ideas in telegrams to Truman during May. On May 11 he cabled:

> The proposed withdrawal of the United States Army to the occupational lines which were arranged with the Russians and Americans in Quebec and

which were marked in yellow on the maps we studied there, would mean the tide of Russian domination sweeping forward 120 miles on a front of 300 or 400 miles. This would be an event which, if it occurred, would be one of the most melancholy in history. . . .

It is just about time that these formidable issues were examined between the principal powers as a whole. We have several powerful bargaining counters on our side, the use of which might make for a peaceful agreement. First, the Allies ought not to retreat from their present positions to the occupational line until we are satisfied about Poland and also about the temporary character of the Russian occupation of Germany, and the conditions to be established in the Russianised or Russian-controlled countries in the Danube valley particularly Hungary, Austria and Czechoslovakia and the Balkans.[53]

Despite the compelling reasons given by Churchill to substantiate his position, Truman still would not agree.

The Debate Reaches EAC

The debate was by no means confined to the two heads of government. By mid-May it had become a vital issue among the military authorities and in the EAC. In the EAC the debate appeared in a slightly modified form. Here it concerned Winant's proposal that the four Allied commanders in chief meet in Berlin in early June to sign and issue the declaration of surrender. The crux of the proposal was that upon signature of the declaration, the four Allied representatives would *ipso facto* constitute the Control Council and begin the establishment of the control machinery. It would then be the task of the Control Council to decide upon the procedures and dates of the withdrawal of forces to the prescribed zones of occupation and the entry of Western garrisons into Berlin. It is evident that underlying Winant's proposal was the administration's conviction that a Western presence must be established in Berlin at the earliest possible moment. Unless the Western Powers were able to get into Berlin somehow, no control machinery would be set up, no agreed policies for the uniform treatment of Germany could be executed, and there would be a rapid consolidation of mutually exclusive zones of occupation, or in other words, a *de facto* partitioning of Germany.

Once in EAC the debate also vitally concerned the Soviet government. At the meeting of May 29 Gusev strenuously expressed objections to Winant's proposal.[54] He pointed out, quite rightly, that Article 6 of the September 12 protocol on zones of occupation provided for that protocol to come into force upon the signature by Germany of the surrender instrument. Consequently, in his opinion, the protocol on zones was now in force. Why were the Western forces not already withdrawing to their assigned zones? Gusev continued that Paragraph 2 of the November 14 agreement on control machinery strongly implied to him that the establishment of the control machinery would take place after the occupation of the assigned zones had been completed.* In any case, he did not believe that the four commanders in chief could constitute the Control Council unless the agreement on control machinery had been declared in force by the date of their meeting.

Gusev's arguments were difficult for Winant to rebut, since they seemed to be legally sound. Winant could merely point out in reply that the gradual establishment of the control machinery and the movement of the Allied forces into their respective zones and into the joint Greater Berlin zone would require an extraordinary amount of close coordination on the part of the commanders in chief. Such coordination could most usefully develop if the commanders met soon in Berlin and thereafter sat together as the prescribed Control Council.

By this time the issue was much more than an argument between Churchill and Truman. Now it concerned the vital interests of all four governments. On May 30 Winant telegraphed the State Department that he had discussed his proposal with Eden and had emphasized the necessity of getting the control machinery operating in Berlin without attempting first to decide the timing of withdrawal of the U.S. and U.K. forces into their zones. He stressed the point that using slow withdrawal for bargaining purposes at the planned meeting of the Big Three "would depend not only on the timing of the withdrawal but on the timing of that meeting; except with grave risk to the Big Three in cooperation in Germany, the delay in that withdrawal could not be longer than could be justified on military and logistical grounds." Winant then reported that Eden had finally adopted his point of view on the question and had also "brought Strang in line."[55]

Western Commanders Arrive in Berlin

Having gotten Strang's agreement on his proposal, Winant continued to press for French and Soviet approval. Finally, on June 4, Gusev informed the Commission that the Soviet government could now agree. The four military commanders met in Berlin on June 5 to formally sign and issue the Declaration Regarding the Defeat of Germany and the Assumption of Supreme Authority with Respect to Germany by the Governments of the United States, the Union of Soviet Socialist Republics, and the United Kingdom, and the Provisional Government of the French Republic. Simul-

---

*Article 2 of the Agreement on Control Machinery in Germany reads: "Each Commander-in-Chief in his zone of occupation will have attached to him military, naval, and air representatives of the other two Commanders-in Chief for liaison duties." *F. R. U. S., Conferences at Malta and Yalta*, pp. 124–125. For Gusev the key phrase was probably "in his zone of occupation." The presence of this phrase in the sentence could logically be taken to imply that each commander in chief would be in occupation of "his zone of occupation" by the time the whole apparatus of control machinery had begun to operate.

taneously two statements, both prepared by EAC, were issued to notify the Germans officially of the protocols now applicable to them: a Statement on Zones of Occupation in Germany and a Statement on Control Machinery in Germany.

The meeting of June 5 was the Western commanders' first opportunity to see with their own eyes the proud capital now reduced to ashes, the city which would serve as headquarters of a military occupation regime. Berlin on June 5, 1945, was a shocking sight to see. General Clay gives a moving description of the ride from the airport to the headquarters of the Soviet High Command:

> Wherever we looked we saw desolation. The streets were piled high with debris which left in many places only a narrow one-way passage between high mounds of rubble, and frequent detours had to be made where bridges and viaducts were destroyed. Apparently the Germans along the route, which was lined with Soviet soldiers, had been ordered to remain indoors, and it was only at intersections that a few could be seen on the streets which crossed our route. They seemed weak, cowed, and furtive and not yet recovered from the shock of the Battle of Berlin. It was like a city of the dead. I had seen nothing quite comparable in western Germany, and I must confess that my exultation in victory was diminished as I witnessed this degradation of man. I decided then and there never to forget that we were responsible for the government of human beings.[56]

At the June 5 meeting Marshal Georgy Zhukov, the commander in chief of the Soviet Forces of Occupation in Germany, made it abundantly clear that disposition of the troops into their respective zones was a Soviet *sine qua non* to the operation of the Control Council.[57] On June 6 Robert Murphy, the United States political adviser for Germany, cabled the secretary of state: "I feel that we witnessed yesterday a Soviet effort to bargain for the removal of our forces from the zone which has been approved by the governments as theirs. In that respect their position seems to be sound."[58]

General Eisenhower also added his recommendation to the list of those urging President Truman not to delay withdrawal for bargaining purposes. On June 6 he telegraphed the Joint Chiefs that: ". . . the fact remains that there is some justification for Zhukov's position that he is unable to discuss administrative problems in Germany when he is still not in control and hence not familiar with the problems of the zone for which he will eventually be responsible. As a result of my discussion with Zhukov I am optimistic that the Russians will join in some form of control machinery when withdrawal is accomplished and will agree to our forces entering into Berlin concurrently with our withdrawal from their zone."[59]

On June 7 Harry Hopkins met with General Eisenhower in Frankfurt for a discussion of the problems involved in dealing with the Russians as the military government of Germany was set up. He fully agreed with Eisenhower that delay in the withdrawal would be unwise. After the meeting he sent a telegram to President Truman stating his judgment:

> I am convinced that present indeterminate status of date for withdrawal of Allied troops from area assigned to the Russians is certain to be misunderstood by Russia as well as at home.
>
> It is manifest that Allied control machinery cannot be started until Allied troops have withdrawn from territory included in the Russian area of occupation. Any delay in the establishment of control machinery interferes seriously with the development of governmental administrative machinery for Germany and with the application of Allied policy in Germany. . . . Delays now may make withdrawal at a later date appear to have resulted from Russian pressure. I urge that prompt action be taken to dispose of this issue.[60]

Churchill Continues His Quest

There were apparently no high administration officials in Washington urging Truman to use delay in withdrawal for bargaining purposes. The fact, however, that official Washington seemed to be in agreement with the president did not solve the fundamental difference with the British government. Churchill was strongly convinced that early withdrawal could lead to a disastrous wreckage of Allied policy in Germany and Europe, and he used all the power of his mind and language to convince Truman that his judgment was correct. On June 4 he cabled the president: "I view with profound misgivings the retreat of the American Army to our line of occupation in the Central Sector, thus bringing Soviet power into the heart of Western Europe and the descent of an iron curtain between us and everything to the eastward.

"I hoped that this retreat, if it has to be made, would be accompanied by the settlement of many great things which would be the true foundation of world peace. Nothing really important has been settled yet you and I will have to bear great responsibility for the future."[61]

Churchill hoped to persuade Truman to delay troop withdrawals at least until discussions could be carried out by the Big Three in person at the forthcoming Potsdam Conference in July. He was also concerned about the increasingly tight Soviet control over Berlin and was inclined to doubt that the Soviet authorities would permit a Western military entry into Berlin simultaneously with Western withdrawal from the Soviet zone. The difficulties encountered by General Flory on his reconnaissance mission to Vienna convinced the prime minister even more strongly that the Soviet government was intending to sovietize Eastern Europe as rapidly as possible and would use any possible means to achieve this goal.

The EAC had been unable for several weeks to reach agreement on zones of occupation in Vienna because of Soviet insistence that only the smaller pre-1938 city of Vienna should be divided, not the Greater Vienna area of 1945. The Russians also insisted that their zone in Vienna should be enlarged to include considerably more territory than they had originally proposed, owing to the vast destruction in the area originally proposed. After considerable difficulty and delay the Western governments finally persuaded Stalin to allow an Anglo-French-American military reconnaissance mission to travel to Vienna in order to survey facilities in the city. The information gathered by the mission was to be used not only to help the Western governments formulate equitable proposals on zones in Vienna, but also to assist the European Advisory Commission in reaching a speedy agreement. After General Flory's arrival in Vienna on June 4, he was informed that the mission would not be allowed to inspect any airfields east of the Danube River and was expected to leave Vienna by June 10. These circumstances prompted Churchill to state the following in a telegram to Truman on June 9:

> "Here is the capital of Austria which by agreement is to be divided, like the country itself, into four zones: but no one has any powers there except the Russians and not even ordinary diplomatic rights are allowed. If we give way in this matter, we must regard Austria as in the Sovietized half of Europe." (See *F. R. U.S., 1945–III*, p. 132.)

Churchill sent another urgent telegram to Truman in early June imploring him to delay the withdrawal of American troops from the Soviet zone.[62] Truman had, however, by this time definitely made up his mind that that policy alternative was unwise and would have to be rejected. On June 11 he informed Churchill that:

> In consideration of the tripartite agreement as to zones of occupation in Germany approved by President Roosevelt after long consideration and detailed discussion with you, I am unable to delay the withdrawal of American troops from the Soviet zone in order to use pressure in the settlement of other problems.
> Advice of the highest reliability is received that the Allied Control Council cannot begin to function until Allied troops withdraw from the Russian zone.
> I am advised that it would be highly disadvantageous to our relations with the Soviets to postpone action in this matter until our meeting in July.[63]

The debate was now clearly at an end, and Truman had won for better or worse. Churchill was left with no choice. On June 14 he replied to Truman: "Obviously we are obliged to conform to your decision, and necessary instructions will be issued. . . . I sincerely hope that your action will in the long run make for a lasting peace in Europe."[64]

The same day Truman cabled Marshal Stalin proposing that the two heads of state issue orders to their commanders in chief to begin withdrawal into their respective zones on June 21. These arrangements should include "simultaneous movement of the national garrisons into Greater Berlin and provision of free access by air, road, and rail, from Frankfurt and Bremen to Berlin for U.S. forces."[65] Stalin replied that the troop movements should be postponed until July 1, since Berlin had not yet been cleared of mines and Marshal Zhukov, commander in chief of the Soviet Forces of Occupation, would have to be in Moscow in late June for a session of the Supreme Soviet.[66] His telegram made no mention of simultaneous entry of Western forces into Berlin or of access. It could only be assumed or hoped that his idea of the troop movements included appropriate provisions for these matters. In a message to Stalin dated June 18, Truman stated that he had issued instructions to the American commanders to begin their redeployment on July 1.[67] The troop redeployments took place July 1–5, with the leading elements of the United States 2nd Armored Division entering Berlin on July 4. Considerable difficulties and delays were experienced by General Parks in getting some of the troops through to Berlin. And once there, military possession of the American sector of occupation had to be accomplished in part simply by ousting Soviet personnel and confronting the Soviet military administration with a *fait accompli*.[68] Token French forces accompanied American and British forces to Berlin, even though the French sector of the city had not yet been agreed to.

Power and Law: Differing Perspectives of Churchill and Truman

It is perhaps impossible to come to any valid historical judgment as to the wisdom of the alternative courses desired by Churchill and Truman. We know which course was chosen and what the results of that choice were. As with any historical event, we cannot turn back the clock and view the results that would have come about had the opposite choice been made. We know now, of course, that many of Churchill's gloomy predictions about Soviet domination of Eastern Europe came to pass. What we cannot know is how differently things would have turned out had the Western Allies delayed the withdrawal of their forces in order to bargain with the Soviet Union.

Churchill felt that by withdrawing forces promptly a golden opportunity was being lost to pressure the Soviet Union into keeping the Yalta agreements and into keeping her policies in Germany in some kind of balance with those of the Western Powers. Truman, together with Hopkins, Winant, Eisenhower, and others, was convinced that delayed withdrawal would work only to destroy a basis of confidence with the Soviet Union and thereby render difficult if not impossible a workable cooperation with the Soviet government in operating the machinery of control and working out uniform policies in the Control Council for the treatment of Germany.

The debate arose in part from the differing perspectives from which the two leaders approached the problem. Churchill's perspective was deeply political in nature and content, stressing the factors of pressure, influence, and coercion in bringing about a desired outcome. Truman's perspective, on the other hand, rested more upon a legal basis and stressed such factors as observance of prior agreements, the setting up of legally constituted organs, and development of a minimum level of international confidence as a basis of a new legal order in the postwar era. These differing perspectives may illustrate to some extent the differences between law and power as conceptual bases from which international phenomena can be viewed.

The telegrams from the State Department to Ambassador Winant characteristically emphasized setting up the control machinery and implementing the EAC agreements as the matters of highest priority. Consider, for example, the department's telegram of June 9 to the ambassador in Italy, similar in every respect to the telegrams to Winant. The telegram states that the "Dept considers our main objective in Austria now to be completion and entry into force of the formal EAC agreements for zoning and control machinery which would assure us full equality of authority as well as responsibility."[69] Since the situation in Austria forms a close parallel to the situation in Germany, the telegram can be considered a valid example of the department's ordering of priorities. What is striking is that the objective to be achieved is the completion and entry into force of the agreements. An underlying assumption of this point of view is that the agreements, once in force, will be a more significant regulator of international behavior than any measures of coercion or power politics. The department and the president wanted most of all to get the agreements declared in force and the machinery set up and operating smoothly. Once this was accomplished, they assumed that a requisite level of international confidence would have been established so as to enable the Four Powers to work together successfully in carrying out the agreements. Confidence is, of course, the backbone of law and of any legal order. Truman felt that until and unless a level of minimum confidence was established among the Great Powers, no arrangements for a postwar order could work. Coercion and power plays were bound to fail. Only in scrupulously carrying out carefully negotiated agreements was there any hope. If the Western Powers were to fail to carry out the agreements or should they threaten to do so by delaying the withdrawal of forces into the agreed zones, there would never be a basis for reliable postwar cooperation. It was the "entry into force of the formal EAC agreements" which "would assure us full equality of authority as well as responsibility."[70] This is essentially a legal point of view.

Such a point of view can be contrasted sharply with that propounded by Churchill. The prime minister was little interested in the entry into force of agreements which, as he pointed out, were "outlined rather hastily at Quebec," at a different period of time and in different circumstances. He apparently felt that such international agreements could effectively determine the nature and shape of the postwar order only to the extent that one or more of the nations possessed sufficient bargaining power to ensure their proper enforcement. Churchill showed little enthusiasm for the agreements or the machinery *per se*. Agreements or machinery meant nothing unless backed by sufficient will and power to make them work. As he pointed out in his telegram of April 18, he was "quite prepared to adhere to occupational zones." But he did "not wish our Allied troops or your American troops to be hustled back at any point by some crude assertion of a local Russian General."[71] There is no evidence that Churchill wished to scrap the agreement on zones of occupation. The telegram of April 18 states precisely the opposite. What Churchill did wish to do was pressure the Soviet government, bargain with it, persuade, induce, or perhaps even coerce it to keep the Yalta agreements and align its policies in Germany with those of the Western Powers. He felt that the bargaining position of the Western Powers was relatively advantageous, since Western forces had overrun a substantial portion of the Soviet zone. It would be a waste not to use this bargaining position to maximum advantage.

Truman stressed the efficacy and value of written agreements, properly carried out, while Churchill stressed the efficacy and value of power and of a bargaining position. Truman's perspective was oriented more toward a legal basis conceptually, while Churchill's perspective was oriented more toward a political basis. There were, of course, two different views of the interests involved. To some extent, moreover, interests were divergent. There were also certain vested interests which had to be protected. Both Winant and Mosely agreed with the president that withdrawal must not be delayed, that the agreements should be declared in force and the control machinery set up as soon as possible. The members of the American delegation to EAC were undoubtedly sincere in their views. They were also, however unconsciously, protecting the prestige of the Commission and the results of many months of laborious effort. Certainly it would have been contrary to their interests to find that the agreements were not carried out. This could mean only that the EAC was a failure and that the many months of painstaking negotiations at Lancaster House had been a meaningless effort and a waste of time. Quite naturally, Winant and Mosely were protecting their own interests and the prestige of their work by urging the president to implement immediately both of the agreements on Germany. More fundamentally, however, both Winant and Mosely shared the president's conceptual approach to postwar relationships. They felt very strongly that if the Western Allies publicly and dramatically scrapped the few weak agreements that had been so laboriously worked out with the Russians, the United States would be committing itself to a posture based simply on force in the postwar period, giving the Russians adequate reason to believe that they could never rely on the United States to keep promises or abide by treaty commitments. Winant and Mosely were also convinced that it would be extremely difficult to explain to British and American publics that violation of wartime agreements was the best way to guarantee orderly procedures and a rule of law in postwar relations among the wartime Allies.[72]

Whether or not Churchill's proposal would have been the wiser course is a question we cannot answer here. It is likely that the judgments of historians will remain in conflict for a long time to come. It can, however, fairly be said that Truman's decision was perhaps based too heavily on simplistic legal considerations without taking into account the broader political implications. On the other hand, it can be asserted with equal validity that Churchill's view, while realistic in its assessment of the political factors and grand in its sweep of historical perspective, was not sufficiently pruned and sharpened by certain key legal considerations, such as the prompt observation of agreements and the building of confidence, which are the cornerstones of any legal or political order. An analysis of the two views is instructive, at any rate, in demonstrating the danger inherent in viewing international phenomena either too strongly in terms of power politics or of cold law. In this situation, as elsewhere in the international arena, the problem at hand involved considerations both of law and of politics and should have been analyzed from both perspectives at once. To demand such balanced judgments from statesmen in times of extreme crisis is, however, asking perhaps more than realistically should be expected.

A Proposal Not to Propose

Once the dismemberment issue had been laid to rest and once it was certain that the Western forces would begin withdrawal to the agreed zones of occupation on July 1 with simultaneous movement to Berlin, the European Advisory Commission once again turned its attention to the problem of delimiting a French sector of occupation in Berlin. As noted above, the Commission, in the course of its deliberations on the formation of a French zone in Germany, had considered various British and French proposals for a division of Berlin into four parts. No agreement was reached, and the subject had scarcely been discussed at all since late May. What discussion had been held took place outside of EAC meetings in informal contacts among delegations.

Toward the end of June a suggestion was made that the EAC decline to determine a new division of Berlin into four parts, since it would be manifestly impossible to make such a division without full knowledge of local conditions.[73] Since EAC lacked this knowledge, it was suggested that rather than attempt the unwise, the Commission should merely state in its report transmitting the amended agreement on zones that no new division of Berlin had been decided upon. The suggestion proposed that the draft report read as follows: "In view of the physical conditions prevailing in the area of Greater Berlin, the Commission has not attempted to delineate an area in Greater Berlin to be occupied by forces of the French Republic. It recommends that the four Govts instruct their respective Commanders in Chief in Germany, acting jointly, to determine the area in Greater Berlin to be assigned to occupation by forces of the French Republic."[74]

The proposed draft paragraph may have represented a victory for the American military authorities. If adopted by EAC, it would place the task of redividing Greater Berlin squarely in the hands of the military commanders, which is precisely where the Civil Affairs Division of the War Department believed such authority should have been placed from the start. On the other hand, it is possible that certain members of the Commission were not averse to abdicating their authority on this issue because of the many complex problems involved. If the EAC could manage to complete a new quadripartite zonal division of Germany and at the same time leave the division of Berlin in the hands of the military commanders, it could be said to have completed its work successfully, even though it had passed the hottest potato of all on to other hands. Most probably, however, as noted below, the draft paragraph represented a Western effort to transfer the question to a level where its outcome might be decided more favorably for the West. (See Annex 10 for further proposals regarding the last paragraph of the report.)

On June 28 Winant reported to the State Department that, although the French government was willing to approve the draft paragraph, the French representative on EAC feared that failure to define the French area in Berlin in the agreement might mean that French forces would not be able to enter Berlin with U.S. and U.K. forces. The Soviet government might insist that French forces wait until the French Berlin area had been defined. Comte de Leusse, Massigli's assistant, was asking assurance that the U.S. military authorities were planning to include a French contingent with the Allied forces which would first enter the city.[75] The State Department answered Winant the following day that the War Department was giving serious consideration to the French request and that instructions would follow as soon as possible.[76]

The Soviet Delegate Balks

The draft paragraph was first discussed at the June 29 meeting.[77] Gusev began the debate by announcing to his colleagues that he presumed that the three commanders in chief would agree that the determination of a French area in Berlin was not the concern of the Soviet commander. Strang's assistant, Viscount Samuel Hood, immediately took issue with the Soviet representative by saying that surely this was a matter concerning all four commanders. Comte de Leusse then observed that the French delegation would accept the paragraph, since it was evident that the EAC did not have sufficient information regarding actual conditions in Berlin. He was certain that the four commanders would have to settle the issue. In reply Gusev pointed out that the Commission had had even less information when it had reached the first agreement on Berlin in the fall of 1944. His delegation liked the decision made at that time and felt that the question of a French zone did not concern the Soviet commander in chief.

Gusev's statement, of course, pointed up some of the holes in the argument put forth by the Western delegations. The Western hesitancy to decide the issue because of a lack of sufficient information was not only a weak argument, but also patently an attempt to transfer the issue to the military level for decision, where it was hoped the military commanders would have more leverage to bargain with the Soviets over space for the French in Berlin. This was also the reason for the desire of the Western delegations to include the draft paragraph in the report transmitting the amended agreement on zones to the four governments.

Even if the Western delegations had obtained Gusev's agreement to include the draft paragraph, there still would have remained the crucial issue of how many commanders would decide the question—three or four. This issue was fundamental, because if the Soviet commander were excluded from the decision, this would naturally mean that none of the territory of the French sector would be taken from the Soviet sector.

In an attempt to prod Gusev on the matter, Lord Hood said that he presumed the three commanders in chief would not want to make a recommendation which might involve an alteration in the Soviet zone without the participation of the Soviet commander. That is why it was essential for the Soviet commander to be involved. Gusev, refusing to give an inch, replied that although the Soviet commander would surely be prepared to give any information or advice, the question of the allocation of a French zone in Berlin was the same as that of the allocation of a French zone in Germany. Gusev meant, of course, that the French sector in Berlin would have to be taken entirely from the British and American sectors, leaving the Soviet sector unchanged.

While the EAC was intently discussing the draft paragraph on June 29, another meeting was being held in Berlin at Marshal Zhukov's headquarters. Present were the marshal and his chief deputies; General Lucius Clay and U.S. representatives; and Lieutenant General Sir Ronald Weeks, the deputy British military governor, and his assistants. At this meeting all the technical arrangements were made for the withdrawal of the Western troops to the western zones and the entry of Western troops into Berlin. It was decided that withdrawal should begin July 1 and should be completed within four days. Western troops would move into Berlin on July 4th, the last day of the withdrawal from the Soviet zone. Much of the discussion at this meeting concerned the routes of access to be utilized in the move to Berlin. A fuller discussion of the meeting appears in the following chapter.

At the EAC meeting of June 30 Mr. Gusev inquired what the French contingent would do upon arrival in Berlin in view of the fact that the city was still divided into only three parts, not four. Comte de Leusse replied that he thought one of the other Powers might provide temporary accommodations in its zone for the French forces pending final agreement on the French area. In reply to Gusev's insistence that there be some definite agreement on that issue, Lord Hood observed that Gusev's desire pointed to the urgency of reaching an early agreement on the four sectors of the city, and the quickest way of obtaining such agreement would be to turn the question over to the four commanders in chief. He assumed that agreement on the French area in Berlin would be reached before the full complement of French forces actually arrived in the city. Comte de Leusse then reminded the Commission that his delegation obviously was most concerned with this problem and that his delegation was strongly convinced that the matter could be handled most expeditiously by referring it to the commanders in chief on the spot. When it became evident that no progress on the matter could be achieved, the meeting was simply adjourned.[78]

The Negotiations on Vienna

The French sector in Berlin was only one of several issues being discussed in the EAC at the time. Ever since mid-April the Commission had been devoting a great deal of its time and attention to the task of delimiting the zones of occupation in Austria and Vienna. These negotiations are beyond the purview of this study. It is relevant, however, to point out, by way of comparison with the Berlin negotiations, a few of the salient features of the negotiations on Vienna. It must be remembered, first of all, that the setting for the Vienna negotiations was quite different from that for the Berlin negotiations. The city of Vienna was liberated by the Red Army before the negotiations on Vienna were even begun in EAC. The Berlin negotiations, on the other hand, had originally been completed long before the Allied armies set foot on German soil. This situation made it perhaps inevitable that the character of the Vienna negotiations would be quite different from that of the Berlin negotiations.

With the Red Army in physical occupation of Vienna, and after May 8 of Berlin also, it became obvious to the Western delegations to EAC that there were some major gaps in the agreements on Germany and Berlin. As noted earlier, the agreements contained no provisions for access to Berlin. And it will be recalled that at the meeting of July 17, 1944, the Western delegations had made a concession to the Soviet delegation that no paragraph providing for joint use of important facilities in Berlin would be included in the German agreement.

Attempts to Fill In the Gaps

It is evident that during the Vienna negotiations some members of Western delegations were having second thoughts about the Berlin situation. On July 2 the U.S. delegation submitted a new version of a draft paragraph which the Western delegations insisted must be included in the report transmitting to the governments the agreement on zones of occupation in Austria. The paragraph stated: "The Commission assumes that the efficient operation of Allied occupation in Austria requires freedom of transit throughout

Austria by road, rail, air and water, for the goods and supplies required by the forces of occupation in Austria, including those forces allotted for the occupation of Vienna, and by the Allied Commission, and likewise common use of transport and communication facilities and public utility services in the City of Vienna. The Commission considers that the regulation of the common use of such facilities is a function of the Allied Council."[79]

In pressing for the inclusion of this paragraph in the report accompanying the Austrian agreement, it can be fairly presumed that the Western delegations hoped that the principles of free access and joint use of facilities would have to apply to Berlin as well as Vienna. The discussion at the EAC meetings in late June and early July bear this out. While discussing the situation in Vienna, repeated references were made to Berlin by the Western negotiators, and oftentimes the phrase "Vienna and Berlin" was used in the presentation of arguments for the necessity of such a paragraph. In a very real sense the discussions on Austria and Vienna, particularly on the draft paragraph above, represent a sort of last-ditch effort by the Western delegations to fill in some of the gaps in the Berlin agreements, even if only by analogy.

At the meeting of July 6 Gusev informed his Western colleagues that he had carefully studied the American formula to be included in the report transmitting the Austrian agreement, but had concluded that nothing should be included in the report with respect to the matter. Lord Hood countered that even though the principles of free transit and common use of facilities might be obvious to all the members of EAC, they might not be so obvious to others not sitting in on the discussions. He felt there certainly should be no harm in stating the obvious.

Gusev replied that he had previously pointed out that the principles stated in the paragraph "naturally must apply," but there were also a number of other questions which would have to be considered by the Allied Council which were not included. That was the reason for not including these provisions in the report. They should be left to the Allied Council. "I suggest that we could put off consideration of these principles until the Commanders have had experience in applying these principles in Berlin."[80]

Gusev's comments point up the fact that the Berlin problem formed a sort of backdrop for the negotiations on Vienna. They also point to the fact that the Soviet government wished to stand pat on the matter. Such provisions had not been included in the German agreements in reference to Berlin, and the Soviet delegation did not think it necessary to include them now in the Austrian agreements for Vienna. If such measures as free access and joint use of facilities were implemented to a great extent by the commanders in Berlin, now that the Western troops had recently entered the city, there was every reason to believe they would also be implemented in Vienna when the Western forces were sent to occupy that city. However, if such principles were not widely or freely observed in Berlin, it would not be wise, from the Soviet viewpoint, to have them written into the Austrian agreements.

Gusev Stands Firm

In the further discussion of July 6 Gusev refused to be budged. He often resorted to the diplomatic device of replying to questions with comments which seemed slightly to miss the point. At any rate, however, he refused to assent to any agreement that would have the effect of making these principles official recommendations of the EAC. Part of the discussion is reproduced below, since it is not only historically very important, but also highly instructive for purposes of analysis:

Massigli: If the question had never been raised it could be settled by the Allied Council. But, the question having been raised, I am profoundly convinced that the omission of a statement of the principles by the EAC is an admission that the principles are not accepted by the Allied Powers.

Gousev: That is not the case. My proposal is that the EAC has recommended leaving this question to the Allied Council.

Lord Hood: Do you, by inference, Your Excellency, accept my formula of July 4? [Identical in all major respects to the American formula of July 2.]

Gousev: I say that this particular paragraph should not be included in the covering report. It must be left to the consideration of the Allied Council.

Massigli: Could you accept sending these principles as a specific recommendation in a separate letter which would not be included in the covering report? . . .

Gousev: I have in mind that each Delegate should communicate to his Government the proposals as made here and discuss what took place so that each Government will be fully informed.

Massigli: This means that the principle is not even recommended to the Governments. . . .

Gousev: Each of us can report independently to his Government. It is obvious that this must be brought to the notice of the Governments since it has been brought up in the EAC. Regarding the actual discussion, each of us will report the form in which the discussion appeared to him. . . .

Lord Hood: It is not in effect the practical arrangements but the question of free transit that we are discussing here . . . the Chairman has said that we have been proceeding on the assumption that we accept these principles. Unless the EAC has been proceeding on a false assumption, I cannot see that any Delegate would have any difficulty in agreeing on any formula which includes acceptance of these principles.

Mosely: If we were to recommend the report without any reference anywhere to the extent to which we are agreed, it might, as M. Massigli has pointed out, leave the presumption that the principle really was rejected. . . .

Lord Hood: The difficulty which the Soviet Representative finds in including the statement that the principles are accepted by the four Governments awakens suspicion in my mind that our discussion hitherto has proceeded on false assumptions. If that is the case, I am not sure we can carry

NEGOTIATIONS IN 1945

on this discussion any further in the EAC. We may have to use other channels to clear up the matter.

Gousev: What false assumptions have you in mind? I have stated more than once that the EAC cannot settle all questions for the Allied Council. . . . If we consider the Agreement on the Zones of Austria from a strict viewpoint, all these questions have really nothing to do with zones. We have drafted an Agreement on the Zones in Austria and on the areas in Vienna, but if each one of our Delegations makes all kinds of proposals we will never be able to reach an agreement. . . .[81]

A careful reading of the discussion discloses that the situation in Berlin was very present in the minds of the negotiators as they discussed Vienna. Lord Hood's comments reveal that by this time the Allies were deeply suspicious of Soviet motives in Vienna. There was also a fear that the arrangements made so long ago for Berlin might not work well, that there really would not be freedom of movement and free access to all facilities and services in the city, and that the sectors might become mutually exclusive regimes. The fact that the entire conversation concerns Berlin as well as Vienna is clearly demonstrated by one of the statements made to the Commission by Mosely on July 4: "The July 2 U.S. draft does not lay down instructions or recommendations. It merely states the assumption of freedom of transit under which the EAC has conducted its deliberations. This draft is for the purpose of informing the Governments and the Commanders-in-Chief in *Germany and Austria* as to the assumptions made by the EAC. . . ."[82]

It is interesting to note that Mosely said the commanders "in Germany and Austria," not merely "the commander in Austria." In other words, the assumption of freedom of transit under which the EAC had conducted its deliberations should apply to both Germany and Austria, to Berlin and Vienna, even though no mention of such a principle was made in any of the agreements on Germany or in the covering reports transmitting those agreements to the governments. There can be no doubt that at this late stage of the game the Western delegations were not only making a hard-nosed effort to get these principles stated in some form in the covering report transmitting the Austrian protocol on zones, but were also attempting to fill in the gaps in the protocol on Germany. If the assumption applied to the EAC deliberations on Vienna, it applied also to Berlin, at least by analogy. This point might be useful to the Western Powers in legal argumentation with the Soviet Union later; it might also serve as a point of reference in planning political policy.

Disputes Over the French Berlin Sector

Following the extensive discussion of the covering report to the Austrian protocol at the July 6 meeting, the delegates once again turned the deliberations to the subject of the EAC's responsibility in respect to a French sector of occupation in Berlin. At the outset of this discussion Mr. Massigli reiterated that his government had originally made an informal suggestion for redividing Berlin and had planned to make a definite proposal later. This decision had been altered because "after visiting Berlin and after our experience in Vienna, we thought it important to make a practical proposition, that is, that the assignment should be left to the four Commanders-in-Chief."[83] Once again we can note the connection made between Vienna and Berlin.

Lord Hood continued the discussion by emphasizing that a definite agreement had been reached at Yalta to invite the French to participate in the control machinery and in the occupation of Germany and that the EAC was charged with working out the arrangements for French participation. At this point the crucial issue became whether or not it had been the intention of the Big Three at Yalta that the French sector in Berlin should be carved out of the British and American sectors alone, leaving the Soviet sector unchanged. Again the actual dialogue is highly relevant:

> Lord Hood: I agree that the procedure for delimiting the French zone in Germany was laid down in the Crimea Conference which stated that the French zone should be apportioned out of the British and American zones, but no mention was made of the French area in Berlin. When the three Governments agreed to invite a fourth Government to join, it seems to me that the natural assumption is that each of the three Governments should be prepared to facilitate the participation of the fourth invited Government. Neither the American nor the British Government suggested that the Soviet Government should contribute to the zone in Germany to be given to the French, but we see no justification for the view that because the procedure was laid down for the apportionment of the French zone that this same procedure applied to Berlin. It seems clearly right and appropriate that the three Governments should make a contribution toward the French sector. Indeed, I might argue that since the Soviet Government made no contribution to the French zone, they therefore now should make a larger contribution toward the French sector in Berlin. The creation of a fourth sector within such a limited area as Berlin must invite a readjustment of all the other three areas. . . .
>
> Gousev: There is no such instruction in the decision of the Crimea Conference, which stated that the French should be invited by the three Powers and if they wished to accept a zone and take part in the control machinery they could do so. This refers equally to the zones in Germany and Berlin. The Commanders-in-Chief will be in Berlin. The fact that the French are on the Control Council assumes that they shall have a zone [i.e. sector in Berlin]. The Crimea Conference said that this should be agreed to by the three Governments through their representatives on EAC.
>
> Mosely: I am glad to confirm the interpretation which the Soviet Representative has presented regarding the decision of the Crimea Conference on the determination of the French zone in Germany. However, the Crimea Conference decision contains no similar provision regarding the determina-

tion of the French area in Berlin. On behalf of my Government I must reject any attempt to expand the Crimea decision by implication or to read such a meaning into it by analogy. Any such extension or interpretation of the meaning of the Crimea decision, with regard to the settlement of the French area in Berlin, is, it seems to me, a matter which would require further and specific agreement between Governments. The United States Delegation has no instructions which would allow it to accept such an extension or interpretation of the Crimea decision regarding the French zone in Germany.

Lord Hood: The Soviet Government reads the Crimea decision that the Soviet Government will make no contribution whatever toward facilitating French participation. The Soviet Government do not wish the sector allotted to them under the agreement of September 12 to be altered in any way.

Gousev: I think that the Soviet Government have made contributions in this matter. Greater Berlin has been liberated by the Soviet forces and now the other Powers are invited to take part in the occupation.[84]

Gusev's last statement deserves special consideration. The fact that he views the ordering of events in this peculiar fashion is interesting. He says that Berlin was liberated by the Red Army and now the other Allies "are invited" to take part in the occupation. One should not, of course, read too much into his comment. The very fact, however, that he mentions the Soviet liberation of the city and speaks of the other Powers being invited to share its occupation is perhaps a very faint initial indication that much later the Soviet government might claim that the Western Allies were present in Berlin by sufferance of the Soviet Union.

As discussed earlier, the fact that the Yalta communiqué made no mention of the disposition of Berlin was problematic. There were, however, several members of the American and British delegations who felt privately that the Soviet position was basically sound that the French sector of Berlin should be formed from the American and British sectors.[85] Despite any personal opinions, the Western negotiators quite naturally made use of every possible argument in hard bargaining in an attempt to maximize the position of the Western forces in Berlin and to win from the Soviets a more equitable division of the city. Mosely wrote, "Personally, I felt that the Soviet position was based on a valid analogy, but of course I argued strenuously on the basis of the instructions of my government."[86] He felt that it was basically unwise for the Western delegations to keep insisting that one Bezirk be detached from the Soviet sector in the face of such unrelenting Soviet opposition.

Conclusion of the Austrian Zones Protocol

On July 9 the Commission held two meetings, one at 11:45 in the morning, the other at 8:30 in the evening. At the morning session the delegates again took up the thorny problem of the covering report for the Austrian protocol on zones of occupation. To the surprise of the Western delegations,

Gusev announced that in the interest of arriving at agreement on Austria his delegation could accept the paragraph proposed by his colleagues with some modifications. The Soviet redraft read as follows: "The Allied Council will make the necessary arrangements for transit in Austria by road, rail, air and water for the goods and supplies required by the forces of occupation in Austria, including those forces allotted for the occupation of the City of Vienna and the personnel of the Allied Commission, and likewise for the common use of transport and communication facilities and public utility services in the City of Vienna."[87]

Lord Hood pointed out that the Soviet redraft substituted "transit" for "freedom of transit." Dr. Mosely commented that in practice this did not seem to make any great difference, since the statement that "The Allied Council will make the necessary arrangements for transit" surely meant that there would be all necessary transit rights. Following this exchange the Commission accepted the Soviet draft, completing agreement on the text of both the Agreement on Zones of Occupation in Austria and the report transmitting that agreement. The documents were formally signed at the evening meeting.

A careful reading of the Soviet redraft indicates that the Western delegations received much less than they had endeavored to obtain. Even though the agreed paragraph provided that "The Allied Council will make the necessary arrangements for transit," it was entirely possible that such arrangements might turn out to be minimal indeed. Also, the provision for "the common use of transport and communication facilities and public utility services in the City of Vienna" might turn out to be extremely weighted in favor of the Soviet military administration. These provisions are a far cry from a clear statement that the EAC assumed that the occupation would *require* complete freedom of transit and common use of facilities. Nevertheless, it was better for the Western delegations to accept what was finally offered reluctantly by the Soviet Union than to delay signature of the agreement indefinitely and risk getting no statement at all in the covering report. Furthermore, the statement finally accepted represented at least a minimal basis from which certain claims could be made against the Soviet occupation authorities if necessary, claims to the effect that "necessary" transit rights and "common use" of certain facilities would have to be granted. The West could also, by logical analogy if not by legal agreement, extend such claims to the occupation circumstances in Berlin.

Impasse on Berlin

The evening session of EAC on July 9 convened at 8:30 P.M. and lasted until well after midnight. The entire meeting was devoted to discussing formula after formula for resolving the impasse over the French sector in the city of Berlin.[88] As the hours wore on the impasse seemed to become more and more complete. At the beginning Mr. Gusev, as acting chairman, read a new proposal which had just been submitted by the French delegation. The proposal read: "The Commission has further been informed that a French contingent is already in Berlin and will remain there until this question has been finally settled.

In these circumstances the Commission, before submitting to Governments recommendations for the delimitation of the French sector, would like to receive information on the physical conditions prevailing in Berlin which it at present lacks and to be notified of any recommendations which might be formulated by the Allied Representatives on the spot."[89]

The Commission now had before it two official draft proposals for the final paragraph of the covering report transmitting the amended protocol on zones in Germany. The American draft provided that the commanders in chief delimit the French area in Berlin themselves, while the French draft merely asked the commanders for information which could be used by the EAC in making the decision.

Mr. Gusev felt that neither draft brought the Commission any closer to solving the problem of the French Berlin sector. The French draft, he thought, was largely irrelevant. If the Commission agreed that the proper procedure was for each representative to ask his government to procure additional information from the commanders and relay this to London, then the procedure should merely be carried out; there was no need to state it in the report. Also, he felt that the problem of delimiting the French sector could not be defined only in terms of physical conditions in Berlin. He pointed out that, although the representatives possessed no information at all, they had succeeded in dividing Berlin into three parts a long time ago. Now, when representatives of all Three Powers were actually in Berlin, it would be difficult to explain the matter to the governments by saying that the Commission could not reach any agreement because it did not have enough information about physical conditions.

Gusev was no more favorably inclined toward the American proposal. He felt that in view of the procedures laid down at Yalta, it was absolutely improper for the Commission to recommend that the four commanders in chief in Berlin allocate the French sector; the matter had nothing whatsoever to do with the Soviet commander. Mr. Winant asked if the last sentence in the American draft would be acceptable to the Soviet delegation if the word "four" and the words "acting jointly" were omitted. The last sentence of the draft would then read: "The Commission recommends that the Governments instruct their respective Commanders-in-Chief in Germany to determine the area in Greater Berlin to be assigned to occupation by forces of the French Republic." (See Annex 10 for original American draft.) Gusev's reply was, "Mr. Winant is very considerate but I suggest we use the word 'three' instead of 'four' in the American draft." Lord Hood then added that "There is some merit in being vague about this."

As the discussion continued it became increasingly evident that Gusev was stalling on any and all proposals. Suggestion after suggestion was made by various members of the Western delegations, yet Gusev could not accept any of them. The Western negotiators were of course aware of why Gusev was stalling. Before agreeing to anything he was determined to extract a commitment from the Western delegations that the French area in Berlin would be taken out of the British and American areas. To get some kind of commitment to this effect it now looked as if Gusev might refuse to agree to any version of the disputed paragraph of the covering report. If the Commission could not clear the report, the amended agreement on zones could not be transmitted to the governments. Gusev conducted the negotiations with skill and finesse. He refused to be pinned down, often by managing to miss the point of his colleagues' comments, yet he made his conditions quite clear as is shown in the following exchange:

> Winant: It would seem to me fair to ask that, since the U.S. and British Governments have agreed to allocate out of their zones an area to be occupied by the French, this paper should be forwarded to our Governments containing that information. This paper fixes the boundaries to be occupied by all four Powers in Germany.
>
> Gousev: I can only welcome the agreement that has already been reached and I would certainly welcome an agreement which concludes the allocation of areas in Greater Berlin provided it was made between the other three Delegations.
>
> Lord Hood: I would welcome at least the agreement on the zones in Germany.
>
> Gousev: But there is no agreement on the areas in Berlin.
>
> Winant: Suppose we just made this statement in the covering report:
>
> > 'The Commission has not yet delineated an area to be occupied by the forces of the French Republic.'
>
> Gousev: But how does that bring us any nearer to the solution of the problem?
>
> Winant: The whole body of the document in which we are in agreement would bring us that much further ahead in our work.
>
> Gousev: Do I understand correctly that the Delegations wish to separate the question of the French zone from the question of the allocation of the French area in Berlin?
>
> Winant: Mr. Chairman, that is not the idea I wish to convey.[90]

It was obvious that the Soviet representative was not about to be moved from his position or to make any concessions. The amended zones agreement was grounded on the Commission's table until some headway could be made on the last paragraph of the report. The day following the long July 9 session Winant telegraphed the State Department that he had noted a marked shift in the Soviet approach and that he assumed this shift was based on instructions from Moscow. Gusev was objecting not only to the last sentence of the final paragraph of the report, but to any draft of the entire paragraph. Winant believed that the Soviet government might have the intention of leaving the question unsettled until the forthcoming Potsdam Conference with a view to insisting at the conference that the French area in Berlin be formed from the U.S. and U.K. areas.[91] Gusev was leaving for Moscow the same day.

Freezing of the Soviet Position

The EAC held its last lengthy debate on the Berlin problem the afternoon of July 12 with Mr. Georgii F. Saksin serving as chairman of the meeting in Mr. Gusev's absence.[92] Mr. Saksin began by stating that the Soviet delegation had asked its military authorities for information on conditions in Berlin. The information received indicated that although the entire city was heavily devastated, the destruction had been much the heaviest in the Soviet sector of the city. This was true not only because of the heavy bombing of the eastern sector but because of the fierce fighting which had taken place when the Red Army advanced through the eastern part of the city. On the basis of this information the Soviet delegation was now ready to state much more definitely its views on the area to be allocated to the French. For convenience sake the Soviet delegation had prepared a proposal to take the place of the last sentence of the draft last paragraph of the covering report submitted by the American delegation. The new paragraph read:

> In view of the physical conditions prevailing in the area of 'Greater Berlin', the Commission has not attempted in Article 7 of the present Agreement, to delineate an area in 'Greater Berlin' to be occupied by forces of the French Republic. The Commission recommends that the question of determining the boundaries of the French area of occupation in 'Greater Berlin', which area, in consequence of the Soviet zone of the City having undergone greater destruction, will be formed out of the American and British areas in 'Greater Berlin', should be referred to the Control Council in Berlin for consideration.[93]

Lord Hood replied to the Soviet proposal by noting that as a practical question the examination and assessment of the relative damage between the sectors in Berlin was a matter of fact which would be very difficult for EAC to ascertain but much easier for the Control Council on the spot. If the French zone were to be delimited by the Control Council, the EAC should certainly leave the Control Council a free hand in accomplishing its task. Lord Hood continued that he did not want to underrate the importance of the factor of destruction and was sure it would be taken into consideration by the Control Council in making the decision.

Mr. Massigli then attempted to work out a compromise solution. He noted that the British recommendation was to refer the matter to the Control Council with no qualification whatever, while the Soviet proposal was for the Control Council to decide the question on the basis of the greater destruction in the Soviet sector of Berlin. The French representative asked if both delegations could compromise and take a midway position. The EAC could then recommend that the question of delimitation be referred to the Control Council and in addition that the Control Council give consideration to the relative destruction in the various sectors in arriving at its decision. Saksin replied that the important point of the Soviet proposal was that the French sector be taken from the two western sectors. If this were omitted and he accepted Massigli's suggestion, there would be nothing left of the Soviet proposal. He felt that the French proposal would be completely misunderstood by Marshal Zhukov, who had supplied much detailed information on the destruction in the Soviet zone. If the French formula were referred back to Marshal Zhukov, he would be puzzled and doubtful about whether his information had been considered by the EAC. Saksin then suggested that the British and American delegations follow the lead of the Soviet delegation and request detailed information from their military authorities in Berlin. Pending receipt of this information the question of agreement on the French sector should be left open.

It will be recalled that Winant had communicated with the military authorities concerning fixed sector boundaries a year previously in mid-July of 1944. At that time he had been informed that a fixed, inflexible delimitation of the three sectors in Berlin would be acceptable to the American military authorities provided that portions of Berlin's population could be moved out of the American or British sectors if necessary in order to accommodate the occupation troops. No conclusion was ever reached in EAC concerning movements of the German population, but the British and American delegations had acquiesced to the Soviet delegation's refusal to provide for any adjustment of the sector boundaries. Now, a year later, the Western delegations were faced with a similar Soviet refusal to make any changes in the boundary of the Soviet sector. Certainly the Western negotiators must have wished that some provision for boundary readjustment had been written into the agreement in 1944. On the other hand such provision may have made little difference now, since the Soviet delegation based its refusal to modify the Soviet sector on the great destruction suffered in the Soviet sector, essentially a question of fact, not law. Mr. Saksin's suggestion that the Western delegations obtain more information from their military authorities in Berlin could not bring much help to the Western negotiators. Mosely noted that anyone who had an opportunity to observe carefully could see that, as a matter of objective fact, the eastern sector of the city was much more extensively damaged than the western sectors. The maps of aerial bombardment available to the Western delegations showed that the borough of Mitte was almost entirely flattened and that most other sections of the Soviet sector were in relatively worse shape than the western sectors.[94]

Following the tea interval, the representatives continued their discussion of the proper procedure for delimiting the French sector. Winant continued to urge that the agreement on zones, as already approved, should be signed and transmitted to the governments with some provision either in the agreement or the covering report that the agreement was "without prejudice" to the positions of the four governments in regard to the settlement of the French zone in Berlin. Mr. Saksin replied that the agreement on zones in Germany and sectors in Berlin should not be split into two parts and that he saw no reason for not concluding the covering report on the basis of the Soviet draft. The result was once again a complete impasse, as is seen from the following exchange:

> Saksin: I doubt that the Governments would greet with enthusiasm an open-ended recommendation regarding Berlin. The question of the French occupation was referred to the EAC a long time ago and events, such as the arrival of French troops in Berlin and French participation in the Komendatura, have left the EAC far behind. For the EAC to make a vague recommendation now will be incomprehensible to the Governments. My Delegation feels that the EAC has full information from Marshal Zhukov on which to base an agreement in principle on the division of Berlin. The EAC would not decide on particular districts but would emphasize the principle of forming the French area out of the U.K. and U.S. areas. That would facilitate a decision of the Commanders-in-Chief better than a vague recommendation which would lead to repetition in the Control Council of the same arguments as presented here. At the first meeting of the Control Council the Soviet Commander-in-Chief would simply repeat that because of the destruction in the Soviet area the French area should be formed from the U.K. and U.S. areas. If we fail to include a definite recommendation in principle, we shall lose valuable time and fail to fulfill the mandate set for the EAC.
>
> Winant: If the U.S. Delegation had suggested that the French area be formed out of the Russian and British areas, I would understand the reluctance of my colleagues to acquiesce without having information regarding the destruction which has occurred in their areas. I sympathize with the Soviet suggestion that we find out the degree of destruction in the U.K. and U.S. areas. In my proposal made earlier to sign that part of the agreement which is settled and to define the U.S., U.K. and French zones in Germany, I felt that we were trying to keep up with events by signing those things on which we are already agreed. Differences in viewpoints and instructions have led to an impasse here. The Soviet Delegation is unable to accept one part of the document and my Delegation is not able, without consulting its Government, to agree to form a French area out of the U.K. and U.S. areas.[95]

The deadlock in EAC now seemed to be complete. Following the meeting, Ambassador Winant cabled the State Department that he believed there was little hope that the Soviet representative would secure any reversal of the formal instructions he had received the previous day from Moscow.

Winant continued, "I believe it would now be wise for our military authorities in Berlin to examine concretely whether delimitation of French area requires adjustment of all three present areas because of physical conditions. Such recommendations from U.S. military authorities in Berlin supported by substantial evidence would greatly facilitate conclusion agreement on French zone."[96]

The Deadlock Resolved at Potsdam

The question was finally resolved at the Potsdam Conference. Mosely recorded that when he first arrived at the conference he found that the representatives of the War Department "at the working level" were still insistent that the French sector be formed by taking one Bezirk from each of the three previously assigned sectors, including the Soviet sector. A few days later, however, the War Department representatives changed their position and abandoned their insistence on detaching one Bezirk from the Soviet sector. Mosely believes that this change of position resulted chiefly from a delayed reaction in realizing the full implications of the food and fuel agreement which had been reached about ten days earlier.[97]

During June and July American military authorities had been urging that the Russians take responsibility for meeting the economic needs of Berlin, including the most vital needs of food and fuel. The traditional sources of food for Berlin had been the agricultural provinces now allotted to the Soviet zone of Germany. Marshal Zhukov, however, refused to accept the suggestions of the Western military commanders. The matter was finally settled at a meeting between General Clay, General Weeks, and Marshal Zhukov, at Berlin on July 7. At this meeting Zhukov insisted that coal for Berlin be made available from the Ruhr and that sufficient food for the western sectors be supplied from the western zones. After some hesitation General Clay agreed that the United States would accept the responsibility of supplying the American sector, subject to the establishment of a common ration in all the sectors of Berlin. General Weeks would seek approval of the British government to supplying the food needs of the British sector from the British zone and to providing a fair share of the city's fuel needs from the Ruhr. Since July 15, 1945, the West has in fact ensured the supply of food and fuel to the civilian population of the western sectors of Berlin.[98]

It was probably a few days after the beginning of the Potsdam Conference before the full implications of the food and fuel agreement became fully evident to the representatives of the War Department. There could be no doubt that American resources, as well as supplies from the Ruhr, would be needed to supply the food and fuel needs of the British and French sectors of Berlin as well as the American sector. Faced with this inescapable conclusion the War Department representatives abandoned their demand that one Bezirk be detached from the Soviet sector to form the French sector.

NEGOTIATIONS IN 1945

It is difficult, of course, to speculate on the course of events had the Russians agreed to supply the food and fuel needs of Berlin. Quite possibly, however, Berlin's position could have been dangerously vulnerable later when the gradual breakdown of quadripartite administration became an established fact. Mosely concluded that, "If their [the Western military commanders'] proposal had been accepted, this would have resulted in the economic amalgamation of Berlin with the Soviet zone. It was Soviet insistence, in July 1945, which established Berlin as a separate economic area in addition to being a separate area of Allied occupation."[99]

On July 17 an agreement was finally reached at Potsdam between General Clay, deputy military governor of the American zone, and General Weeks, deputy military governor of the British zone, that the French area of occupation in Berlin would be formed from the sectors originally allocated to the United States and the United Kingdom. (See Annex 11 for comparison of the final draft of the paragraph submitted by the Soviet delegation in EAC with the final version approved at Potsdam.) The agreement was cabled to Assistant Secretary of State James C. Dunn in Washington by Assistant Secretary of War John J. McCloy the same day.[100] It is interesting to note that this troublesome problem, which had perplexed the representatives to EAC for weeks, was settled at Potsdam at the working military level. There is no evidence that the heads of state, the foreign secretaries, or the senior military commanders were vitally involved in the discussions of the French sector at Potsdam. It must be assumed, however, that the agreement between Clay and Weeks was approved by President Truman and Secretary of State Byrnes, as well as by General Eisenhower. (On July 3, 1945, James F. Byrnes succeeded Edward R. Stettinius as secretary of state.) The fact that the issue was settled at the working military level perhaps reflects a general feeling that the problem itself was mainly a military problem which concerned mostly matters of fact. In addition, it would seem that both the British and American governments were not inclined to insist that one Bezirk be taken from the Soviet sector in the face of the unrelenting stand taken by the Soviet government on this issue.

One might wish that the problem of the French sector in Berlin, indeed the whole nexus of problems centering on Berlin, had been accorded more time and attention at Potsdam. There was already evidence that all was not well in Berlin and that deep conflicts of interest between the Allies could surface at any time. Quite naturally, the subject of Allied policy towards Germany as a whole commanded the lion's share of attention at the conference. However, there was perhaps a lack of foresight on the part of the chief representatives in not being able to anticipate the fact that Berlin was a microcosm of the German problem at large, that policy conflicts and relationships between occupation authorities in Germany would be reflected most vividly and indeed magnified in Berlin, especially since Berlin constituted a special enclave within one of the zones.

Secretary of State Byrnes telegraphed Ambassador Winant from Babelsberg, a suburb of Potsdam, on July 18, authorizing him to accept the Soviet formula of July 12 for the final sentence of the covering report as soon as the U.K. representative had instructions to do so.[101] Similar instructions, however, were not immediately forthcoming to Sir Ronald Campbell from the British Government. There was evidently some strong opinion within the British Foreign Office that since agreement had been reached to form the French sector of Berlin from the western sectors, this agreement should be embodied in the amended agreement on zones by defining the boundaries of the new French sector in that document.[102] (Sir Ronald I. Campbell had succeeded Sir William Strang as the British representative to the EAC on July 3. After Strang's departure the negotiations were handled largely by Lord Hood, though Sir Ronald had the responsibility of making any final decisions. Sir William Strang was reassigned to Germany as political adviser to General Weeks, the deputy military governor of the British zone.)

On July 19 the secretary to the American delegation to EAC, Mr. E. Allen Lightner, Jr., had a conference with Lord Hood at the British Foreign Office. Mr. Lightner emphasized that the American delegation wanted to get the agreement on zones signed as soon as possible and felt that this would be delayed too long if the EAC itself had to define the exact limits of the French sector. Lord Hood agreed wholeheartedly and stated that he would telephone or wire Potsdam at once for authorization to accept the Soviet paragraph in the covering report. He also showed Mr. Lightner a telegram which had just been received from Potsdam by the Foreign Office. The telegram went into considerable detail regarding the possible area to be allotted to the French and stated that it was hoped the French would be satisfied with the borough of Reinickendorf but that in case they should demand additional territory the British and Americans would undoubtedly be able to give them parts of other districts.[103]

The memorandum sent to Winant by Mr. Lightner reporting on his conference with Lord Hood may have been Winant's first clue as to what the military authorities in Potsdam were doing in regard to the formation of a French sector in Berlin. Mosely has reported that during both of the major conferences in 1945, Yalta and Potsdam, the American delegation to EAC received almost no communications from the representatives at the conference. The British delegation, on the other hand, received lengthy reports daily. Because of the cordial relations between members of the two delegations, the British representatives to EAC were kind enough to brief the American representatives fairly often in regard to the proceedings of the conferences.[104] Here again is potent evidence that the Commission ranked much higher in London than in Washington and that the American delegation was not given the requisite attention or authority to accomplish its task by the highest officials of the American government.

At the meeting of July 23 the Commission remained immobilized, since the British delegation still had not received full authority to accept the Soviet draft final paragraph of the covering report.[105] The same day, however, General Eisenhower reported to the War Department that Generals Clay and Weeks had consulted with General Koeltz and had been able to reach an agreement on the delimitation of the French sector of Berlin. General Koeltz, acting with full authority to effect a settlement, had agreed to accept the districts of Reinickendorf and Wedding as the French sector of the city. Eisenhower recommended that this assignment be approved by the American government and presented to the Control Council for approval. Weeks was recommending the same course of action to the British government.[106]

The Agreement Is Completed

The British government promptly approved the recommendation and notified Sir Ronald Campbell that he should accept the Soviet draft last paragraph of the covering report. Now that all the delegations were authorized to approve the Soviet paragraph, the amended agreement and the covering report could be officially signed by the Commission. It should be noted that the French sector, as agreed to at Potsdam, was taken entirely from the sector previously allocated to Great Britain in the September 12, 1944, Protocol on Zones of Occupation in Germany and the Administration of "Greater Berlin." The British sector now consisted of four districts rather than six. Although we have no way of knowing what transpired in the negotiations among the generals at Potsdam, it can perhaps reasonably be surmised that the British military authorities somehow became more than impressed with the full implications of the food and fuel agreements of July 7. Even as the American military authorities abandoned their insistence upon detaching one district from the Soviet sector, the British military authorities overcame any aversion to abandoning responsibility for two districts to the French government.

The EAC held a formal meeting on July 26 to give official approval to the agreement amending the protocol of September 12, 1944, as well as to the report transmitting the agreement to the governments.[107] The amending agreement readjusted the boundaries of the British and American zones of occupation to provide for a French zone of occupation. Article 7, however, was modified merely by adding the French Republic to the enumeration of the Powers administering Berlin. As Mosely has pointed out, the amended protocol on zones in Germany now contained an inbuilt legal contradiction. Although Article 7 provided for French participation in the occupation of Berlin in principle, the original division of the city into only three sectors was left unchanged.[108] The covering report stated that the

Control Council should decide upon a new division and that the French sector would be taken from the American and British sectors. However, the new division into four sectors approved by the Control Council on July 30 was never incorporated into the September 12, 1944, agreement as an official amendment. This minor divergence between law and fact, although interesting, was never a point of issue in the misunderstandings that later developed among the Allies over Berlin. The reason is of course clear: the divergence had nothing to do with the Soviet Union, since the Soviet sector of Berlin as defined in the September 12, 1944, agreement was left unchanged.

Ambassador Winant notified his colleagues on the European Advisory Commission on July 29 that the United States government had officially approved the July 26th amending agreement together with the report. Similar notification of approval was given by the United Kingdom on August 2, by the Provisional Government of the French Republic on August 7, and by the Soviet Union on August 13. Meanwhile the military commanders were already making provisions to carry out the new arrangements.

The Control Council held its first meeting in Berlin on July 30. At this meeting General Eisenhower, Marshal Zhukov, Field Marshal Montgomery, and Lieutenant General Koenig gave official approval to the assignment of Reinickendorf and Wedding as the French sector of occupation. It was further agreed that the details regarding the occupation of the French sector would be worked out by the deputies to the British, French, and American commanders respectively.[109]

With the French now confirmed in their sector of occupation in Berlin, the protocols on Germany negotiated in the European Advisory Commission were in full force legally and practically. The remaining five meetings of the EAC were devoted to a discussion of the final report on the work of the Commission to be submitted to the four governments. At the Potsdam Conference it had been agreed that the EAC should be dissolved when it had completed the task of amending the September 12, 1944, agreement on zones of occupation. In its place a new Council of Foreign Ministers was created to make the necessary preparations for the peace settlements.[110] On August 31, 1945, the European Advisory Commission held its last meeting.[111] Its work was now complete.

BERLIN: ZONES OF OCCUPATION

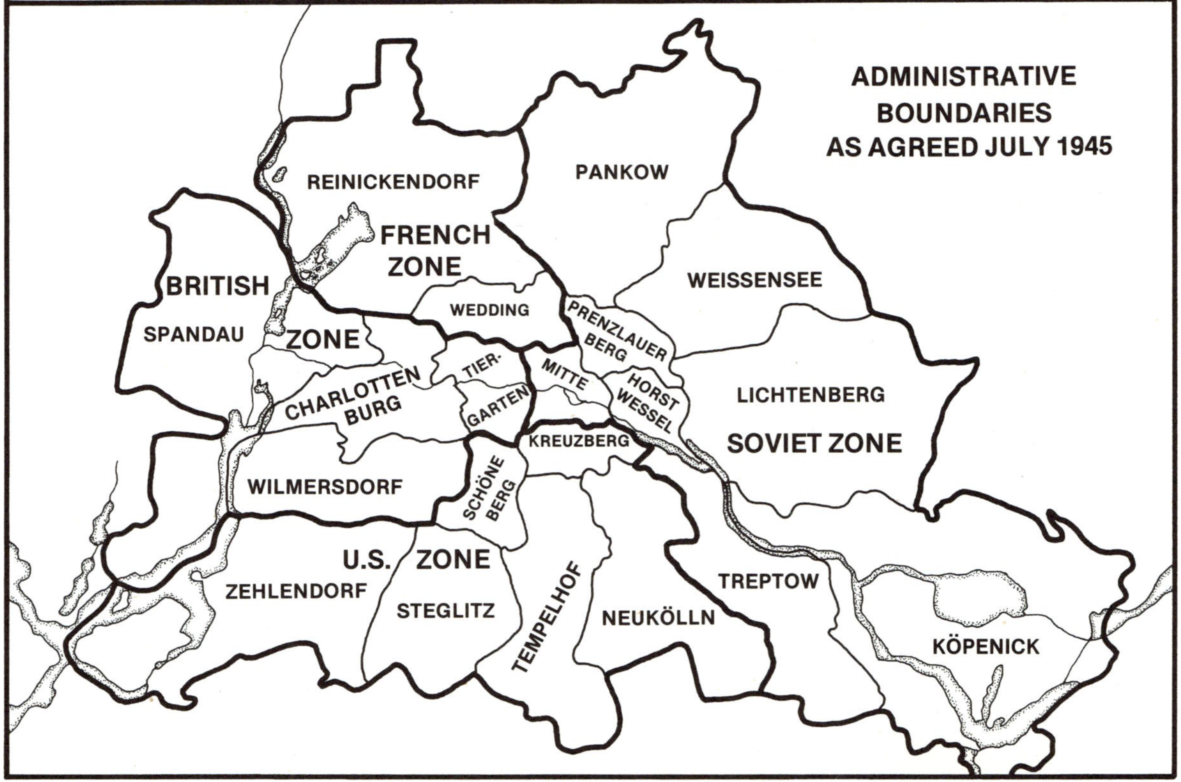

SIX

THE SPECIAL PROBLEM OF ACCESS IN WARTIME AND POSTWAR NEGOTIATIONS

In any discussion of the postwar status of Berlin the problem of access to the city for the Western occupying Powers assumes central importance. This is true for two reasons. In the first place, the geographical fact of Berlin's location as a specially administered enclave 110 miles within the Soviet zone meant that the Western Powers must traverse Soviet territory somehow, by rail, road, or air, in order to establish and maintain a physical presence in the city, either civilian or military. Secondly, the legal right of the Western Powers to occupy three sectors of the city as established in the EAC protocol on zones of occupation could not be given effect in actual fact unless the Western Powers possessed ways and means of regular access to the city through the Soviet zone.

A Perplexing Question

In a study of the creation of Berlin's postwar international status the subject of Western access to the city deserves special treatment. As we have seen the European Advisory Commission prepared through careful negotiations the documents which established the regime of Four Power zonal occupation and administration of Germany and Berlin after the war. Interestingly enough, however, the EAC throughout the entire course of the negotiations dealt with the subject of access only peripherally and was never instructed by the governments to prepare articles of agreement on access or to incorporate provisions for Western access into the two protocols on Germany. From a legal standpoint this situation seems highly irregular for the simple reason that provisions for access to a piece of territory, especially an enclave, would seem to be an integral part of any agreement or series of agreements which have the effect of establishing a new political and legal regime with corresponding rights and duties. The fact that provisions for Western access to Berlin were not negotiated in the European Advisory Commission does not mean that no rights of access were created. Such rights were created in a legal sense by the protocols which established the Four Power regime in Berlin and gave the Western Powers the right to occupy three sectors of the city. The legal rights were in fact given practical effect by various agreements made in 1945 between representatives of the Western Powers and representatives of the Soviet Union.

In this chapter we shall trace the development of various provisions for Western access to Berlin during the year 1945. Though often seriously challenged by the Soviet Union, the agreements made at that time form the basis of the arrangements which have, for the most part, been in effect since that time and which have over the years given rise to a profound controversy between the Soviet and Western governments as well as between various lawyers, scholars, and writers on the two sides. In our discussion we shall have to give particular attention to the question as to why the arrangements for access were not negotiated within EAC and included in the protocols on Germany. This analysis necessarily leads us to inquire into the actual status of the access arrangements. Does the fact that they were made by the military commanders in Germany rather than the plenipotentiary representatives in EAC affect their legal standing or validity? Did the Western governments make a major blunder by not settling the matter of access in the EAC agreements? These particular questions, as well as others to be discussed later, would seem to require that the subject of access to Berlin be accorded special consideration and analysis in a chapter separate from those which chronicled the history of the negotiations on the military occupation and zonal division of Berlin.

Concern Within EAC

Despite the fact that the Western delegations to EAC never explicitly raised the question of access to Berlin with the Russian delegation, certain of the Western representatives were quite aware and concerned about the problem from the outset of the negotiations. As related in Chapter Three the State Department's Country and Area Committee for Germany had prepared a paper on zones of occupation in Germany in late 1943. Dr. Mosely, then a key member of the committee, had prepared an alternative version of the paper which provided for a corridor to connect the prospective western zones with Berlin. The CAC proposal was forwarded to the Working Security Committee in early 1944 but encountered an immediate and resolute rejection by the Civil Affairs Division of the War Department on the grounds that provision for areas of occupation was a strictly military matter which would have to be dealt with at the appropriate time by the proper military authorities. (See pages 34–36.) Presumably the corridor proposal evaporated without being considered seriously either by the highest authorities in the State or War Departments or by the president, whose thinking at the time evidently incorporated Berlin in the American zone. The proposal was an unfortunate victim of the protracted struggle between the State Department and the Civil Affairs Division of the War Department over whether the Working Security Committee and the European Advisory Commission should even be functioning, much less giving consideration to zones of occupation in Germany.

It will also be recalled that Mr. Winant raised the question of access with representatives of the War Department during his visit to Washington in May, 1944. Although the representatives of the Civil Affairs Division had by this time recognized the competence of EAC to negotiate the protocol on zones in Germany and had of necessity accepted President Roosevelt's approval of the Soviet zone boundary as set forth in the original British proposal, these representatives refused to authorize Mr. Winant to discuss any provisions for access to Berlin with the Russians in EAC. (See pages 44–45.) Dr. Mosely recalls from conversations with Winant after his return to London that the ambassador was highly dismayed by the position taken by the Civil Affairs representatives but realized that it would be impossible to table any proposals concerning access in EAC without the explicit approval of the WSC.[1]

During the month of July, 1944, the draft agreement on zones in Germany and Berlin was actively negotiated and agreed to article by article by the representatives in EAC. Mr. Winant was prevented from introducing the access issue by the conflicting crosscurrents in Washington and the resulting gap in his instructions. A careful reading of the record shows no evidence at all, however, that the British delegation either introduced any proposal entailing access provisions or attempted to raise the issue with the Russian delegation at any time. And it must be remembered that it was the original British proposal, as drawn up by the Attlee Committee, which placed Berlin as an enclave within the Soviet zone. This proposal, which was approved by EAC with only slight modifications, contained no mention of any provisions for access, and Sir William Strang evidently felt that such provisions were unnecessary and could only serve to exacerbate the negotiations with the Russians. William Franklin observes that, "Considering the military situation, the British proposal as it stood was farsighted and timely, for it had obtained Russian recognition of the right of the Western Powers to be in Berlin on a footing of parity with the Russians even though the indications were that the Soviet Army would get there first."[2]

The French delegation was not present in EAC during the July, 1944, negotiations. After the French joined the EAC in November, Mr. Massigli did not make any attempt, as far as is known, to press the issue of access with either of the Western delegations or with the Soviet delegation, although Dr. Mosely explained to the French ambassador in detail why the protocol on zones of occupation contained no provision for access to Berlin. Consequently, if it is true that the absence of provision for access to Berlin in the EAC protocols was a mistake and that the Western delegations should be faulted for this, it must be said that the blame cannot be placed solely to the account of the American ambassador. Mr. Winant seems to have been much more concerned about the problem of access to Berlin than anyone in the British delegation, and after the protocol on zones was signed the French delegation never made any attempt to urge the two other Western delegations to fill in this loophole.

Why the EAC Was Excluded

There are several reasons that the problem of access to Berlin was not dealt with in the European Advisory Commission and that no provisions for access were included in the EAC protocols. In the first place, the necessary assumptions which formed the basic foundation for the entire process of negotiation in EAC made the problem of access seem much less important at the time than it later came to be. During the basic negotiations on Germany and Berlin in mid-1944, the Commission assumed that after the surrender whatever was left of the German government and central administration in Berlin would continue to operate, only under the stringent control of the Allied military authority. The zones of military occupation were looked upon primarily as necessary divisions for the convenience of the Allies in stationing their occupation troops. Germany as a country would still be a going concern; the primary tasks of the Allies would be to punish, control, and rehabilitate that country. It was not foreseen at the time, or at least not really expected, that the entire German government and central administration would vanish into thin air with Germany's collapse. These assumptions are clearly reflected in the Agreement on Control Machinery. The agreement states that the chief functions of the Control Council would be "to initiate plans and reach agreed decisions on the chief military, political, economic and other questions affecting Germany as a whole . . . ," and "to control the German central administration. . . ."[3]

Since the zonal divisions were not considered to be of crucial significance, the matter of providing for Western access to Berlin was not viewed as an absolute necessity. The members of the Commission expected that there would be freedom of movement across zonal boundaries for all the Allied military and civilian staffs in Germany and that some freedom of movement for proper purposes would be granted to the German population. If there were any need to reach more concrete agreements concerning Allied transit within and between zones, such agreements could easily be made later by the military authorities. There was no pressing need to include them in the basic protocols on Germany. Strang states that, "It was not our expectation that the zones would be sealed off from one another. (This was a Soviet conception which only became apparent in the late summer of 1945, when the occupation was an accomplished fact.) It seemed to us therefore

SPECIAL PROBLEMS OF ACCESS

that any necessary arrangements for transit could be made on a military basis by the Commanders-in-Chief when the time came."[4] Strang concludes that Mosely was correct in emphasizing that "the duty of reaching allied agreement which would provide for adequate access to Berlin was, by decision of the American military staff, left for direct negotiation among the allied military commanders in Berlin."[5]

Assumptions About the Postwar Order

The assumptions under which the European Advisory Commission worked in drafting the protocols on Germany may appear shortsighted to us today. It may intelligently be asked why the Western delegations to EAC did not foresee major difficulties with the Soviet Union in the operation of a quadripartite regime in Germany after the war and why more adequate safeguards for the position of the Western Powers in Berlin, especially regarding transit rights, were not a matter of highest priority. This can be understood only in the context of the times, which made it necessary that certain basic assumptions about the postwar order be adopted in order that any planning for the postwar order could be accomplished. Almost inescapably the Western Powers had to assume that at least a minimum of cooperation with the Soviet Union would be forthcoming in the prodigious task of establishing some kind of coherent order from the wreckage in Europe after the war. This was, however, by no means a blind faith. Many officials in London and Washington, notably Churchill, Murphy, Winant, and Mosely, were deeply apprehensive concerning Soviet motives and intentions once the military victory over the Axis had been achieved. What must be realized is that the acceptance of the contrary assumption, namely, unrelenting conflict with the Soviet Union after the war, would have blocked any coherent efforts at planning for the postwar order and would have left the Western Allies with a hostile Soviet government and a hopeless situation in Europe. In 1944-45 it was only reasonable to hope that a satisfactory, perhaps even profitable, level of cooperation with the Soviet government could be achieved. William Franklin observes that, "The assumption of at least reasonable cooperation was the foundation for the entire structure of occupation in Germany and Austria; it was not peculiar to the drawing of zonal boundaries. If the assumption had been postwar hostility rather than cooperation, undoubtedly a great many negotiations with the Soviet Union would have been handled differently, including zonal boundaries."[6]

Without a doubt the Western negotiators felt that to push for clearly defined provisions for access to Berlin might lead to a breakdown of the delicate negotiations on the zonal division of Germany, or might lend credibility to the assumption that each zone would be a sealed off geographic entity. Indeed it might be concluded that the Western delegations accomplished a skillful *coup de maitre* in gaining Soviet assent to Western occupation of a part of Berlin and the division of the city into four zones of occupation. However this may be, it can also be argued that there was no real need, from a legal point of view, to insist that articles providing for Western transit rights to Berlin be included as an integral part of the protocol on zones of occupation. According to this argument the Soviet government necessarily recognized a right of transit for Western forces across Soviet territory when it recognized the right of those forces to occupy a portion of Berlin. Franklin asserts that ". . . the need of the Western Powers for access to Berlin across the intervening Soviet zone was utterly apparent. Once the Soviet government accepted the right of the Western Powers to be in Berlin, it thereby acknowledged the self-evident corollary of their right to go to Berlin."[7]

Unanswered Questions

Although this argument undoubtedly holds true from the viewpoint of international law, it does not answer all questions. One might well ask why then it was necessary for the U.S. delegation to undertake protracted negotiations to secure transit rights across the British and French zones to the landlocked American zone. Was there not in this case also a self-evident corollary of free transit rights because of the established fact of American occupation of a certain geographical location? Concerning this problem Franklin writes: "Transit rights across the British and French zones for the landlocked American Army in south Germany had to be pledged in writing precisely because such rights did not otherwise exist. But the right of the Western Powers to be in Berlin was expressly guaranteed in the protocol; so the right of access followed as a matter of course."[8]

To this argument it might be rejoined that the right of American forces to occupy the southern zone of Germany was also expressly guaranteed in the protocol; so the right of access to this zone through other intervening zones followed as a matter of course. If the British and French governments accepted the right of American forces to be in south Germany, they necessarily recognized the self-evident corollary of their right to get there and to be properly supplied. Why is the case of the American zone different from the case of the Berlin zone in theory? In a very real sense Berlin, as an area of joint occupation not part of the Soviet zone, constituted a fifth zone. Transit rights to any enclosed zone through intervening zones should have been a self-evident corollary of the fact of physical presence in and occupation of that zone.

To this question, as to many other complex questions surrounding the problem of Berlin, there is perhaps no definitive answer. At any rate it is somewhat peculiar that protracted negotiations were conducted among the Western Allies over American transit rights across the British and French zones while nothing was done about transit rights across the Soviet zone to Berlin. Whatever the merits or demerits of this set of circumstances, this

SPECIAL PROBLEMS OF ACCESS

arrangement occurred at the insistence of the Western military authorities. Mr. Winant received detailed instructions concerning negotiations with the British and French delegations over transit rights through the British and French zones; he was never authorized to approach the Russian delegation about transit rights to Berlin. In this situation it is almost ironic that Mr. Gusev, in an attempt to urge the Western delegations to settle their differences, felt compelled to state at the meeting of November 6, 1944, that transit arrangements similar to those that the Americans were demanding of the British would be granted by the Soviet Union, giving United States and British forces full access to Berlin across the Soviet zone. (See pages 69–70.) One of the primary reasons, in fact, for the failure of the Western Powers to insist upon access rights to Berlin was the protracted struggle over transit rights through the British zone to the American zone. This dispute so occupied the energies of the Western negotiators and so distracted attention from so many other important issues that to have added another debate over transit rights through Soviet territory to Berlin would certainly have doomed the entire set of negotiations on Germany to breakdown and failure.

The year 1944 saw no concrete efforts by the Western governments to secure from the Soviet government a recognition of rights of access to Berlin. Only after the protocol on zones of occupation had been signed, amended, and approved did the Western governments show any vital interest in the access problem. During 1945 several attempts were made, mostly through military channels, to plug this loophole and secure some Soviet recognition of transit rights to Berlin.

The Mosely Memorandum

Even though the American delegation to EAC was not authorized to take up the issue with the Russians, some members of the delegation remained highly concerned over the problem. In the early months of 1945 Dr. Mosely, with Ambassador Winant's approval, prepared a memorandum and draft agreement on access provisions. In preparing this draft Mosely writes that he felt it was particularly important to keep in mind "the difficulties and chicaneries which the Russians had inflicted on American military missions in the countries of Eastern Europe since August 1944."[9] The draft agreement provided that the American commander in chief could choose any two rail lines and any two highways as lines of access for American military persons and goods traveling to and from Berlin. One railroad and highway would connect Berlin with the British zone, the other lines would lead from Berlin to the American zone. Provisions were included which would authorize the American commander to carry out "any repairs to railroads, roads, signal systems and bridges which he might deem necessary, and to maintain gasoline pumps, repair patrols, rest stations, and communications points along these facilities."[10] If any of the routes designated by the American commander were found to be unusable, the Soviet commander would be obligated to make alternative facilities available at once.

Unfortunately the Mosely draft was not presented to the Soviet delegation in EAC due to a lack of instructions from Washington. Mosely hoped, however, that since negotiations on access were being handled through military channels, the draft might provide useful material to the American military authorities in formulating proposals. In mid-May, 1945, an American representative from SHAEF, Colonel Kootz, visited London for a thorough briefing on the progress of the EAC negotiations.[11] In lengthy conversations Dr. Mosely attempted to point out that it would be wise for the Western Powers to secure rights of access to Berlin in the form of signed protocols with the Soviet Union rather than to leave the matter as a purely military settlement, as no one could foresee how important these provisions might turn out to be later. He also stressed the point that the withdrawal of American forces from the Soviet zone into the American zone should take place simultaneously with the entry of American forces into Berlin. When Colonel Kootz departed from London he took with him a copy of the Mosely memorandum and draft agreement back to SHAEF headquarters.[12] There is no way of knowing whether the memorandum was discussed at SHAEF headquarters and whether it influenced the thinking of the military authorities in subsequent discussions with the Russians. At any rate, the draft agreement was never presented to the Soviet government.

Discussions at Yalta

On February 1, 1945, the American Joint Chiefs of Staff met with the British Chiefs of Staff at Malta. Although the subject of zones of occupation in Germany was examined, the question of Berlin or of access to the city was not discussed. At another pre-Yalta meeting at Marrakech, French Morocco, Secretary of State Stettinius, together with his chief advisers from the State Department, apparently agreed that the question of Western access to Berlin was one which should be handled by the military authorities.[13]

The first serious examination of the access problem by the military authorities appears to have taken place in the early stages of the Yalta Conference. On February 6 the American Joint Staff, a staff group working under the Joint Chiefs of Staff, completed a memorandum which they proposed should be sent to the British Chiefs of Staff and the Soviet General Staff. The text of the memorandum read: "The U.S. forces in Berlin and certain other areas will be isolated from the main areas of U.S. occupation by territory occupied by other than U.S. forces. There will be need for regular transit by road, air, and rail across the intervening territory. The U.S. Chiefs of Staff propose that the general principle be accepted of freedom of transit by each nation concerned between the main occupied area and the forces occupying

SPECIAL PROBLEMS OF ACCESS

Berlin and similar isolated areas. They further propose that the details be worked out by the local commanders."[14]

The memorandum was discussed by the American Joint Chiefs at a meeting on February 7. They concluded that before the paper was forwarded to the British or Soviet military authorities it should be redrafted along broader lines to provide for freedom of transit for military purposes across all zonal boundaries. The memorandum as redrafted would then apply to Vienna as well as Berlin and would establish a more logical and coherent basis for access to all the zones of occupation in Europe after the war. Since the American government, after prolonged persuasion by Churchill, Winant, and others, had decided in January to accept a zone of occupation in Austria and Vienna, the Joint Chiefs apparently realized that they now had a problem of access to American areas of occupation across two pieces of Soviet occupied territory—in Austria and Germany.

Unclear Views of the Joint Chiefs of Staff

Since the paper was returned to the staff group for reworking, it was not discussed with either the British or the Russians during the Yalta Conference.* The Joint Staff planners promptly set to work redrafting the memorandum, and by the latter part of the month a new draft, considerably broader in scope, had been prepared. The new draft provided as follows:

> United States forces in zones of tripartite occupation will require regular access by air, road and rail to the main United States zones of occupation. In addition, all United States forces of occupation will require access to other parts of Europe across British and Soviet zones of occupation. It appears that similar access will be required by Soviet and British forces.
>
> The United States Chiefs of Staff propose that the general principle of freedom of transit across zones of occupation and zones of tripartite occupation, be accepted. Details of transit shall be worked out between the local commanders.
>
> The foregoing is proposed as an interim military measure pending general agreements as to transit which may be expected from the European Advisory Commission.[15]

The reference to the European Advisory Commission is puzzling. According to its own terms the memorandum should serve as "an interim military measure pending general agreements as to transit which may be expected from the European Advisory Commission." As we have seen, the

---

*Feis, p. 533, states that the subject of access was raised with the British and Russian military authorities at Yalta, but that the matter was dropped when the Russians proved reluctant to discuss it. Franklin, pp. 26–27, states on the other hand that the subject of access was not raised at Yalta, since the American Joint Chiefs of Staff felt that the memorandum should first be redrafted. The Franklin account would seem to be more authoritative.

American delegation to EAC had never received any authorization to conduct negotiations relating to matters of transit or access, and this situation was primarily the result of the view held by the War Department and the Joint Chiefs that access was purely a military matter which must be dealt with at the military level. The two protocols on Germany were silent on the subject of access to Berlin. The JCS memorandum may indicate that by this time the Joint Chiefs were rethinking their position concerning the jurisdiction of the EAC in matters of transit. At the time the protocols on Germany were signed the United States had not agreed to participate in the occupation of Austria or the quadripartite occupation of Vienna. Now, however, the problem of access involved two cities—Vienna and Berlin. In addition, there were the arrangements which had been worked out concerning American transit across the British zone in Germany, and the military authorities were now involved in another complicated dispute over transit rights across the French zone. Similar arrangements would also have to be worked out for Austria. In view of all this the Joint Chiefs may have concluded that it might be wise if the EAC concluded some general arrangements on transit provisions which could cover all these situations at once. This would naturally involve some abdication of military responsibility in such matters and a diminution of the role of the Joint Chiefs of Staff. In view of the increasing complexity of the matter, however, the JCS might have been only too happy to pass some of the responsibility on to the EAC.

If such is the case, this would presumably be done by drafting certain new "quadripartite directives," not by amending the protocols on Germany. One of the tasks of the EAC not discussed in this book was the preparation of so-called "draft directives" which, after approval by the four governments, would serve as instructions to the Control Council and to the four commanders in chief in the management of German affairs. Since the staff of the U.S. delegation to EAC was at this time deeply involved in discussions of the various directives, the JCS memorandum probably meant that the EAC would be empowered to draft certain new directives embodying general principles of transit. Franklin states that, "the feeling was that the military paper would suffice for the immediate future and that the longer-range needs would be met by one of the quadripartite directives that were being drawn up in the EAC for the future guidance of the Allied Control Council for Germany."[16]

If such was the intention of the Joint Chiefs, it was never carried through. In the coming weeks and months the American delegation to EAC still did not receive any instructions from Washington to undertake any negotiations relating to transit arrangements. To a certain extent this reflects again the lack of coordination in Washington between the State and War Departments which had plagued the American representatives from the very beginning of EAC's work. On the other hand, the fact that the JCS memorandum was ignored by the Soviet General Staff may mean that the Joint Chiefs subsequently decided that they could not yet permit the subject of transit arrangements to be handled through the EAC.

The JCS memorandum was transmitted to the Combined Chiefs of Staff for consideration on February 27. Simultaneously it was presented to the Soviet General Staff through the U.S. Military Mission to the U.S.S.R.[17] Franklin writes that the American delegation to EAC and probably the British delegation was informed of this move and that there were discussions as to how to proceed.[18] The British Chiefs promptly stated their concurrence in a memorandum of March 9, 1945, but no answer was ever received from the Soviet authorities. There the matter rested for the time being. Ambassador Winant received no further instructions, and the EAC did not proceed to work out a directive embodying general principles of transit or freedom of access to Berlin or Vienna.

Access Linked to Withdrawal

By the time of the German surrender on May 8, Allied forces had driven deep into areas of Thuringia and Saxony which were allotted to the Soviet zone by the terms of the protocol on zones of occupation. Since these forces remained in place pending further instructions to General Eisenhower from Washington, the question of access to Berlin and Vienna became closely linked with the question of the withdrawal of Allied forces from Soviet territory. Both Berlin and Vienna had been overrun by the Soviet army. Quite obviously the Soviet government could now refuse to permit Allied garrisons to occupy the designated areas of Berlin and Vienna unless and until Allied forces had withdrawn from the territories allotted to the Soviet Union. And conversely, the Western Powers could refuse to withdraw their forces from territories allotted to the Soviet Union until Western forces had occupied their sectors of Berlin and Vienna.

In April the great debate had begun between Churchill and Truman over whether withdrawal should be used as a means of pressure on the Soviet government to settle a number of outstanding questions. (The story of this debate and its outcome is recounted in the previous chapter.) Churchill felt that maximum political mileage should be derived from this favorable military situation, while the American president was convinced that a delayed withdrawal of Allied forces would only serve to exacerbate relations with the Russians and prevent the machinery of control from being put into operation. On June 8 the president received an urgent message from Harry Hopkins, who was at the time in Germany on his return from consultations in Moscow. Hopkins' message read:

> It is manifest that Allied control machinery cannot be started until Allied troops have withdrawn from territory included in the Russian area of occupation. Any delay in the establishment of control machinery interferes seriously

with the development of governmental administrative machinery for Germany and with the application of Allied policy in Germany. . . .

As a concurrent condition to our withdrawal we should specify a simultaneous movement of our troops to Berlin under an agreement between the respective commanders which would provide us either unrestricted access to our Berlin area from Bremen and (*or?*) Frankfurt by air, rail, and highway on agreed routes.[19]

On June 13 Ambassador Winant sent a telegram to the president, the secretary of state, and the secretary of war reporting that the British government had agreed to the withdrawal of Allied forces into their assigned zones. In his telegram he also strongly emphasized the importance of linking withdrawal from the Soviet zone with the entry of Allied garrisons into Berlin and the importance of "provision of free access" to Berlin.[20]

In line with these recommendations President Truman decided that the question of withdrawal of Allied forces from the Soviet zone should clearly be coupled with Soviet agreement on three other questions: simultaneous movement of Allied forces into Berlin and Vienna, the provision of free access for U.S. forces to and from Berlin and Vienna, and the prompt establishment of the Allied control bodies in both Berlin and Vienna. These conditions were explicitly set forth in his telegram of June 14 to Marshal Stalin proposing that both sides issue appropriate instructions to their commanders to effect these objectives.[21] Stalin's reply of June 16 clearly acknowledged that Allied withdrawal from the Soviet zone would be accompanied by simultaneous entry of Allied garrisons into Berlin. No mention was made, however, of any provisions for access to Berlin or Vienna or the setting up of the control bodies in those cities.[22]

The next efforts to negotiate some provision for free access to Berlin and Vienna were made through military channels. On June 26 General John Deane, head of the U.S. Military Mission at Moscow, reported that he had discussed the matter of free access to Berlin and Vienna with the Soviet military authorities and that he anticipated no difficulty in settling the matter. On June 27 Deane cabled that Marshal Zhukov would meet with General Clay in Berlin on the subject of access. In his telegram of June 28 Deane stated: "It is my opinion that when our representatives meet with Zhukov there will be little difficulty in arranging for free access for our troops to Berlin, and that, if I am correct in this, the same principle will apply to Vienna."[23]

The Meeting of June 29, 1945

The single most important conference concerning the problem of Western access to Berlin was the now-famous meeting of General Clay and General Weeks with Marshal Zhukov on June 29, 1945. The meeting began at 2:30 in the afternoon at Marshal Zhukov's headquarters in Berlin. Clay records

SPECIAL PROBLEMS OF ACCESS

that Zhukov was "polite, even affable, with a sense of humour and with the obvious desire to seem friendly. I liked the marshal instinctively and never had reason to feel otherwise. . . . He conducted the negotiations personally and appeared to be in full control of the Soviet position."[24] At the outset of the conference General Clay suggested that the withdrawal of Allied forces from Soviet territory be accomplished in three phases taking nine days, with Soviet troops moving in right behind the withdrawing Allied forces.[25] Marshal Zhukov thought this was much more time than necessary and inquired if the difficulty was that the American forces couldn't move more rapidly or that the Soviet forces couldn't follow more quickly. Clay replied that this was a tentative arrangement which had been worked out with the Soviet field commanders.

As the discussion continued Clay volunteered that six days might be enough to effect the American withdrawal. Zhukov still thought this was more time than necessary and emphasized that the quicker the Americans withdrew from the Soviet zone, the quicker they would be able to enter Berlin. After much more discussion it was finally agreed that the British would take one day for withdrawal from their northern sector and two more days for withdrawal from their southern sector. Pending confirmation with General Omar Bradley the following day, General Clay agreed that the American forces would complete their withdrawal in four days. Zhukov agreed that the Americans could send reconnaissance parties to Berlin on July 1, the first day of the withdrawal, and that the main body of troops would enter Berlin on July 4, the day the American forces completed their withdrawal from the Soviet zone.

The discussion then turned to the routes of access to Berlin from the western zones of Germany. Marshal Zhukov stated that he had received requests for three rail lines, Berlin to Hamburg and Bremen, Berlin to Stendal and Hannover, and Berlin to Brandenburg-Magdeburg and Hannover. He had also received a request for two highways, one from Berlin to Dessau-Halle-Erfurt-Eisenach-Kassel and Frankfurt, the other from Berlin to Magdeburg and Braunschweig, and a request for air lanes from Berlin to Bremen as well as Berlin to Frankfurt. Zhukov continued that since all these routes cut across the Soviet zone and it was his responsibility to protect them, he would have an extremely difficult administrative problem to deal with. He therefore felt that one rail line and one highway should certainly be adequate for the feeding and supply of a small garrison of 50,000 troops, the overall combined figure of British and American forces. He stated in addition that he could not agree to two air lanes.

General Clay continued to defend the requests for several highways and rail lines and for two air lanes. He emphasized that the American forces in Berlin would be faced with an exceedingly difficult supply situation. The Americans' sole port was Bremen in northwest Germany, the American occupation zone was in southwest Germany, while Berlin, the administrative occupation zone, was surrounded by the Soviet zone. It would therefore be necessary to have freedom of access and rights on several different access routes. Clay stressed that the Americans were not asking for exclusive use of the routes, but must have the right to use them as much as needed. Finally, after much lively discussion, Clay agreed to accept the Magdeburg-Berlin rail line with the understanding that the British would not make further demands for the Hamburg-Berlin rail line. The Magdeburg bridge would be rebuilt with American material and Russian engineers. It was further agreed to accept the autobahn from Hannover to Magdeburg-Brandenburg and Berlin for use by both British and American forces. General Clay accepted the one highway but stated that he reserved the right to reopen the question in the Control Council in the event that the one road was not satisfactory. Zhukov agreed that possibly all the points discussed at the conference might be changed later. Concerning traffic on the autobahn Zhukov stated that it would be necessary for vehicles to be governed by Russian road signs, military police, and document checking, but that there would be no inspection of cargo, since the Russians were not interested in what was being hauled, how much, or the number of trucks moving. Both Clay and Weeks agreed to these provisions.

When the discussion turned to air lanes, General Hill of the British delegation asked for authority to fly "in an arc bounded by Hamburg, Berlin and Frankfurt, using whatever direct route to Berlin was required depending on originating point of flight without restriction and authority to fly 50 miles east of Berlin for instrument landing." Apparently, however, Zhukov was not authorized by the Soviet government to grant anything more than one main air lane from Berlin to Magdeburg with possible branches northwest and southwest from that lane. At any rate Clay and Weeks finally agreed to use the main air lane from Berlin to Magdeburg. From Magdeburg two lanes would be used, one to Frankfurt in the American zone, the other to Hannover in the British zone. In effect, therefore, two air corridors over Soviet territory would be in use. Marshal Zhukov stated that he would report to his government that the Americans and British had accepted the air lane with the understanding that they operate under U.S. and British regulations, notifying Soviet authorities with the same notice given American and British authorities. Clay and Weeks acceded to the Soviet request to notify the Russians one hour before takeoff or arrival over Soviet territory, giving the number of aircraft and destination.

General Clay writes that when he went to the conference he "did not wish to accept specific routes which might be interpreted as a denial of our right of access over all routes. . . . The import of the issue was recognized but I did not want an agreement in writing which established anything less than the right of unrestricted access."[26] Once at the conference table with Zhukov, however, Clay found that he had little alternative but to accept the specific access routes offered by the marshal. Furthermore, Clay records that he found merit "to the Soviet contention that existing routes were needed for demobilization purposes." Faced with the necessity of securing the use of at least some access routes for supplying the immediate needs of the forces in Berlin, Clay accepted what he could get at the moment and what was probably the most that Zhukov was authorized to offer anyway. Clay writes: "Therefore Weeks and I accepted as a temporary arrangement the allocation of a main highway and rail line and two air corridors, reserving the right to reopen the question in the Allied Control Council. . . . While no record was kept at this meeting,[27] I dictated my notes that evening and they include the following: 'It was agreed that all traffic—air, road and rail, . . . would be free from border search or control by customs or military authorities.'"[28]

Was it a mistake that the assignment of these access routes was not formalized in a written agreement? There is certainly merit to Clay's suggestion that nothing less than the right of unrestricted access should have been formalized in writing. On the other hand, it may quite realistically be posited that a right of "unrestricted" access was never in the cards; Zhukov or the Soviet government would never have agreed to such a condition, and it would have been folly for Clay or the American government to have insisted on it. Following this line of argument one might insist that General Clay and the highest officials of the American government should have had enough political discernment to realize this circumstance and should have attempted therefore to formalize in writing the access routes which were assigned at the June 29 meeting.

There are several reasons why the understandings were made orally rather than in writing. In the first place, both General Clay and Marshal Zhukov apparently thought at the time that the allocation of these routes was only a temporary measure. Clay reserved the right to reopen the question in the Control Council, and Zhukov stated at one point that perhaps all the points discussed at the meeting might be changed. There was of course not much point in formalizing such temporary arrangements in written agreements. Secondly, these arrangements were reached at the military, not the diplomatic level. The question of access, rightly or wrongly, was dealt with as an operational military question, not a question for diplomatic negotiation by duly appointed governmental representatives. Written agreements between governments are not usually negotiated and signed by military figures. Although both Marshal Zhukov and General Clay were fully authorized by their respective governments to negotiate on the question of access and reach certain understandings, it is probable that neither of them was authorized to prepare and sign a written agreement on the matter. Indeed it can be forcefully argued that if any written agreements were reached on the problem of access they should have been negotiated and signed in the European Advisory Commission, the proper diplomatic forum at the time, and submitted by the EAC to the governments for approval.

Another reason that the access routes were not formalized in a written agreement is the fact that the American government did not really realize the importance which the routes of access might have in the future. Clay writes that, "we had a large and combat-experienced army in Germany which at the moment prevented us from having any worries over the possibility of being blockaded there (in Berlin)."[29] This shortsightedness would seem to be the result of a rather naive confidence on the part of the American administration that the mere existence of a right of access to Berlin was what really mattered. The physical routes of access were only a military technicality arising from the basic right of access which was guaranteed by the fact that American forces would be present in Berlin. It is perhaps unfortunate that the highest figures in the American administration were not able at the time to realize the deep political or legal implications of the access question, implications which became tragically evident within so short a time.

The Matter of Responsibility

General Clay hoped to secure the assignment of more access routes when the question was discussed in the Control Council. In this matter his judgment was mistaken. He readily admits this, which says much about his ability to be candid. He writes, "I must admit that we did not then fully realize that the requirement of unanimous consent would enable a Soviet veto in the Allied Control Council to block all of our future efforts."[30] It may seem strange to us that General Clay did not at the time foresee the difficulties which would plague negotiations in the Control Council. He was, however, inexperienced in the game of negotiating with the Russians, and he was unfamiliar with the intricate techniques of diplomacy. If responsibility must be pinpointed for this shortsightedness, it certainly cannot be put to the account of General Clay alone. The president, the secretary of state, the secretary of war, and many other high administration officials underrated the importance of securing clearly recognized access routes from the outset. Both Presidents Roosevelt and Truman seemed completely amenable to the urgings of the military authorities that the question of access was an operational military question. Official Washington seemed to expect that General Clay would have no difficulty making the appropriate arrangements with the Russians, and no one seemed to suspect that there would be major trouble over the issue in the Control Council negotiations. Naturally this attitude was partly the result of the almost inescapable assumption, or at least hope, of successful postwar collaboration with the Russians. If, however, someone must be faulted for the myopic way in which the matter of access was handled, it is the entire administration in Washington, and probably that in London as well, not General Clay alone.

Necessity of Written Agreements?

There is a danger in assuming too readily that the Western Powers committed a major blunder by not securing written agreements on routes of access to Berlin in mid-1945. It should not be presumed that any written agreement or series of agreements could have obviated the difficulties that later arose or that the blockade of 1948 could have been avoided if written agreements on access had existed. A treaty or written agreement, to be sure, establishes certain legal consequences for certain courses of action. It does not, however, determine the political choices which dictate the courses of action selected. It may have some influence upon those political choices, but it does not determine them. A written agreement on access routes would certainly not have prevented the Soviet Union from precipitating a crisis over Berlin whenever it chose to do so for the achievement of certain political goals. General Clay writes, "I doubt very much if anything in writing would have done any more to prevent the events which took place than the verbal agreement which we made. The Soviet Government seems to be able to find technical reasons at will to justify the violation of understandings whether verbal or written."[31] Sir William Strang records that he fully agrees with this point of view.[32] At best a written agreement on access routes would have given the Western Powers a more solid legal basis for making certain claims against the Soviet Union and would have lent legal justification to certain political actions taken by the Western Powers. It would not have lessened the gravity of the basic political crisis over Berlin between East and West in the years following 1945.

The Position of EAC

As we have seen, the European Advisory Commission was concerned with the problem of access to Berlin only peripherally all during the year 1945. Mosely emphasizes the fact that he and Ambassador Winant were anxious to negotiate with the Russians on the issue and strongly desired to include some provisions for access to Berlin in the EAC protocols on Germany, if this were possible. It was the insistence of the War Department that access to Berlin was a purely military matter which kept this issue beyond the purview of EAC.[33] After June, 1945, the American representatives on the Commission received no further communications from Washington concerning the access problem. They were evidently not informed of the Truman-Stalin exchange of letters in mid-June or of the negotiations on access at the military level between Clay, Weeks, and Zhukov on June 29 and subsequently.[34] This is hardly surprising, in view of the fact that even the State Department assumed that after the German surrender, most decisions would pass to the competence of the Allied Control

Council, as soon as it was set up, and to intergovernmental negotiations; the EAC would be phased out as soon as possible.

Even if the Western delegations to EAC had been given clear instructions to attempt to negotiate some provisions for access to Berlin in the amendments to the protocol on zones in Germany, it is by no means certain that they would have been successful in the endeavor. Strang writes: "It may also have been a mistake not to try for a clause about access to Berlin in one of the European Advisory Commission's protocols. But in my judgment, it would not have been possible to secure Gusev's agreement to this: he would have maintained that these were self-evident matters which it would be for the military commanders to settle."[35]

The Question of Access to Vienna

Even though the EAC was not involved at all in the negotiations on access to Berlin, it was, as we have seen in the previous chapter, concerned to an extent with the negotiation of provisions for free access to Vienna in the negotiations on Austria. It will be recalled that Dr. Mosely, with the full support of the British and French delegations, attempted to get the Soviet delegation to agree to provisions for free transit to Vienna, freedom of movement for the occupation forces throughout Austria, and joint use of facilities in Vienna in the covering report transmitting the Austrian protocol on zones. After protracted discussion the Commission was finally able to agree to a paragraph satisfactory to both sides on July 9.* Strang recalls that it was only with great difficulty that the Soviet delegation could be brought to agreement on this paragraph.[36] The paragraph provided that the Allied Council would "make the necessary arrangements for transit in Austria by road, rail, air and water for the goods and supplies required by the forces of occupation in Austria, including those forces allotted for the occupation of the City of Vienna. . . ."[37] Although the paragraph contained only a rather weak statement concerning transit to Vienna and although it appeared in the covering report rather than in the agreement itself, it was at least a clear statement that a right of Western access to Vienna existed and would have to be carried out practically by arrangements reached in the Allied Council. Franklin states: "The significance of the paragraph was larger than its actual wording, since by repeated statements the Soviet representatives had asserted that these principles applied to Berlin as well as to

---

*See pages 102–105, 107–108. In a written memorandum to the author, August 30, 1970, Mosely states that the American delegation to EAC always seemed to have more leeway on Austrian matters and more opportunity to formulate proposals. Replies from Washington also seemed to be more prompt, resulting in greater American effectiveness in the Austrian negotiations than in the German negotiations. Since most of the proposals concerning Austria were actually formulated in London, the U.S. delegation to EAC could play the veto game against the War Department in SWNCC.

SPECIAL PROBLEMS OF ACCESS

Vienna. In this curious fashion the Western negotiators did achieve—at long last—a formal statement of principles on transit rights across the Soviet zone in Austria to Vienna and, by specific analogy, across the Soviet zone in Germany to Berlin."[38] Mosely states that the negotiations on transit through Austria were not conducted with the express purpose of setting up an analogy for access through Germany to Berlin. The analogy came to be drawn for two reasons: the Soviet obstruction encountered on General Flory's mission to Vienna, and Gusev's attempt to omit the question of access to Vienna on the grounds that the German protocols had not contained express provisions for access to Berlin.[39] Whether or not it was the intention of the Western negotiators, however, the analogy between Vienna access and Berlin access was by now clear to everyone at Lancaster House.

New Studies Are Made

The question of access remained settled for all intents and purposes following the conference of June 29 and the completion of the agreements on Austria in July. During the following months, the three Western Powers utilized the various access routes to and from Berlin day after day without serious incident. No change in the access routes was made until November, when the number of air corridors to Berlin was increased from two to three. There is no published record of any Four Power discussions having been held on the question of access routes between July and November.

In the fall an Air Directorate was established subordinate to the Coordinating Committee as part of the control machinery in Germany. The Directorate's Aviation Committee undertook a comprehensive study of the aviation needs of the occupying Powers in Germany. Working with requests from the American, British, and French representatives for the setting up of a system of air corridors radiating all directions from Berlin, the Aviation Committee prepared and submitted a paper to the Air Directorate in November. The paper proposed the creation of six corridors over Germany: Berlin-Hamburg, Berlin-Hannover (Bückeburg), Berlin-Frankfurt-on-Main, Berlin-Warsaw, Berlin-Prague, Berlin-Copenhagen.[40]

During the discussion of the paper in the Air Directorate, the Soviet representative, Lieutenant General T. F. Kutzevalov, stated that he could agree to the creation of the three corridors from Berlin to the West: Berlin-Hamburg, Berlin-Bückeburg, and Berlin-Frankfurt-on-Main, as these were clearly necessary to provide for the needs of the Western occupation troops in Berlin. He felt, however, that the corridors Berlin-Warsaw, Berlin-Prague, and Berlin-Copenhagen, as well as a seventh corridor Bückeburg-Prague proposed by the British representative, were not related to securing the needs of the occupying forces in Berlin and could not therefore be discussed in the Air Directorate without instructions from higher authorities. In addition, he felt that the present rules of flight in the second group of air corridors were suitable to all and did not need to be changed. In the report of the Air Directorate to the Coordinating Committee, dated November 22, 1945, the directorate asked for confirmation of the three western corridors. Regarding the three eastern corridors and the Bückeburg-Prague route, the directorate requested the committee either to decide in principle the creation of these corridors or transmit the question to appropriate higher authority. In addition, the directorate asked for permission to compile rules of flight and means of safeguarding flights along any corridors approved.[41]

Decisions in November and December

The report of the Air Directorate was considered by the Coordinating Committee at its twenty-third meeting held on November 27, 1945.[42] General Robertson explained that it was "absolutely essential for the British to have air corridors both for flights from Berlin to Bückeburg, Headquarters of the British Army of the Rhine, and from Berlin to Hamburg, where this headquarters had a number of branches."[43] General Clay pointed out that the Americans also considered the Berlin-Bückeburg air corridor essential, since it was the logical connection for the Americans' primary port city of Bremen. To these suggestions General Sokolovsky had no objection. At the conclusion of the meeting the committee approved the creation of the three western corridors, but decided that the question of the three eastern corridors plus the Bückeburg-Prague route did not fall within its competence. Since these routes traversed other than occupied German territory, a decision at the governmental level would be needed to effect their creation.[44] The approval of the Coordinating Committee was then remitted to the Control Council for final decision. At its thirteenth meeting held on November 30, 1945, the Control Council gave final approval to the creation of the three corridors from Berlin to the western zones: Berlin-Bückeburg, Berlin-Hamburg, and Berlin-Frankfurt-on-Main.[45] Confirmation of the three western air corridors was now complete.

In the final months of 1945 further arrangements for use of ground access routes were made by various organs of the control machinery. There is no published record of the negotiations on these arrangements. A review of such negotiations would, however, exceed the bounds of this study, since they were concerned largely with technical matters. It was agreed that Western military personnel and military freight might use the Helmstedt-Berlin railroad track through the Soviet zone, and the Marienborn-Berlin autobahn route.[46] Barge traffic into Berlin was the subject of separate agreements between the British and Soviet zones.[47]

On March 6, 1946, the U.S. member of the Coordinating Committee submitted a memorandum requesting additional air corridors for commercial aviation, since it was felt that the three existing corridors were not adequate to provide for safe, economical operation of aircraft over Germany.

SPECIAL PROBLEMS OF ACCESS

The request was discussed at a meeting of the Air Directorate on April 30, 1946. In adamantly refusing to accede to the request the Soviet delegate stated that: "The Soviet Delegation thinks that the existing system of air routes through the Soviet Zone of Occupation in Germany is fully sufficient, not only to meet the requirements of the Allied Troops in the Sector of Greater Berlin, but also to carry out successfully all the Allied transportation needs for commercial cargoes regardless of their volume."[48] As a consequence, no agreement could be reached on increasing the number of air corridors.

The various agreements on access routes, both formal and informal, were carried out with little controversy until the Berlin blockade of 1948. Concerning the agreements of June 29, 1945, between Clay, Weeks, and Zhukov the U.S. political adviser for Germany, Robert Murphy, stated in a letter of April 7, 1948, to the State Department that, "as you understand, this agreement was never formalized, each party having made his own notes. However, during the interval that has elapsed since June 29, 1945, the lines of agreement have become established by daily usage and practice."[49] The lines of agreement were indeed quite well established. Until March 30, 1948, traffic flowed over all the access routes without interference by Soviet authorities and without restriction other than compliance with established traffic and safety regulations. It was not until the institution of the Berlin blockade that the routes of access suddenly became the subject of an explosive political clash.

SEVEN

POST-MORTEM ON THE WORK OF EAC

Having completed our review of the Allied negotiations which determined the postwar fate of Berlin, it is perhaps appropriate to attempt to make some overall assessment of the work of the European Advisory Commission in reference to the Berlin settlement. Such an assessment is difficult to make and must probably remain highly tentative for several reasons. First of all, the Berlin negotiations represent only a small segment of the total range of negotiations on Germany during the war years; thus, the problems surrounding the Berlin situation are inextricably interwoven into the nexus of problems connected with the larger question of what to do with Germany after the war. Any mistakes that might have been made in deciding upon the postwar fate of Berlin must be somehow related to the mistakes that were made in the disposition of Germany as a whole. Secondly, the negotiations on Germany and Berlin were not confined to the European Advisory Commission. Negotiations at the military level always formed a kind of second tier to the negotiations in EAC itself, and many of the basic decisions reached at the military level profoundly influenced the results arrived at by the Commission. Indeed the negotiations at the military level were sometimes even more determinative than those in EAC as can be seen from the British plan for deployment of troops in RANKIN and the June 29, 1945, arrangements on transit. Hence the work of the EAC can never be evaluated in the abstract; the EAC operated in a rather restricted context and was only one of the myriad bodies involved in postwar planning, even though it was the crucial body in the case of Germany and Berlin.

The Isolation of Berlin

Perhaps the primary question in any assessment of the protocols negotiated by EAC concerns the decision as to the geographical location of the capital city in the regime of zonal occupation. Was it not a basic mistake to leave Berlin as an enclave in the Soviet zone? Could not some settlement have been reached which placed Berlin within a western zone or which at least gave the Western Powers territorial access to Berlin? The answers to these questions are made somewhat simpler when one takes a basic map of Germany and studies it for a few moments. Berlin is located well within the eastern third of Germany even when the 1937 boundaries of Germany are taken into account. Once the regime of three separate zones of occupation had been decided upon, the almost inevitable conclusion was that the Soviet Union would occupy the eastern zone. It would have been senseless to propose that one of the Western Powers occupy eastern Germany while the Soviet Union occupy a zone in the west. This would have meant that the Soviet Union would have to travel across an intervening zone to supply its own zone, while a Western Power would have to traverse the Soviet zone to get to the east. In addition, it is unthinkable that Britain would ever have agreed to bringing a Soviet presence into Western Europe clear up to the borders of Belgium and Holland. With this alternative necessarily shelved, the only other way to give the Western Powers any kind of direct territorial access to Berlin would have been to place Berlin at the point of confluence of the three zones. Such an idea was considered in the early stages of planning for Germany by various planning staffs in the Department of State but was ultimately rejected as infeasible. Whether or not such a plan was given serious consideration within the British government is unknown. The first proposals of the Attlee Committee presented to EAC by Sir William Strang in January, 1944, concluded that Berlin should be located wholly within the Soviet zone but should be "a separate Combined zone."[1] At any rate any attempt to divide Germany so that the zones of occupation would come together at Berlin would assuredly have produced a bizarre, unrealistic division of the country with the zonal lines in total disregard of any of the traditional German administrative boundaries. Planning staffs in both the British and American governments concluded at an early stage that zonal divisions should correspond as far as possible with the state and provincial frontiers in Germany.

The logical assumption from the outset of the EAC negotiations was that the Soviet Union would occupy the eastern zone of Germany. What is actually rather amazing about the results of the work of the Western delegations is that the delegates worked for and achieved a Soviet agreement to make an exception of Berlin to the general scheme of zonal occupation. Thereby they created the right of the Western Powers to set up and maintain a physical and political as well as token military presence in Berlin. The Soviet government could have steadfastly refused to accede to any Western presence in Berlin from the very beginning. Strang emphasizes that, "The moral effect in Germany as a whole of the undivided control of their capital by the Soviet forces is not easily measured, but would have been far-reaching; and the free world would have lost the asset, uneasy and precarious though it may be, of having a foot in Berlin and of establishing an oasis of freedom in the middle of the desert of the Soviet zone."[2] The Western delegations to EAC deserve considerable credit for gaining Soviet assent to an agreement which gave the Western governments an unequivocal foothold in the capital city located so far within the eastern part of Germany.

The fact that Berlin constituted an enclave within the Soviet zone in the EAC agreements may seem a terrible error to later observers with all the benefits of hindsight. The alternatives were, however, few indeed: either some kind of territorial corridor connecting the western zones with Berlin, an alternative which was probably unattainable after the submission of the British proposal on zones very early in the negotiations in January, 1944; a mixed-force occupation of all of Germany, a solution early rejected by all Three Powers; or no Western presence in Berlin at all. The decision making Berlin an enclave must be seen in the light of the circumstances at the time the decision was reached. It gave the Western Powers a foothold in the capital city. The fact that Berlin was entirely surrounded by the Soviet zone was not envisaged as a serious situation. The occupation zones were conceived of by the EAC representatives as being important chiefly for administrative purposes in the stationing and billeting of occupation troops. The economic, social, and administrative unity of Germany as a whole would not be seriously disturbed. The EAC anticipated that there would be free movement between zones for all occupation personnel and for the German population for proper purposes. Consequently, Berlin's placement as an enclave did not appear either dangerous or unwise to the Western delegations.

Troubled Times and Difficult Circumstances

The EAC agreements on Germany and Berlin might have emerged in quite different form if the circumstances surrounding the EAC's work had been different. At the Moscow Conference the three foreign ministers had decided that some special body should be established "for dealing with questions requiring current and close collaboration." The EAC was given a mandate to "study and make joint recommendations to the Governments upon European questions connected with the termination of hostilities. . . . "[3] The clear expectation was that the representatives on EAC would possess a rather wide latitude in studying various alternative solutions to certain pressing problems of the postwar order and in formulating viable joint recommendations to forward to the three governments. The expectation remained unfulfilled. From the very beginning the EAC was forced to operate within a highly restricted context. It is possible that had the EAC been accorded the wide discretionary limits originally envisioned for it, the representatives to that body could have developed some far-reaching and imaginative solutions to the problems connected with military victory over Germany, solutions never even studied or debated within the respective governments. As it turned out the EAC was obliged to negotiate only on the basis of proposals developed and fully approved within each of the respective governments separately. It never possessed, nor was it able to develop, a real mandate of its own.

Part of our task, since we have reviewed carefully the negotiations on Berlin in EAC, is to discover some of the reasons for the difficulties which constantly plagued the EAC in its vital work. As we have seen, the British government seemed ready and willing to give the EAC full support in the accomplishment of its objectives. The frustrations and setbacks endured by the EAC must, therefore, be laid mostly to the account of the United States and the Soviet Union. The Soviet government was apparently loathe to give Mr. Gusev any meaningful room for maneuver in his dealings with the Western delegations. Characteristically he seemed to be chained to his briefcase in his insistence that a certain point was nonnegotiable from the Soviet point of view. From time to time he kept the work of the EAC at a standstill for days, even weeks, by refusing to proceed with the agenda or to yield on any point. At other times he stated that he could not proceed because he lacked appropriate instructions from Moscow. Mr. Gusev seemed personally eager to contribute to the success of the EAC negotiations, but it was obvious that often he did not have the full support of his government. Whereas Winant and Mosely could take initiatives toward Washington, Gusev could not take similar initiatives toward Moscow; all he could do was report U.S. and U.K. proposals to Moscow and wait for instructions. Gusev often complained to Mosely privately that he was unable to get answers from Moscow and was consequently unable to negotiate meaningfully at EAC meetings or permit meetings to be held. Molotov, he said, was busy "building tanks" until eleven at night and dealt with foreign policy matters after 11:00 p.m. (Written memorandum from Philip E. Mosely to the author, August 30, 1970.) Stalin, like Roosevelt, was never enthusiastic about EAC and was unwilling to let it develop a preeminent role in the process of planning for the postwar order.

Washington Policymaking: EAC's Major Affliction

Whatever the difficulties in Moscow, it still must be realized that the rivalries and contradictions in Washington constituted perhaps the major hindrance to the efficient functioning of the EAC. While Gusev was often intransigent, Winant was downright embarrassed. We have already spoken at some length of the manifold delays and reversals endured by Mr. Winant. Could these have been avoided? Could the whole process of policy formulation have been sufficiently rationalized so that Mr. Winant received promptly full guidance and instructions based on a concurrence of views in the relevant departments in Washington?

The major difficulty involved in the clearance of instructions to Winant was of course the chronic quarrel between the State and War Departments. The War Department tended to view the EAC as a child of the State Department and consequently refused to contribute to the child's upbringing. When the Working Security Committee was set up to provide interdepartmentally coordinated policy instructions to Mr. Winant, the War Department designated representatives at such a low level that they lacked any authority to approve anything or make any vital contribution to the consultations. The major difficulty lay with the representatives of the department's Civil Affairs Division. Kennan writes that, "The main source of the trouble was, quite clearly, the Civil Affairs Division of the War Department, which refused initially even to take part in any interdepartmental discussion looking to the instruction of the American representative on the EAC, and which later, having grudgingly consented to take part, did so in a manner so lacking in both candor and enthusiasm as to give the impression of sabotage."[4] The Civil Affairs representatives defended the interests of the military authorities with extreme tenacity, as if they were lawyers defending the interests of a client in court. Any suggestion which they felt was contrary to military interests or interfered with military jurisdiction was rejected summarily. This narrow, partisan point of view was not only immature and unnecessary but produced needless difficulty and delay in any attempt to get an interdepartmental meeting of the minds on important policy issues. Had the Civil Affairs representatives been able to realize that neither the War Department nor the Joint Chiefs of Staff possessed a monopoly of truth and that postwar political and economic policy in Europe was also a logical concern of the State Department, the ambassador in London could have been spared a great deal of grief. Perhaps the greatest errors on the part of the Civil Affairs Division were the refusal to give Mr. Winant any direction whatever in the negotiations relating to the delimitation of sectors in Berlin and the refusal to permit the matter of access to be negotiated in EAC at all. Kennan notes that, "As conduct on the part of people sharing responsibility for the instructing of an American envoy on major subjects of international negotiation, I find this irresponsible and seriously reprehensible."[5]

The Subordinate State Department

On the other hand, it must be emphasized that the wartime snarl in Washington was not entirely the fault of the Civil Affairs Division of the War Department. The State Department must also take a share of the blame. The department had at its disposal a sizeable number of well-trained experts and planning staffs who produced a number of carefully researched policy studies for the postwar order. Unfortunately, however, all during this period the State Department seemed singularly inept at making a coherent case for its well-documented policy studies either in the halls of the White

House or in the offices of important departmental chiefs. Part of the trouble was that neither Cordell Hull nor Edward R. Stettinius was a dominant, powerful secretary of state. Neither of these men stood as close to the president as such personal advisers as Harry Hopkins and Admiral William D. Leahy. An influential secretary of state could perhaps have done much more to impress upon the president the merit of the policy aims and goals which emerged from State Department studies. On the other hand, President Roosevelt was not the easiest man to work for in the State Department post. He tended to act as his own secretary of state much of the time, and on many occasions he simply ignored the State Department by withholding from the secretary vital information relating to the conduct of the war or the policy goals being considered by the administration. Despite the president's attitude toward the department, however, a shrewd and dominant secretary of state could have done much to cajole or coerce the War Department and the Joint Chiefs to cooperate with the WSC in a more realistic manner and could have influenced much more vitally the thinking of the president in matters of postwar foreign policy. The preeminence of ideas emanating from the military quarters need not have gone unchallenged for such long periods of time. The State Department largely abdicated its responsibility in March, 1944, by transmitting to Ambassador Winant with no comment at all a document of the Joint Chiefs which "made no substantive sense and was not even responsive to the known realities of the situation."[6] George Kennan comments incisively on the State Department's subordination to the military during the war years:

> I think it may well be asked whether responsible officials of the Department of State were justified in enduring this state of affairs and in collaborating, as they did, in the farcical and near-tragic confusion to which it repeatedly led. . . .
>
> Presumably, the standing instructions or understandings under which the Department of State was then operating gave it no formal right to intervene in such matters. But surely there are limits to such passivity and such a formal disclaimer of responsibility. . . . Why it should have been left to a junior officer such as myself to jeopardize his own career by going directly to the President on these two separate occasions—why the Department of State could not have taken upon itself this minimal responsibility—was a mystery to me at that time. It remains a mystery to the present day.[7]

President Roosevelt: The Final Responsibility

The inability of the State Department to articulate its views forcefully and the deplorable infighting between the State and War Departments in WSC and SWNCC were circumstances which gravely embarrassed the American ambassador at Lancaster House and which caused delay and uncertainty in the EAC negotiations. Ultimately the final responsibility for this regrettable state of affairs must rest with the American president.

There can be no doubt that Franklin Roosevelt handled the awesome responsibilities of the presidency during these tumultuous years with extraordinary, near superhuman capacity. He was a man with a keen mind, a dominant personality, and an exceptional ability to cope with grave crisis situations. When it comes to his handling of the negotiations on postwar Germany, however, his brilliant record is marked with some fatal flaws.

At the Moscow Conference in 1943 the American government assumed a solemn commitment to work out an agreed plan for the postwar disposition of Germany in concert with Britain and the Soviet Union. The body to which this grave responsibility was entrusted was the European Advisory Commission. Unfortunately Roosevelt placed America's commitment to EAC under constant suspicion. He was never enthusiastic about the EAC and he made known his displeasure with the Commission at the Yalta Conference and in repeated memoranda to the secretary of state. His virtual suspension of the work of EAC in October, 1944, could easily have worked to destroy the Commission completely had it not been for the patience and persistence of the representatives of all Three Powers on the Commission. If the Commission had broken up at that time, the United States would have had to bear the responsibility for failing to honor an international commitment duly entered into.

If Roosevelt did not approve of the direction in which EAC moved or of the policy aims it worked to implement, the question must be asked why he took no steps to correct the situation. He could have recalled Mr. Winant to Washington at any time for consultation or briefings. In addition he could have supplied Winant from time to time with a full expression of his views either directly or through the secretary of state. This he failed to do, leaving Winant in a position of constant uncertainty concerning the relationship of the EAC negotiations to the policies of the administration.

One of Mr. Winant's chief problems was the lack of instructions or guidance with which he was so often confronted. The conflicting lines of policy formulation in Washington led to repeated deadlock in WSC and often prevented that body from clearing any papers for transmission to London. Even worse, the papers which were eventually forwarded more than once represented a complete reversal of the instructions Winant had received only a short time before. The responsibility for this deplorable state of affairs also rests ultimately with the president. It is not to Roosevelt's credit that the lines of policy formulation in reference to postwar Germany remained incredibly tangled and confused throughout his administration. There was only one man who could have removed the tangles and established clear, coherent procedures for the formulation and transmission of policy alternatives to the ambassador in London. Only Mr. Roosevelt could have ironed out the competing jurisdictions of the War Department, the Joint Chiefs, and the State Department and rationalized the process of policy formulation in reference to postwar Germany. That he failed to do so and left Mr. Winant in a constantly vulnerable position at the EAC negotiating table is regrettable indeed.

The process of formulating policies for the postwar order was made unduly difficult partly because of Roosevelt's own ideas in reference to the conquered enemy state. One of the reasons that the State and War Departments were able to continue their struggle for the president's attention over such a protracted period of time was that Roosevelt's views on Germany and postwar Europe were never clearly defined and tended to vacillate a great deal. The president often tended to permit his prejudices against Germany and Germans, prejudices he may have acquired during his days as a young tourist in Germany, to influence his thinking to an unwarranted degree. On the one hand he favored a harsh, repressive policy in Germany after the war. On the other hand he was on occasion quite amenable to policy views developed in the State Department which looked forward to the reconstruction of Germany as a peaceful member of the international community as rapidly as possible. Throughout the year 1944 the president wavered in his thinking from one general approach to the other, inadvertently giving full rein to the competing jurisdictional struggles between departments.

Morgenthau's Ill-Fated Plan

Perhaps Roosevelt's greatest error in the handling of the German problem was to allow the Treasury Department to become involved in questions which normally would have been totally beyond its jurisdiction. The president's close personal relationship with Secretary of the Treasury Henry Morgenthau had the effect of giving Morgenthau undue weight in matters of foreign policy as a close adviser of the president. The ill-fated Morgenthau Plan for the pastoralization of Germany was vigorously fought by the State Department, and the precepts of the plan ran counter to basic foreign policy premises adhered to by many other branches of the federal bureaucracy. Secretary of War Stimson and Assistant Secretary McCloy opposed the plan rather promptly. Secretary of State Hull wavered at first but then joined Stimson in opposing the plan. The Civil Affairs Division of the War Department, on the other hand, liked much of the plan and managed to get substantial portions of it absorbed into JCS 1067, the Directive to the Commander in Chief of U.S. Forces of Occupation outlining basic policies for the military occupation of Germany. The army really did not abandon the spirit of the Morgenthau Plan until April, 1946, after the level-of-industry agreement had been negotiated in the Allied Control Council in Berlin. (Written memorandum from Philip E. Mosely to the author, August 30, 1970.)

The plan held a great deal of attraction for President Roosevelt, who continued to press hard for its adoption as official Allied policy from time to time until his death. Undoubtedly Roosevelt's liking for the plan stemmed in part from his great confidence in Mr. Morgenthau's judgment as confidant and adviser. It does, however, point up quite plainly the fact that Roosevelt's ideas about postwar policy in Germany were ill-conceived to an extent. It is difficult to understand how the president could favor a plan which was opposed by almost all knowledgeable experts on international affairs at the time and which certainly would have resulted in the creation of a power vacuum in the industrial heart of Europe after the war.

The president's approval of the Morgenthau Plan and his periodic attempts to persuade other Allied leaders to accept parts of the plan cast a continuous shadow of doubt over the proceedings in the European Advisory Commission. So also did the president's approval of the dismemberment idea. The representatives on the Commission could never be quite sure of the efficacy and long-range value of their work so long as the American president refused to give his full support to the negotiations and continued to espouse ideas which ran counter to the policy aims and goals which the Commission hoped to achieve in Germany. The American representative was effectively barred from making any vital contribution to the negotiations or participating in any effort to develop intelligent, far-sighted, long-range plans for postwar Germany as long as the president allowed the departmental infighting and bureaucratic logjams in Washington to continue. It was much to the detriment of the delicate negotiations at Lancaster House that the foreign policy process in Washington, at least as far as the subject of postwar Germany was concerned, remained in a state of disarray.

Criticism and Countercriticism

It remains for us to attempt to make some assessment of the results of the work accomplished by the EAC and of the reasonableness of the agreements negotiated by the Commission. In this connection it is relevant to ask whether the agreements signed by the EAC could have been written so as to obviate some of the dismal events of subsequent years, such as the development of mutually exclusive regimes and the occurrence of crisis after crisis over Berlin. Professor Jean Smith believes that the EAC agreements were by and large ill considered. He suggests that, from the viewpoint of the West's interests, it was a great mistake to draw the boundaries of the occupation zones so as to locate Berlin one hundred and ten miles within the Soviet zone. He apparently believes that the outcome of the negotiations on zones could have been much more satisfactory to the security needs of the United States and suggests that the major part of the blame for the unsatisfactory terms of the agreements belongs to the State Department and the U.S. delegation to EAC.

Unwittingly, the United States had become a party to an agreement to which the responsible Administration at that time was opposed. If the gov-

POST-MORTEM ON THE EAC

ernmental machinery had been able to translate this opposition into effective action in London, that agreement would not have been reached. If the State Department had proven itself capable of following Administration direction in the years before the war, the situation probably would not have arisen in the first place.

When the boundaries of the Soviet zone were first proposed, the conflict in Washington prevented President Roosevelt's ideas from being transmitted to London. When the Administration position later was forwarded, the opinion of the London delegation prevented it from being introduced into the proceedings.

The total inability to translate the policy announcements of President Roosevelt on the *Iowa* into effective action at the scene of the negotiations in London exposes a weakness in our governmental process which recent events have shown to be a luxury we can hardly afford.[8]

These statements require careful analysis. Smith faults the State Department and the U.S. delegation to EAC for not adhering closely to the directives of the president in the negotiations in London. This criticism would be entirely justified, had it not been for the tangled, bifurcated policy process in Washington which initially prevented the transmission of any directives at all to London for several weeks in early 1944. This delay was hardly the fault of Winant or the American delegation. And it must be remembered that the document which Winant finally received in March, 1944, was a military directive to the Combined Chiefs of Staff which made no sense politically and could not even be presented to the Commission without extensive redrafting. (See pages 40–43.) The American Joint Chiefs insisted that the directive represented the wishes of the president. It cannot be assumed, however, that the president's wishes as expressed on the *Iowa* were eternally fixed and not subject to revision in response to changed military or political circumstances. When George Kennan pointed out the altered set of circumstances in his interview with the president in April, Roosevelt was not at all averse to giving his approval to the zonal boundaries as proposed by the British delegation, provided the United States would occupy the northeast zone. Later in the year the president was persuaded by Churchill to change his mind on that question also. In view of the president's remark to Kennan that the directive received in London represented only "something I once drew on the back of an envelope,"[9] it is not correct to assert that the president's policy pronouncements were callously disregarded by the State Department and the American delegation to EAC.

It can be posited in response to Smith's criticism that the State Department and the American delegation to EAC were under a kind of moral and political obligation to attempt to secure a modification of those precepts in the president's thinking which contradicted the political realities of the time and which represented a patently unsound negotiating position for the U.S. delegation in the proceedings of the Commission. In attempting to influence the president's thinking concerning U.S. policy in postwar Germany and in working quietly and patiently to bring U.S. policy recommendations into some kind of balance with those being developed by the British and Soviet delegations, the American ambassador was rendering that kind of international service which we must expect and demand of an experienced diplomat.

It may be correct to point out that President Roosevelt was never quite happy with the provisions of the agreement on zones of occupation. In addition, Professor Smith is perhaps quite correct in his assertion that the agreement would never have been reached if the president's initial opposition to the boundaries as proposed by the British had been translated into effective action in London. The fact of the matter is, however, that if the president's opposition had been stressed too actively or too long by Mr. Winant, there may well have been no agreement at all. It is a mistake to believe that the zonal boundaries could have been drawn much more favorably to the West, perhaps even including Berlin in a western zone, if only Mr. Winant had acted swiftly and vigorously in presenting the JCS directive which approximated Roosevelt's ideas on zonal boundaries. As we have seen, the British and Soviet delegations had both approved the British proposal for the future Soviet zone and had done so long before Winant received the JCS directive from Washington. Furthermore, the boundaries suggested in the JCS memorandum were so incomprehensible and formed zones of such unequal proportions that the document was a source of acute embarrassment to the American delegation, so much so that Ambassador Winant took the unusual step of sending Kennan back to Washington to explain to the president why it was impossible to present the document to the EAC. It cannot be thought that Roosevelt's ideas on boundaries as sketched on the National Geographic map or as described in the JCS memorandum ever stood the slightest chance of acceptance by the EAC. Consequently it is not really fair to fault Winant or the State Department for failing to heed Roosevelt's directions. Indeed, as shown by the Roosevelt-Kennan meeting, the president was quite ready to accept the boundary proposed for the Soviet zone in the British draft after Mr. Kennan had pointed out to him the confusion which had been caused by the JCS memorandum. Taking these considerations into account, it is perhaps appropriate to conclude that Mr. Winant and the other members of the American delegation were only fulfilling the responsibilities entrusted to them as diplomatic envoys of the United States by their persistent efforts to influence and inform the president's opinion on matters of postwar policy in Germany.

A Mistaken Assumption

One assumption that would seem to underlie Professor Smith's criticism of the EAC is the idea that if the entire set of negotiations had been handled by the military authorities and the War Department, the outcome would have been much more satisfactory to the interests of the United States and the West.[10] This assumption is not necessarily true. Certainly the planning of occupation policy and the division of Germany into zones of occupation entailed foreign policy interests that far transcended the competence of the military branches of the government. Naturally, the zones of occupation might have looked different if they had been decided upon in May, 1945, after Germany had been conquered and completely occupied by Allied forces. The Western military authorities at that time would have been in an extremely favorable bargaining position because of the territory they controlled. It was not, however, the policy of any of the Allied Powers to leave such important questions as zones of occupation and control machinery for last minute negotiation. One of the reasons that the zones of occupation were decided upon so far in advance was to obviate a mad scramble for territory in Germany between East and West at the end of the war. Given the desirability, indeed the necessity, of reaching advance agreements on such crucial questions as zones of occupation and the disposition of postwar Germany, there is no reason to assume that such negotiations would have been handled more successfully by military authorities. The questions considered by the Commission concerned overlapping interests of a political, economic, social, and military nature which could have been treated only at the highest diplomatic level by a collegial body such as the European Advisory Commission, not by military authorities alone.

The way in which the question of access to Berlin was handled is good evidence that negotiations at the military level were not necessarily bound to succeed more profitably than negotiations in EAC. The history of the military negotiations on access is replete with errors and negligence of the most unfortunate sort. It will always remain somewhat of a mystery that the Western military authorities spent so many months haggling over American access rights through the British and French zones while nothing was done about securing any rights of Western access through the Soviet zone to Berlin. There is no way of knowing whether Mr. Winant could have fared better in the EAC in getting the Soviet government to agree to some provisions for access to Berlin in the German agreements. The negotiations on Austria and Vienna do not necessarily suggest an affirmative answer to that question. One thing, however, is clear: considering the outcome of the military negotiations on the access question, Mr. Winant should have been allowed to try his hand in the EAC. The insistence of the military authorities on handling the access question purely through military channels was not justified from any point of view. Arrangements on access represented one important segment of the total negotiations on the postwar disposition of Germany as a whole and should have been incorporated into the EAC negotiations at an early date, even while keeping military considerations paramount. That military needs and convenience would be taken into account fully in defining the U.S. negotiating position in London was the reason why the State Department took the initiative in setting up the WSC. What the State Department did not foresee was that the Civil Affairs Division of the War Department would twist that effort at coordination into a cast-iron veto on any and all U.S. positions.

Plugging All the Holes

Much of the criticism which has been directed toward the EAC in the postwar years seems to be based upon an assumption which, if examined carefully, is not really tenable. That is to say, many of the critics seem to assume that the EAC should have been able to plug all the holes in the German agreements and should have provided Western defense mechanisms for all the possible sources of conflict with the Soviet Union which might arise after the war. Certainly there were many flaws in the agreements as negotiated by EAC. It is true that the agreements on Germany did not contain many favorable options for the Western Powers in case of conflict with the Soviet Union, but it is also unreasonable to expect the Western delegations to EAC to have been able to foresee and make provision for all possible sources of conflict between East and West in the postwar order. It must be remembered that the EAC had to base its work upon certain basic assumptions about the postwar system in order to proceed at all. One of those assumptions was that after the war there would be sufficient good will and cooperation among the Great Powers to enable them to collaborate successfully in managing the postwar arrangements in Europe. The EAC had to assume that cooperation, not hostility, would be the major cornerstone of the postwar order; otherwise it would not have been able to proceed at all. Since the Commission operated on this basic assumption, it viewed its task as one of finding reciprocally acceptable solutions for the disposition and treatment of postwar Germany, not one of devising means for the mitigation of postwar disputes. To expect the Western representatives on EAC to have provided satisfactory options for the West in all disputes that might arise over Germany and Berlin after the war is to misrepresent the context in which EAC operated and to demand more than has been accomplished by any Western negotiating body in recent times.

An Important Omission

When one considers the specific arrangements that were devised for Berlin in the postwar disposition of Germany, there is perhaps one area in which the work of the EAC remained less than complete. Nowhere in any of the EAC agreements is there any clear statement of the legal relationship of Berlin to the other zones of Germany. Today this appears to be a serious gap, mainly because of the rich legal controversy over the status of Berlin which has developed in the years since the war. The record of the EAC negotiations shows that the representatives spent a great deal of time discussing the legal status of Germany as a nation after the war, the legal status of the German government vis-à-vis the Allied Control Authority in the occupation regime, and the status of German nationality. In addition, lengthy discussions were held on such problems as the status of displaced persons and prisoners of war and the legal accreditation of foreign missions in Germany. When it comes to Berlin, however, the discussions were almost exclusively political in tone and content with little or no recognition given to legal considerations.

There are, of course, good reasons for the omission. First of all, the EAC was a body for political negotiations, not a legal commission of jurists; it existed to reach certain political settlements, not to define legal relationships. Secondly, there appeared no real need at the time to define precisely the legal relationship of Berlin to the other zones, since all the zones of occupation, including Berlin, were looked upon mainly as administrative divisions of the Allied Control Authority. Thirdly, the most serious postwar legal tangle, namely, the status of the access routes to Berlin, was not a concern of the Commission, since the access question was not negotiated through EAC.

Nevertheless, one might wish that the EAC had given more serious consideration to legal considerations in the negotiations concerning Berlin. Berlin's actual relationship to the other zones of occupation is left rather vague and indefinite by the language of the protocol on zones which stipulates that, "Germany, . . . will, for the purposes of occupation, be divided into three zones, . . . and a special Berlin area, which will be under joint occupation by the three Powers." At no point in the protocol is Berlin referred to as a "zone"; the language refers only to the "Berlin area" or simply to "Greater Berlin" throughout. In the actual discussions at the EAC negotiating table, however, the representatives repeatedly talked about the "Berlin zone." The representatives must have been aware that the subtle difference between the word "zone" and the word "area" in the written protocol might later give rise to controversy over the actual legal status of Berlin in relation to the other zones of occupation. The failure of the representatives to face this problem head-on and to define the relationship more precisely is regrettable in the light of the political developments which have taken place in Berlin since 1945. At the time, however, such political developments could not be foreseen, and the representatives probably felt that the language of the protocol was sufficiently clear to allow a workable regime to be established. Legal relationships could be defined in actual practice as time went on. In addition, to engage in lengthy discussions at the negotiating table on Berlin's legal relationship to the other zones might have opened still another can of worms which could have delayed agreement on the zones protocol even further. The consequences of the lack of a precisely defined relationship between the Berlin area and the other zones, however, have been unfortunate. Legal controversy involving considerable acrimony as well as inaccuracy has flourished since the early days of Berlin's quadripartite occupation. In addition, the Western Allies later found it difficult to make strong remonstrances to the Soviet Union against the total absorption of East Berlin into the East German regime and against the building of the Berlin Wall in the eastern sector of the city.

The Verdict

Considering the work of the European Advisory Commission as a whole in reference to Berlin and Germany, it is clear that the Commission produced a series of agreements which were given full effect by the Four Powers when the appropriate time came and which worked admirably in regulating the occupation regime in Germany for nearly three years. The agreements concerning Berlin continue to be observed to a significant extent to this day, albeit not without important modifications.

Considering the exceedingly difficult circumstances in which the EAC had to work and the minimal support given its work by two of the governments sponsoring it, it is remarkable that the Commission was able to produce in so coherent a fashion the documents which were later approved by the governments and went into effect as international treaties regulating the postwar disposition of Germany and Berlin. Had it not been for the patience, perseverance, and persistence of all three representatives on the EAC, it is likely that the documents would never have been produced. The chaotic circumstances of conquest at the end of the war in that case would have been left entirely to impromptu military settlements, with all the unpredictable results attached thereto. This is, in essence, the real value of the work of the EAC. Indeed it is probably no exaggeration to say that, as a collegial body working quietly behind the scenes at the highest levels of diplomacy, the European Advisory Commission came as close as any body in recent history to laying the foundation stones of trust, confidence, and respect which are the indispensable elements of any workable international system.

EIGHT

THE BERLIN NEGOTIATIONS AND WARTIME ALLIANCE DIPLOMACY

Our purpose in this final chapter is to give consideration to the broader aspects of the Berlin negotiations as an exercise in wartime alliance diplomacy. Though we have necessarily had to give a certain amount of attention to the policy process in Washington as an input and regulator of the proceedings in London, we should nevertheless remember that the negotiations in London were international negotiations, part and parcel of the dynamic process of international diplomacy. If our interest had been to retrace the evolution of American policy in reference to postwar Germany and Berlin, we would have had to keep our attention focused on Washington. Our interest, however, has been in the evolution of an international, more specifically Allied, policy in reference to postwar Berlin, thus keeping our attention focused primarily on Lancaster House in London. Insofar as an inter-Allied plan for postwar Germany and Berlin was worked out, it was achieved largely within the framework of the European Advisory Commission. And insofar as postwar arrangements for Berlin were concerned, the EAC seems to be the only body where such matters were ever discussed among the Allies, excepting the access problem, at least until the Control Council and the Kommandatura, themselves creations of the EAC negotiations, began to function in the summer of 1945.

Success or Failure?

It might be concluded that the settlement on Berlin was a diplomatic disaster for the West and that the processes of international diplomacy concerning Berlin in and through the European Advisory Commission were therefore a sham. What the West received as a result of the negotiations was only a piece of a divided city wholly within the Soviet zone of Germany. This conclusion, though certainly possible, would seem too hasty and too simple. As pointed out in the previous chapter, the possible alternatives were few indeed, and the remarkable fact about the negotiations is that the Western Powers succeeded at all in getting the Soviet Union to agree to a Western presence in Berlin. We know, of course, that the Western hold on West Berlin was extremely precarious for many years and that the situation remains far from settled today, despite the quadripartite agreement on Berlin of September 3, 1971. Still, however, we must not overlook the fact that for over thirty years the Western Powers have been able to maintain an oasis of Western civilization and culture deep within the territory of the repressive East German regime. Even today West Berlin remains a symbol of vibrance and strength throughout the entire world. These considerations would at least tend to temper a hasty conclusion that the Berlin settlement was a diplomatic debacle for the West.

Nevertheless, the conclusion is almost inescapable that the European Advisory Commission did not succeed in creating a truly viable set of arrangements for Germany or Berlin for the postwar period. Quadripartite administration of Germany as a whole and Berlin as a special area rapidly deteriorated into a system of hermetically sealed, mutually exclusive regimes. Even before the end of 1946 the Greater Berlin area was in effect split between two rival administrative systems. This outcome leads us to inquire into the pitfalls of diplomacy among the members of a wartime alliance in general and more specifically into the difficulties of alliance diplomacy through a quasi-collegial body such as the European Advisory Commission.

It is perhaps impossible to arrive at any definitive assessment of the quality of EAC diplomacy in reference to Berlin. After all, the Berlin settlement occupied only a small percentage of the EAC's total working time, and it represented only part of a much more inclusive set of arrangements for Germany as a whole. In order to arrive at a truly valid assessment it would be necessary to produce a great number of parallel studies of the Allied wartime negotiations, both in and out of EAC, covering all the major subjects of negotiation. In the absence of such voluminous work, however, the Berlin negotiations in EAC can be instructive in pointing up a number of limited conclusions and speculations.

The Need for Top-Level Agreement

In the first place, the Berlin arrangements negotiated by EAC show clearly that international diplomacy is a delicate and precarious art, a process which threatens to break down at every difficult juncture. Even among allies bound together in a wartime military coalition against a common enemy, diplomacy is a hazardous course. When the coalition partners include members of opposing economic and social systems, the process of diplomacy is made even more complicated. Several times in the Berlin negotiations, as we have seen, the conversations were broken off or suspended for considerable lengths of time, sometimes for reasons having no connection with the negotiations themselves. On other occasions an impasse was reached which could not be surmounted for days or even weeks. Such an impasse was by no means always an East-West affair; almost as often it seemed to be between the Western Powers themselves, as in the Bremen access dispute. What is important to realize is that the delicacy of diplomacy within EAC was related less to the structure and composition of that body than to the general pattern of relationships between the members of the Allied coalition. The level of agreement achieved in EAC was always a reflection of the level of agreement at the highest levels of government. The prolonged delay in deciding on the French zone in Germany and the French sector in Berlin was obviously related to unresolved issues among de Gaulle, Churchill, Roosevelt, and Stalin. The EAC was perhaps no different from any other intergovernmental negotiating body in this respect. The success or failure of any set of negotiations within any given forum depends ultimately upon the level of consensus at the highest levels of government. If a fundamental agreement on the basic outlines of a peace plan is lacking, then such a plan cannot be negotiated by even the most streamlined negotiating body or the most talented diplomats. And even if the diplomats should somehow succeed in getting a conference agreement on a plan, it would still be nonviable if the will to implement it is absent. Here then is the touchstone of the success or failure of international negotiations.

East-West Suspicions

In the case of the EAC there were severe ruptures in the plaster of the wartime military coalition which constantly impeded the Commission in the course of its work. The EAC needed, in addition to the reservoir of diplomatic skill represented on the Commission, the will of all four governments at the highest level in order to be successful. Such will was not always present. Throughout the course of the war and quite clearly by 1944–1945, there were fundamental suspicions and misgivings between the Soviet Union and the Western Powers which were clearly reflected in the efforts of the EAC to design a status for postwar Berlin. Churchill's series of frantic telegrams to Truman in opposition to withdrawal of American troops from Eastern Germany clearly shows the deep apprehensions of the British government in regard to Soviet behavior after the war. (See pages 88–91, 94–96.) Marshal Chuikov's war memoirs likewise reveal a rather deep mistrust of Western intentions on the part of the highest figures in the Soviet military establishment and presumably also the Soviet government.[1]

These mutual suspicions, which intensified toward the end of the war, would seem to lend credibility to the conclusion that if it had not been for the work of the European Advisory Commission and the basic protocols on Germany and Berlin drawn up within that body during the war, it is quite likely that there would have been a troublesome, perhaps violent, East-West struggle for territory and influence in Germany at the end of the war. Although the debate will undoubtedly continue for many years over the wisdom of Churchill's proposal to postpone the withdrawal of American troops for bargaining purposes with the Soviet Union, the fact still remains that ultimately each of the three major Allies eventually established control only in the zone which had been decided for it long before the Allied armies even entered Germany. Berlin, likewise, became an area of joint responsibility and was militarily occupied by sectors as had been decided by the EAC many months previously. Consequently, we may conclude that even though the arrangements for Germany were far from complete and eventually nonviable, still the EAC contribution to the postwar order was noteworthy. The arrangements drawn up in EAC helped to obviate a chaotic East-West struggle in Germany and Berlin after the war and established at least a basis upon which a coordinated program and policy could have been carried out by the Allies, had they been able to surmount the basic misunderstandings which gave rise to the Cold War.

Failure to Carry Out the Moscow Commitment

The suspicions and apprehensions of the war years weighed heavily upon the work of the EAC and prejudiced the outcome of the negotiations to no small degree. What happened, actually, was that none of the three major Allies carried out in good faith the commitment made at the Moscow Conference in 1943 when the decision was made to establish the European Advisory Commission. Quite clearly, the establishment of EAC was based on the premise that the Commission would work to design the basic outlines of a postwar order in Germany and recommend this plan to the three governments. The Commission would necessarily have to work in difficult and unfamiliar territory; it would need to be innovator, designer, and inventor all at the same time within the limits of its competence. It would proffer to the three governments advice and recommendations which might lead them to a harmonious, rational, and practicable set of arrangements for the postwar period. This role the EAC was never allowed to play. Difficulties within each of the three member governments plus suspicions and apprehensions at the highest level between the Soviet Union and the Western Powers kept the EAC from fulfilling its implicit mandate and from accomplishing the kind of results it could have and should have. This fact was underlined forcefully by the late Professor Walter Dorn: "If one is bent on being critical, one will call this what it deserves—embracing a policy of drift. What is certain is that on both sides of the Atlantic the professional diplomats had been overruled. On both sides of the Atlantic a commitment, implicit in the decision of the Moscow Conference of 1943 to negotiate a tripartite occupation policy, had been abandoned, not, indeed in favor of improvisation as in Italy, but in favor of unilateral instructions of the four governments to their supreme commanders, which was still worse."[2]

Why did the Three Powers, especially the United States, shrink from the full implications of the Moscow agreement regarding the purposes for which the European Advisory Commission had been set up? The reasons are, of course, difficult to pinpoint, but certainly there was a kind of latent fear that the EAC might outdo itself. Due to the cordial nature of personal relationships within the Commission, the governmental leaders perhaps feared that the London diplomats might trust each other more than the respective heads of government, and they might agree to plans considerably more far-reaching than the heads of government themselves were prepared to agree to. In addition, there was perhaps some fear that the EAC might gain too much power and prestige in the long run and might overshadow the processes of decision making in the respective capitals in respect to postwar Germany.

President Roosevelt in particular made various attempts to see to it that the American delegation to EAC never gained any real decision-making competence and was kept strictly subordinate to policy directives sent out from Washington. The president was entirely correct from a procedural standpoint, but the net effect of keeping the American delegation under such severe strictures was a failure, at least in spirit, to live up to the Moscow commitment to work out a comprehensive plan and policy for defeated Germany in concert with the other Allies within the framework of the European Advisory Commission. Premier Stalin, like Roosevelt, never quite trusted the EAC. He was loathe to accord Mr. Gusev much personal attention and attempted to keep EAC affairs on the margins of the Soviet government's official concern. Gusev never possessed the kind of instructions that would have permitted him to engage in comprehensive exploratory conversations on postwar Germany with his colleagues on EAC. Of the three governments represented at Moscow, only the British government seemed inclined to accord the EAC the comprehensive mandate implied in the conference protocol. More than British willingness, however, was necessary for such a mandate to become reality.

The Conceptual Lack of a Master Plan

The failure to carry out the full implications of the Moscow commitment regarding EAC points up a more fundamental circumstance mentioned earlier, namely, the lack of trust between the Soviet Union and the Western Powers which persisted throughout the war years. This lack of trust and the abiding suspicion of either side for the other meant that a real consensus on the basic lines of a settlement for postwar Germany could not be achieved at the highest level of heads of government. And in absence of agreement at the highest level, it could not be artificially manufactured in EAC. The two basic protocols on Germany and Berlin negotiated by EAC, the agreement on occupation zones and the agreement on control machinery, both amended, represent only the skeletal outlines of a plan for the disposition of Germany and Berlin in the postwar period. They provided for the division of Germany into zones of military occupation, including a special and separate Berlin area, and for the basic organs of a military administration, again with a special regime for the Berlin area. What they did not provide was the barest ground plan of a policy program to be jointly implemented by the Allies in the zones of occupation through the control machinery. The EAC agreements were like a new house with no furniture in it. The effort to work out a detailed and comprehensive inter-Allied policy program for defeated Germany in the form of a set of quadripartite directives to be issued to and put into effect by the four zonal commanders never reached fruition in the EAC.

The three, later four, Allied governments succeeded only in building the foundation of the projected new building of postwar Germany. Lack of basic agreement at the highest levels prevented them from completing and furnishing the building. When the EAC was not permitted to complete negotiations on the numerous quadripartite draft directives, it began work, in April, 1945, on a single broad statement of policy. This document finally became part of the Potsdam Agreement as "The Principles to Govern the Treatment of Germany in the Initial Control Period." Unfortunately, however, the Potsdam Agreement came too late and resulted in an artificial construction which rapidly disintegrated. Professor Dorn is essentially correct in his judgment that, ". . . a sustained effort to negotiate a common Allied occupation policy before the end of the war was not made, and when it was made at the Potsdam Conference it was too late."[3]

From beginning to end a conceptual master plan for postwar Germany was lacking. Even more, the Allies did not agree on the outline of even a temporary solution to the German problem after the anticipated victory in war. The EAC did not attempt to negotiate long-range solutions to postwar problems, such as territorial settlements, etc. These were supposed to be settled by a peace treaty. EAC planning was assumed to cover an indeterminate period, perhaps two years or so, between the end of hostilities and the peace settlement. But even here there was a basic failure of wartime inter-Allied policy coordination, and it must be attributed, in the last instance, to the suspicions and disagreements at the highest levels of government and ultimately to the heads of government themselves. We cannot, of course, simply fault Roosevelt, Churchill, and Stalin for failing to agree with each other and develop the needed master plan. There were indeed all manner of reasons rooted in the structure of international politics and the context of the times why they were unable to agree on certain questions. Statesmen, unlike saints, do not operate on faith. The fact remains, how-

THE NEGOTIATIONS AND ALLIANCE DIPLOMACY 161

ever, that the lack of anything resembling a master plan for postwar Germany severely hampered the entire process of negotiation within the EAC.

Preconditions for the Success of International Negotiations

The experience of EAC in 1944–1945 points up some of the basic problems associated with any effort to negotiate during wartime a policy or plan for the posthostilities period. There would seem to be at least two preconditions which must be fulfilled before any such negotiations can fully succeed. In the first place, there must be a high level of confidence and trust between the members of the coalition which extends to the highest levels of government. And in the second place, each member of the coalition must either have or develop some very basic ideas concerning the structure of the postwar order, and these must be of such a nature that they can be meshed or coordinated with the plans of the other members of the coalition. It is not enough that the allies aim to achieve a total military victory over the enemy. If there are not definite and positive objectives, i.e. structural changes in the pattern of international relationships, which are to be achieved above and beyond the military victory, then the war will have been fought in vain. All too often in the history of human conflict the postwar order after a major struggle has turned out to be less satisfactory and less stable than the system which resulted in general international breakdown and gave rise to the war. In the case at hand, the situation in Germany and Berlin after World War II turned out to be less than satisfactory because the Allies gave too much attention to the achievement of victory over Nazi Germany and too little attention to the structure of a vastly altered postwar order. None of the Allies seemed to have a clear idea of the kind of Europe which should result from Germany's defeat, and none of them had anything resembling a master plan for the new Europe which could be discussed with the Allies. Lacking clear vision, the Allied leaders entrusted to the European Advisory Commission the task of drawing up the design for a postwar European order. But having once commissioned the EAC, the Allies then shrank from the full implications of the commitment they had made and declined to accord the EAC the support it needed to fulfill its mandate. We can see now with the wisdom of hindsight that this was not the best way to pursue peace planning during wartime. We can also see that things could have been quite different. As with any historical situation, we can posit a set of proverbial "ifs" which might have produced very different historical results. If the Soviet Union and the Western Powers had developed more confidence in each other for the fashioning of a better future after the war, if they had given a great deal more thought to the development of a blueprint for a rational postwar order, if they had carried out fully and in good faith the commitments made at the Moscow Conference, and finally if they had given the European Advisory Commission full and positive support in all aspects of its complicated work, then the arrangements made for postwar Germany and Berlin might have been more intelligent, more practicable, and more permanent. A word of caution, however, is in order. To ask for the fulfillment of all these conditions may be asking for something like perfection in international affairs, a never attainable condition, and may be suggesting more than was realistically possible in the context of 1944–1945.

The Failure of Governmental Bureaucracies

Deep suspicions and a lack of trust between East and West constitute only one of several reasons for the failure of the Allied governments to agree on the basic premises of a postwar order for Germany and Berlin. There are other reasons also. The failure of governmental bureaucracies to perform rationally is undoubtedly another important reason. In the previous chapter we discussed at length the departmental infighting and bureaucratic logjams in Washington throughout 1944 and 1945 which so often prevented the State Department from cabling instructions to Ambassador Winant in London. The British government was plagued with these conditions to a much lesser degree, but even Sir William Strang often found it necessary to negotiate with less than adequate instructions. In addition, there was the intergovernmental dispute within the British government over the dismemberment issue, with Eden, Strang, and the Foreign Office opposed to dismemberment and Churchill supporting it. Though we do not know much about bureaucratic disputes within the Soviet government at this time, we may safely assume that Mr. Gusev's lack of instructions was not always due solely to Stalin's unwillingness to send instructions. Most probably there were certain communication problems and bureaucratic disputes even in Moscow which prevented the Soviet government from providing Mr. Gusev with prompt and adequate instructions. We do know that during 1943 and most of 1944 the Soviet Foreign Ministry was quite firmly in control of general foreign policy. After November or December, 1944, the military became more heavily involved. When the issue of reparations came into the picture, by the time of Yalta, a special committee directly subordinate to Stalin became very influential. (Written memorandum from Philip E. Mosely to the author, August 30, 1970.)

This leads us to another broad conclusion concerning the efficacy of international negotiations. If a number of governments decide to institute international negotiations on a certain subject or range of subjects, they should not expect the body or forum to which the negotiations are entrusted to achieve notable results unless the diplomats are provided with full and adequate instructions at all times through clear channels of communication to the responsible authorities in the respective national capitals. This is a *sine qua non* of the success of international diplomacy. The quarrels, dis-

THE NEGOTIATIONS AND ALLIANCE DIPLOMACY 163

putes, and confused lines of communication in Washington during 1944–1945 in reference to the London negotiations must be considered entirely inexcusable. They were unnecessary, and they could have been cleared up in short order if the appropriate steps had been taken. As it was, the confusion in Washington seriously impaired Ambassador Winant's effectiveness at the negotiating table and impeded the whole process of diplomacy at Lancaster House.

The Failure of Statesmanship

There is one last factor in the failure of the Allies to develop a viable plan for postwar Germany and Berlin which must not be overlooked. The failure is essentially one of statesmanship. The Big Three—Churchill, Roosevelt, and Stalin—stand permanently in the annals of history as towering statesmen in reference to their work in forging a mighty military coalition which achieved the total destruction of the Nazi Third Reich in World War Two. The record of their work, however, in reference to the establishment of a viable postwar order in Germany and Berlin is less than brilliant. The Allied failure to achieve within EAC a comprehensive postwar plan for Germany occurred not only because of basic East-West disagreement, because of inattention to postwar problems, or because of inefficient governmental bureaucracies. Occasional lack of statesmanship at the highest level also played a role. President Roosevelt persisted until his death in raising objections to the negotiation of a comprehensive postwar German policy agreement with the other Allies. This he did contrary to the advice of many of his trusted advisers and despite the obvious need for a comprehensive plan in order to avert a bitter struggle for influence in Germany after the war. Quite naturally he did not want to tie the hands of the U.S. commanders in Germany after the war and he did not want to limit the options of American policy. On the other hand, however, this amounted to a dangerous policy of drift, an attempt to sweep under the rug the difficult problems of postwar cooperation in Europe in the hope they could be solved by a new general international organization, the United Nations. It is not unfair to suggest that this was not statesmanship at its best.

The long and dreary squabble between Churchill and Roosevelt over occupation of the northwest zone also represented a deplorable lack of real statesmanship. At times it seemed reminiscent of two children quarreling over possession of the same toy. The hard-nosed fashion in which both men presented their nonnegotiable claims over many months' time represented sheer obstinacy rather than statesmanship. Roosevelt's hard-headed insistence upon American occupation of the northwest zone in the face of persuasive arguments that the southern zone would be just as satisfactory served not only to delay the EAC negotiations substantially but also to alarm and irritate the Russians needlessly. The Russians suspected that the U.S.

and the U.K. were stalling in order to avoid any definite commitment on the Soviet zone and perhaps also to see if the German military could succeed in overthrowing Hitler and surrendering to the West. Also, the American president's long attraction for a punitive and repressive peace for Germany and for the idea of dismemberment, which would leave a power vacuum in the center of Europe, places some doubt upon the wisdom of the president's leadership in matters concerning postwar Germany.

The quality of Soviet statesmanship is also open to severe criticism. There can be little doubt that Stalin hoped to use the Allied military victory to add territory to the sphere of Soviet domination in Europe. No one disputes the fact that the Soviet Union began taking action in clear violation of the Yalta agreements almost as soon as the ink was dry on the documents. Soviet refusal in 1945 to give up one inch of the previously allotted Soviet sector of Berlin in the interest of reaching a compromise settlement in the creation of a new French sector strengthens the conclusion that the Soviet leadership was more interested in maximizing the Soviet Union's power in postwar Europe than in devising a rational settlement which might safeguard the peace. Our intention here is not to imply that statesmen should always possess infallible wisdom or should be expected to make choices which turn out to be historically sound. What we are merely trying to suggest is that the failure of the EAC to negotiate a long-term, viable solution for postwar Germany cannot be traced solely to impersonal forces, events, and historical circumstances. There was also human failure, and in the last analysis, a failure of statesmanship at the highest level which contributed significantly to the disappointing results achieved by the EAC.

The Matter of Basic Assumptions

The signature of a new Quadripartite Agreement on Berlin on September 3, 1971, provided an interesting new perspective from which to view the work of the EAC. (The text of the Quadripartite Agreement is reproduced in Annex 12.) If a careful analysis is made of the provisions of the agreement, it becomes evident that the basic assumptions underlying the agreement were very similar to the assumptions espoused by the EAC in the negotiation of the protocols on Germany in 1944–45. For instance, the preamble to the agreement takes note of the fact that the new understanding was reached by the Four Powers "Acting on the basis of their quadripartite rights and responsibilities." This provision effectively negates the long-standing Soviet contention that all wartime agreements concerning Berlin had lapsed and that the Soviet government no longer possessed any responsibility for the Berlin regime, since East Berlin was capital of the sovereign German Democratic Republic and West Berlin was an independent political entity. "Quadripartite rights and responsibilities" means, as the EAC assumed, that the regime in Berlin must be a special joint Four

Power responsibility arising from Germany's defeat in the war and the resulting assumption of supreme authority over the capital by the Allies, a regime that, though modified, remains in force today. Part I, Article 1 of the agreement stipulates that "The four Governments will strive to promote the elimination of tension and the prevention of complications in the relevant area," tension and complications which should not have arisen at all if the EAC's assumption of political cooperation in managing Germany and Berlin in the postwar period had been carried out in good faith by the four governments. Part I, Article 3, stipulates that "The four Governments will mutually respect their individual and joint rights and responsibilities, which remain unchanged," joint rights and responsibilities which were created by the EAC protocols with the expectation, or at least hope, that the occupation regimes in Germany and Berlin would be cooperatively managed until replaced by a peace treaty or a final settlement of the German question.

One of the most significant provisions of the Quadripartite Agreement is contained in Part I, Article 4, where it is stipulated that "The four Governments agree that, irrespective of the differences in legal views, the situation which has developed in the area, . . . shall not be changed unilaterally." Here it would seem that the Four Powers foresee a return to one of the most basic assumptions espoused by the EAC in 1944–45, the assumption that in the collaborative administration of Berlin during the postwar period, joint concordant policies would have to be pursued by all Four Powers, and unilateral action to change the basic foundations of the regime would be unacceptable. Part I, Article 4, thus lends credence to the idea that power plays to absorb pieces of territory into a sphere of influence, especially in Berlin, would only lead to dangerously explosive great power conflicts; hence the only way to manage the situation intelligently is to forswear unilateral action and proceed on the basis of at least a minimum level of political cooperation. This idea is precisely what the EAC had in mind in the negotiations of 1944–45.

As far as access to Berlin from West Germany is concerned, the agreement states in Part II, A, that: "The Government of the Union of Soviet Socialist Republics declares that transit traffic by road, rail, and waterways through the territory of the German Democratic Republic of civilian persons and goods between the Western Sectors of Berlin and the Federal Republic of Germany will be unimpeded; that such traffic will be facilitated so as to take place in the most simple and expeditious manner; and that it will receive preferential treatment." Such arrangements on transit and access were bargained for long and hard by the Western negotiators in EAC in the Austrian protocols, though without complete success, with the implicit idea that such provisions would apply also to Western access to Berlin at least by analogy. A provision similar to Part II, A, was precisely what Ambassador Winant wished so desperately to attempt to insert into the Berlin sections of the German protocols, but he lacked authorization from Washington to negotiate the matter. And certainly General Clay assumed that he had accomplished more or less the essence of Part II, A, in the negotiations of June 29, 1945.

Part II, C, of the Quadripartite Agreement provides that the residents of the western sectors of Berlin will be able to travel to and visit areas of East Germany "for compassionate, family, religious, cultural or commercial reasons, or as tourists, under conditions comparable to those applying to other persons entering these areas." The assumption of more or less normal civilian communications and travel between sectors of Berlin and between Berlin and other areas of Germany was clearly held by the Western negotiators in EAC and even, it would seem, by the Soviet negotiator throughout the Berlin negotiations of 1944–45.

Finally, Annex IV, Section B, Article 2(d) of the Quadripartite Agreement attempts to provide relatively normal participation for West Berliners in international life by the declaration of the Soviet government that no objection will be raised to "The participation jointly with the participants from the Federal Republic of Germany of permanent residents of the Western Sectors of Berlin in international exchanges and exhibitions, or the holding in those Sectors of meetings of international organizations and international conferences as well as exhibitions with international participation. . . ." Quite clearly the EAC negotiators assumed in the Berlin negotiations of 1944–45 that, insofar as the occupation regime allowed, Berliners would participate minimally in international life on the same basis as all other Germans.

The signature of the Quadripartite Agreement of September 3, 1971, was widely viewed by statesmen and scholars throughout the world as a significant new breakthrough in the search for a reasonable settlement to the crisis-ridden Berlin problem. The Quadripartite Agreement entered into effect following the conclusion of detailed implementing agreements by the two German states and the signature of a Final Quadripartite Protocol by the Four Powers. The expectation was widely held that the agreement might lead eventually to a state treaty between the two Germanys, opening the way for United Nations representation for each. It might also hasten the advent of a European security conference, long sought by the Russians as a vehicle to achieve Western recognition of the German Democratic Republic and of the status quo in Eastern Europe. It might also lead to negotiations for mutual and balanced force reductions between NATO and the Warsaw Pact nations. Shortly after the agreement was signed, Time Magazine correspondent Benjamin Cate wrote that "the signing of the Berlin Agreement marks the close of 26 years of East-West tension over the status of West Berlin, tension that often found Americans and Russians muzzle to muzzle. To the Russians, West Berlin was not only a thorn in the Soviet side, but also a place where the West could be squeezed whenever the Kremlin so decided. It was this atmosphere that made West Berlin the short fuse to World War III in Europe. Today West Berlin has been defused."[4]

THE NEGOTIATIONS AND ALLIANCE DIPLOMACY

It was, of course, clearly never the intention of the EAC negotiators that Berlin should become "the short fuse to World War III in Europe." The EAC in fact made every attempt to see to it that the protocols on Germany would lay down the basis for a cooperative occupation regime in Germany and Berlin that might lead to a satisfactory peace treaty and the reconstruction of Germany as a peaceful member of the international community. In a real sense the Quadripartite Agreement of 1971 marked a return by the Four Powers to many of the assumptions espoused by the EAC in the negotiations of 1944–45. Hence, in a way, the painstaking work of the EAC was vindicated twenty-six years after the original protocols on Germany were signed. The Western negotiators in EAC, and probably also the Soviet negotiator to a certain extent, assumed that the only way to accomplish a workable postwar international order in Europe was to draw up a zonal occupation regime in Germany and a sectoral occupation regime in Berlin which could be managed by the Four Powers on a cooperative basis and serve as a prelude to a final postwar settlement of the problem of German power in Europe. They strove to devise protocols that would obviate a mad East-West scramble for territory and influence in Germany after the war. They expected, or at least hoped, that all four allies after the war would pursue fraternal policies based on the EAC quadripartite directives which later became the Potsdam Agreement. Such policies would activate the provisions of the protocols on Germany and Berlin in a harmonious manner and lead to the eventual reconstruction of a peaceful Germany in Europe. As far as Berlin is concerned, the Quadripartite Agreement of 1971 marks a limited but significant return to these basic principles. Berlin was henceforth to be administered on a truly quadripartite basis, indeed on the basis of the quadripartite rights and responsibilities laid down in the original EAC protocols, and in such a fashion as to eliminate tension and promote Four Power harmony and cooperation in the great European city.

The relevant question to be answered here is why the basic assumptions espoused by the EAC in 1944–45 did not lead to the expected results but led instead to the creation of Berlin as the greatest flashpoint in Europe for twenty-six years. Why did the EAC not succeed in creating a viable, workable regime for Berlin in the postwar period? With the wisdom of hindsight the question is now not so difficult to answer. The answer lies partly in the fact that the assumptions espoused by the EAC in the quiet, collegial diplomatic negotiations of 1944–45 created a schizophrenic frame of mind at the highest levels of government of all Four Powers. Churchill, Roosevelt, and Stalin allowed the EAC, begrudgingly and perhaps even unwittingly, to conduct the negotiations and devise the German protocols on the basis of the basic assumptions discussed above. The provisions of the German protocols, clearly reflecting these assumptions, were duly ratified by all four governments. But when it came time to bring the agreements to life and actually set up the occupation regimes in Germany and Berlin, policies were pursued which contradicted the basic assumptions underlying the EAC protocols. Hence, the diplomatic assumptions of 1944–45, apparently approved by all Four Powers, were very early contradicted by the actual policies of 1945–46, policies which worked to render the EAC agreements nonviable and make Berlin the crisis point of Europe. It was not until twenty-six years later, in 1971, that the Four Powers saw fit to negotiate a new Berlin agreement predicated, more or less, on the original EAC assumptions of 1944–45, thus vindicating in a real way the work of the European Advisory Commission. It was the severe schizophrenia found at the highest levels of government in the period 1944–46 which produced a volatile and crisis-prone situation in Berlin for much of the postwar period, not the work of the EAC.

Judging the EAC

Having considered both the positive and the negative aspects of the Berlin negotiations in EAC and having devoted considerable attention to the various factors underlying the Commission's failure to achieve long-term viable results, it remains for us to make some assessment of the utility of a body such as the European Advisory Commission as a forum for peace planning during wartime. We have seen that the EAC was required to carry on its work in extremely adverse circumstances. It never received the full support it deserved from any of the participating governments, and it had to work under a constant cloud of Soviet-Western suspicion. What is really rather remarkable is that the EAC succeeded at all. The fact must be emphasized, however, that the Commission did succeed in negotiating the two major protocols which regulated the status of Germany and Berlin for at least three years and established the border which still exists in Germany today, including West Berlin as an enclave within the German Democratic Republic.

The EAC agreements were by no means perfect documents; they contained certain loopholes and inconsistencies which later gave rise to acrimonious political and legal controversy. And, more serious, they contained no provisions which might have blocked or at least moderated the rapid sovietization of the eastern zone of Germany or the Soviet sector of Berlin. The documents were not, however, designed for this purpose, nor was the EAC a body which had any authority to forecast or hedge against the political developments of the future beyond adopting basic assumptions for the negotiation of the agreements. Essentially the EAC agreements were temporary arrangements for the occupation and control of the defeated enemy. In effect they represented an agreement to agree later on the long-range solution. That the Four Powers have not yet reached a satisfactory solution to the question of the permanent disposition of Germany and Berlin is not the fault of the EAC.

What is striking when one reviews the work of the EAC in reference to the Berlin negotiations is the manner in which the EAC constantly served

THE NEGOTIATIONS AND ALLIANCE DIPLOMACY

as a catalyst in the process of maximizing possible areas of agreement between the major Allies. Often when the top governmental leaders seemed to be locked in an insoluble dispute, the diplomats at Lancaster House continued to negotiate quietly and patiently in an attempt to capitalize on the widest area of agreement which could be found. In this way the EAC negotiations served to induce the governments to find even wider areas of agreement. The EAC always seemed to be, in a way, one step ahead of the governments in the level of agreement achieved. Consequently, it became the task of the chief representatives on EAC to attempt to bring their governments along that extra step and agree to an extra point in order to safeguard Allied unity in EAC and ensure the success of the delicate negotiations. The EAC constantly prodded Washington, Moscow, London, and Paris to expand the area of agreement and to get on with the urgent task of designing the outlines of a postwar order in Europe.

The representatives in EAC were not able to generate agreement in the Commission artificially when such agreement was lacking at the top levels of government. One is impressed with the fact, however, that they did not try to do so. They seemed constantly aware of the fact that it would serve no purpose to write vague, poorly drafted articles of agreement which only masked disagreement at a higher level. Instead they made constant efforts to explain the situation to their respective governments, to inform their superiors' point of view, and to achieve genuine governmental agreement on the issues at hand.

EAC Protocols vs. Potsdam Agreements

The value of the work of the EAC is placed in sharper perspective when the EAC protocols are compared to the Potsdam agreements. The Potsdam agreements were largely the fruit of summit diplomacy, while the EAC protocols were the results of protracted negotiations within a quasi-collegial body of diplomatic plenipotentiaries. The Potsdam agreements are notable for their artificiality. The major reason that they began to fall apart almost immediately after signature is that they were synthetic; they attempted to plaster over enormous cracks in the substance of concurrence. In the absence of genuine agreement on fundamental principles, the governmental leaders at Potsdam resorted to the device of writing an elaborate, but vague and ill-defined protocol to paper over their differences and produce accord when real agreement was in fact lacking.

The difference between the Potsdam agreements and the EAC protocols is qualitative. The Potsdam agreements were artificial; the EAC protocols, on the other hand, represented genuine agreement, but were incomplete. The Potsdam agreements proceeded to fall apart forthwith; the EAC protocols established a quadripartite regime which lasted nearly three years, until the foundation stones upon which they were based began to disintegrate, not to be resurrected again until the Quadripartite Agreement of 1971. To a significant extent the EAC protocols even established a permanent situation in that the borders they established have not been altered. The signature of a Treaty of Cooperation between the Federal Republic of Germany and the Union of Soviet Socialist Republics on August 12, 1970, underlined the permanence of the postwar borders in Germany. Article 3 of the treaty stipulates that both governments "regard the frontiers of all the states in Europe today and in the future as inviolable, as they stand on the date of the signing of the present treaty, including . . . the frontier between the Federal Republic of Germany and the German Democratic Republic." (*New York Times*, August 13, 1970, p. 2.)

The EAC protocols, in contrast to the Potsdam agreements, rested upon a foundation of genuine, though minimal agreement; they extended that agreement to its outermost limits but did not attempt to transcend it. This then is possibly part of the value of diplomacy through a forum such as the EAC.

The Berlin negotiations in the European Advisory Commission demonstrate both the strengths and weaknesses of quiet diplomacy through a quasi-collegial body. The EAC achieved a great deal; it could have achieved even more had it received the full support and confidence of the governments which created it. As it was, the EAC was not able to rise above the swirling currents of wartime diplomacy at manifold levels in order to use its collective imagination in the designing of a comprehensive rational master plan for postwar Berlin, Germany, and Europe. The Commission remained part of those swirling diplomatic currents because of an inability on the part of governmental leaders to trust it completely. We cannot know whether or not the EAC would have achieved salutary results if it had been accorded the full confidence implied by its mandate. We do know, however, that the EAC was certainly one of the most useful and most extraordinary bodies in the history of allied wartime diplomacy.

ANNEXES

[ ] means author's note.

Annex 1

DRAFT PROTOCOL ON MILITARY OCCUPATION OF GERMANY SUBMITTED BY BRITISH DELEGATION TO EAC JUNE 12, 1944

Military Occupation of Germany

1. Upon unconditional surrender Germany, with the exception of the Berlin area and Austria, will be divided for purposes of occupation into three zones. Each zone will be occupied by the forces of one of the three countries, U.S., U.K., U.S.S.R.

2. The boundaries between the three zones shall be as follows:

Eastern Zone: All of Germany to the east of a north-south line running past Lübeck and Brunswick and more particularly described as follows:-
(here take in description)

Northern Zone: All of Germany west of the boundary of the Eastern Zone and north of an east-west line running from Hof past Frankfort-on-the Main (inclusive) to. . . . and more particularly described as follows:-
(here take in description)

Southern Zone: The remainder of Germany.

3. The Eastern Zone, with the exception of the Berlin area, will be occupied by forces of the Union of Soviet Socialist Republics.

4. The forces to occupy the Northern and Southern Zones will be determined by the U.S. and U.K. Governments.

5. The Berlin area, consisting of the City of Berlin and surrounding territory will be occupied jointly by the three countries. A more particular description of the Berlin area to be occupied under this Article is as follows:-
(here take in description)

6. Austria will be under tripartite control.

7. [Article concerning military commanders.]

8. [Article concerning maintenance of law and order.]

9. The territory of Germany referred to in this document means all of Germany as it existed on January 1, 1938.

(signed) _____
_____
_____

Annex 2

DRAFT OF TEXT OF ARTICLE 2 OF PROTOCOL ON OCCUPATION SUBMITTED BY BRITISH DELEGATION TO EAC JUNE 13, 1944

2. The boundaries of the three zones and of the Berlin area, and the allocation of the three zones as between the U.K., the U.S.A., and the U.S.S.R., will be as follows:-

(a) The territory of Germany (including the province of East Prussia, but excluding Schleswig-Holstein), situated to the East of a line drawn. . . . [description of eastern zone]. . . . will be occupied by the armed forces of the U.S.S.R., with the exception of the Berlin area, for which a special system of occupation is provided in subparagraph (d) below.

(b) [description of northwest zone; name of occupying Power left blank]

(c) [description of southern zone; name of occupying Power left blank]

(d) The Gau Berlin (Greater Berlin) will be under joint occupation by the armed forces of the U.K., the U.S.A., and the U.S.S.R.

Annex 3

REDRAFT OF PROTOCOL ON MILITARY OCCUPATION OF GERMANY SUBMITTED BY AMERICAN DELEGATION TO EAC JUNE 19, 1944

PROTOCOL of the Agreement of the Union of Soviet Socialist Republics, the United Kingdom and the United States of America, with reference to the military occupation of Germany after the surrender.

The Governments of the U.S.S.R., the U.K., and the U.S.A. have reached the following understanding with regard to the execution of Article 11 of the Instrument of Surrender of Germany:-

1. Germany, within her frontiers as they were on the 31st December 1937, will, for the purposes of occupation, be divided into three zones, one of which will be allotted to each of the three Powers, and a special Berlin area, which will be under joint occupation by the three Powers.

2. The boundaries of the three zones and of the Berlin area, and the allocation of the three zones as between the U.S.S.R., the U.K., and the U.S.A. will be as follows:-

    Eastern Zone. . . .
    Northwestern Zone. . . .
    Southwestern Zone. . . .
    Berlin Area. . . .

3. The occupying forces in each zone will be under a commander designated by the Government of the country whose forces occupy that zone.

4. Each of the three Powers may, at its discretion, include among the forces

ANNEXES

employed on occupation duties under the command of its Commander-in-Chief, (small or limited?) contingents from the forces of any other Allied Power which has participated in military operations against Germany.

5. The present agreement does not extend to the organization of military government or control in Germany. (?)

Annex 4

REDRAFT OF PROTOCOL ON OCCUPATION OF GERMANY SUBMITTED BY SOVIET DELEGATION TO EAC JUNE 29, 1944

Draft presented by the Delegation of the U.S.S.R. of a PROTOCOL of an Agreement between the Government of the Union of Soviet Socialist Republics, the United Kingdom and the United States of America, on the zones of occupation in Germany and the administration of the City of Berlin.

The Governments of the U.S.S.R., the U.K., and the U.S.A. have reached the following agreement with regard to the execution of Article 11 of the Instrument of Surrender of Germany:-

1. Germany, within her frontiers as they were on the 31st December, 1937, will for the purposes of occupation, be divided into three zones, one of which will be allotted to each of the three Powers, and a special Berlin area, which will be under joint occupation by the three Powers.

2. The boundaries of the three zones and of the Berlin area, and the allocation of the three zones as between the U.S.S.R., the U.K., and the U.S.A. will be as follows:-

The territory of Germany (including the province of East Prussia) situated to the East of a line [description of eastern zone]. . . . will be occupied by the armed forces of the U.S.S.R., with the exception of the Berlin area, for which a special system of occupation is provided below.

The territory [description of northwestern zone]. . . . will be occupied by the armed forces of

All the remaining territory [description of southern zone]. . . . will be occupied by the armed forces of

The armed forces of the U.S.S.R., U.K., and U.S.A. will be brought into the city of Berlin, by which expression is understood the territory of "Greater Berlin" as defined by the law of the 27th April, 1920. For this purpose the territory of "Greater Berlin" will be divided into three zones:-

Northeastern part of the city (districts of Pankow, Prenzlauerberg, Mitte, Weissensee, Friedrichshafen, Lichtenberg, Treptow, Koepenick) will be occupied by the forces of the U.S.S.R.;

Northwestern part of the city (districts of Reinickendorf, Wedding, Tiergarten, Charlottenburg, Spandau, Wilmersdorf) will be occupied by the forces of blank;

Southern part of the city (districts of Zehlendorf, Steglitz, Schoeneberg, Kreutzberg, Tempelhof, Neukoelln) will be occupied by the forces of blank.

The central aerodrome of Berlin, Tempelhof, will be used by the U.S.S.R., U.K. and U.S.A. on equal terms.

3. The occupying forces in each zone will be under a commander designated by the Government of the country whose forces occupy that zone.

4. (a) An Inter-Allied Governing Authority (Komendatura) will be established to administer 'Greater Berlin,' consisting of three commandants—one from each of the Allied powers. The head of the Inter-Allied Governing Authority will be the Chief Commandant, whose duties will be carried out in rotation by each of the three commandants.

Each of the three commandants shall hold office as Chief Commandant for a period not exceeding 15 to 20 days.

(b) The necessary technical machinery, staffed by personnel of the three Allied Powers, will be set up at the offices of the Inter-Allied Governing Authority, and its form will, in general, correspond to the structure of the municipal organizations of 'Greater Berlin.' The Inter-Allied Governing Authority will communicate direct or through this machinery with the municipal organizations of Berlin.

(c) The Inter-Allied Governing Authority for the administration of 'Greater Berlin' parallel with its functions of administering the city, will also exercise day-to-day supervision over the activities of the municipal organizations of Berlin controlling the various departments of the city's daily life.

(d) The Allied forces stationed in the territory of 'Greater Berlin' will also be responsible for the maintenance of public order in the respective zones of 'Greater Berlin' and for the protection both of the Inter-Allied Governing Authority administering 'Greater Berlin' and of all other agencies which may be set up by the Allies in that city.

5. [Article concerning auxiliary contingents]

6. This Protocol has been drawn up in triplicate in the Russian and English languages. Both texts are authentic. The Protocol will come into force on the signature by Germany of the Instrument of Unconditional Surrender.

Annex 5

REDRAFT OF BERLIN SECTION OF
ARTICLE 2 OF PROTOCOL ON
OCCUPATION SUBMITTED BY
BRITISH DELEGATION TO EAC
JULY 5, 1944

The Berlin area (by which expression is understood the territory of "Greater Berlin" as defined by the law of 27th April, 1920) will be jointly occupied by armed forces designated by the three Commanders-in-Chief. These forces will be respectively stationed in sub-areas of "Greater Berlin" which are provisionally fixed as follows:-

North-Eastern Sub-Area (districts of Pankow, Prenzlauerberg, Mitte, Weissensee, Friedrichshain, Lichtenberg, Treptow, Köpenick) will be allotted to the forces of the U.S.S.R.

North-Western Sub-Area (districts of Reinickendorf, Wedding, Tiergarten, Charlottenburg, Spandau, Wilmersdorf) will be allotted to the forces of _____ .

Southern Sub-Area (districts of Zehlendorf, Steglitz, Schöneberg, Kreutzberg, Tempelhof, Neukölln) will be allotted to the forces of _____ .

The limits of these Sub-Areas will be subject to adjustment by the three Allied Military Commanders in the light of the accommodation available at the time of occupation.

In accordance with the principle of joint occupation of the "Greater Berlin" area, all facilities in the area will, as may be necessary, be available equally to the forces and agencies of the Three Powers.

Annex 6-A

REDRAFT OF ARTICLE 2 OF PROTOCOL ON OCCUPATION SUBMITTED BY AMERICAN DELEGATION TO EAC JULY 12, 1944

[This American redraft of Article 2 was considered at the July 12 meeting of EAC paragraph by paragraph. The tentative changes agreed upon by the delegates are indicated as follows: **boldface** means added; ~~strike through~~ means deleted.]

The Berlin area (by which expression is understood the territory of 'Greater Berlin' as defined by the law of 27 April 1920) will be jointly occupied by armed forces of the USSR, UK, and USA ~~designated~~ **assigned** by the respective commanders-in-chief. For this purpose the territory of 'Greater Berlin' will be ~~provisionally~~ divided into the following three parts:- e~~mploying the existing boundaries of the districts hereafter mentioned~~.

North-Eastern part of 'Greater Berlin' (districts of Pankow, Prenzlauerberg, Mitte, Weissensee, Friedrichshain, Lichtenberg, Treptow, Koepenick) will be occupied by the forces of the U.S.S.R.;

North-Western part of 'Greater Berlin' (districts of Reinickendorf, Wedding, Tiergarten, Charlottenburg, Spandau, Wilmersdorf) will be occupied by the forces of the _____ ;

Southern part of 'Greater Berlin' (districts of Zehlendorf, Steglitz, Schöneberg, Kreutzberg, Tempelhof, Neukölln) will be occupied by the forces of the _____ .

~~(5). For purposes of occupation and administration the Staaken airdrome will be included in the 'Greater Berlin' area.~~

~~This division will be made primarily for convenience in billeting and in the maintenance of public order. It may be subject to adjustment by the Inter-Allied Governing Authority for 'Greater Berlin' (as referred to in Article 5) in the light of the accommodations available at the time of occupation. All facilities in 'Greater Berlin' required for use by the occupation authorities and for the conduct of military government will be available jointly to the forces and agencies of the USSR, UK, and USA under the direction and control of the Inter-Allied Governing Authority for 'Greater Berlin.'~~

Annex 6-B

REDRAFT OF ARTICLE 5(a) OF PROTOCOL ON OCCUPATION SUBMITTED BY BRITISH DELEGATION TO EAC JULY 12, 1944

[This British redraft of Article 5(a) was considered at the July 12 meeting of EAC. The tentative changes agreed upon by the delegates are indicated as follows: **boldface** means added; ~~strike through~~ means deleted.]

5(a) ~~A joint~~ An Inter-Allied Governing Authority (komendatura) consisting of ~~the~~ three ~~local Commanders,~~ **Commandants,** ~~one for each Allied Power,~~ appointed by their respective Commanders-in-Chief, will be established to direct **jointly** the administration of the 'Greater Berlin' area.

Annex 6-C

REDRAFT OF ARTICLE 5(b) OF PROTOCOL ON OCCUPATION SUBMITTED BY BRITISH DELEGATION TO EAC JULY 12, 1944

[This British redraft of Article 5(b) was considered at the July 12 meeting of EAC. The tentative changes agreed upon by the delegates are indicated as above.]

5(b) In accordance with the principle of joint occupation of the 'Greater Berlin' area, all transportation, communications, public utilities and ~~other like facilities, including~~ airfields, in the 'Greater Berlin' area will, as may be necessary, be available ~~equally~~ **jointly** to the forces and agencies of the three Powers.

Annex 6-D

DRAFT PARAGRAPH FOR INCLUSION IN COVERING REPORT TO PROTOCOL ON OCCUPATION SUBMITTED BY BRITISH DELEGATION TO EAC JULY 12, 1944

[This British draft of a paragraph for inclusion in the Covering Report transmitting the Protocol on Zones of Occupation was discussed at the July 12 meeting of EAC. The tentative changes agreed upon by the delegates are indicated as above.]

The Commission recommends to the three Governments the following understanding in regard to Art. 2 of the above-mentioned draft Protocol:-

The limits of the three parts of 'Greater Berlin' described in Article 2 of the Draft Protocol on the zones of occupation in Germany and the administration of ~~the City of~~ 'Greater Berlin' ~~will~~ **may**, if necessary, be subject to adjustment by the ~~three Allied Military Commanders~~ Inter-Allied Governing Authority mentioned in Article 5 in the light of the accommodation available at the time of occupation.

Annex 7-A

PROTOCOL BETWEEN THE UNITED STATES,
THE UNITED KINGDOM, AND THE SOVIET UNION
REGARDING THE ZONES OF OCCUPATION IN GERMANY
AND THE ADMINISTRATION OF "GREATER BERLIN"
SEPTEMBER 12, 1944

The Governments of the United States of America, the United Kingdom of Great Britain and Northern Ireland, and the Union of Soviet Socialist Republics have reached the following agreement with regard to the execution of Article 11 of the Instrument of Unconditional Surrender of Germany:-

1. Germany, within her frontiers as they were on the 31st December, 1937, will, for the purposes of occupation, be divided into three zones, one of which will be allotted to each of the three Powers, and a special Berlin area, which will be under joint occupation by the three Powers.

2. The boundaries of the three zones and of the Berlin area, and the allocation of the three zones as between the U.S.A., the U.K. and the U.S.S.R. will be as follows:-

The territory of Germany (including the province of East Prussia) situated to the East of a line drawn from the point on Lübeck Bay where the frontiers of Schleswig-Holstein and Mecklenburg meet, along the western frontier of Mecklenburg to the frontier of the province of Hanover, thence, along the eastern frontier of Hanover, to the frontier of Brunswick; thence along the western frontier of the Prussian province of Saxony to the western frontier of Anhalt; thence along the western frontier of Anhalt; thence along the western frontier of the Prussian province of Saxony and the western frontier of Thuringia to where the latter meets the Bavarian frontier; thence eastwards along the northern frontier of Bavaria to the 1937 Czechoslovakian frontier, will be occupied by armed forces of the U.S.S.R., with the exception of the Berlin area, for which a special system of occupation is provided below.

The territory of Germany situated to the west of the line defined above, and bounded on the south by a line drawn from the point where the western frontier of Thuringia meets the frontier of Bavaria; thence westwards along the southern frontiers of the Prussian provinces of Hessen-Nassau and Rheinprovinz to where the latter meets the frontier of France will be occupied by armed forces of. . . .

All the remaining territory of Western Germany situated to the south of the line defined in the description of the North-Western Zone will be occupied by armed forces of. . . .

The frontiers of States (Länder) and Provinces within Germany, referred to in the foregoing descriptions of the zones, are those which existed after the coming into effect of the decree of 25th June, 1941 (published in the Reichsgesetzblatt, Part I, No. 72, 3rd July, 1941).

The Berlin area (by which expression is understood the territory of 'Greater Berlin' as defined by the Law of the 27th April, 1920) will be jointly occupied by armed forces of the U.S.A., U.K., and U.S.S.R., assigned by the respective Commanders-in-Chief. For this purpose the territory of 'Greater Berlin' will be divided into the following three parts:-

North-Eastern part of 'Greater Berlin' (districts of Pankow, Prenzlauerberg, Mitte, Weissensee, Friedrichshain, Lichtenberg, Treptow, Köpenick) will be occupied by the forces of the U.S.S.R.:

North-Western part of 'Greater Berlin' (districts of Reinickendorf, Wedding, Tiergarten, Charlottenburg, Spandau, Wilmersdorf) will be occupied by the forces of. . . .

Southern part of 'Greater Berlin' (districts of Zehlendorf, Steglitz, Schöneberg, Kreuzberg, Tempelhof, Neukölln) will be occupied by the forces of. . . .

3. The occupying forces in each of the three zones into which Germany is divided will be under a Commander-in-Chief designated by the Government of the country whose forces occupy that zone.

4. Each of the three Powers may, at its discretion, include among the forces assigned to occupation duties under the command of its Commander-in-Chief, auxiliary contingents from the forces of any other Allied Power which has participated in military operations against Germany.

5. An Inter-Allied Governing Authority (Komendatura) consisting of three Commandants, appointed by their respective Commanders-in-Chief, will be established to direct jointly the administration of the 'Greater Berlin' Area.

6. This Protocol has been drawn up in triplicate in the English and Russian languages. Both texts are authentic. The Protocol will come into force on the signature by Germany of the Instrument of Unconditional Surrender.

The above text of the Protocol between the Governments of the United States of America, the United Kingdom and the Union of Soviet Socialist Republics, on the zones of occupation in Germany and the administration of 'Greater Berlin' has been prepared and unanimously adopted by the European Advisory Commission at a meeting held on 12th September, 1944, with the exception of the allocation of the North-Western and South-Western zones of occupation in Germany and the North-Western and Southern parts of 'Greater Berlin,' which requires further consideration and joint agreement by the Governments of the U.S.A., U.K. and U.S.S.R.

Representative of the Government of the U.S.A. on the European Advisory Commission:	Representative of the Government of the U.K. on the European Advisory Commission:	Representative of the Government of the U.S.S.R. on the European Advisory Commission:
JOHN G. WINANT	WILLIAM STRANG	F. GUSEV

LANCASTER HOUSE, LONDON, S.W. 1
  12th September, 1944.

ANNEXES

Annex 7-B

AGREEMENT BETWEEN THE GOVERNMENTS OF THE UNITED STATES OF AMERICA, THE UNITED KINGDOM, THE UNION OF SOVIET SOCIALIST REPUBLICS, AND THE PROVISIONAL GOVERNMENT OF THE FRENCH REPUBLIC REGARDING AMENDMENTS TO THE PROTOCOL OF SEPTEMBER 12, 1944, ON THE ZONES OF OCCUPATION IN GERMANY AND THE ADMINISTRATION OF "GREATER BERLIN," JULY 26, 1945 (EXCERPT)

The Governments of the United States of America, the Union of Soviet Socialist Republics and the United Kingdom having, pursuant to the decision of the Crimea Conference announced on 12th February, 1945, invited the Provisional Government of the French Republic to take part in the occupation of Germany,
the Governments of the United States of America, the Union of Soviet Socialist Republics and the United Kingdom and the Provisional Government of the French Republic have agreed to amend and to supplement the Protocol of 12th September, 1944, between the Governments of the United States of America, the Union of Soviet Socialist Republics and the United Kingdom on the zones of occupation in Germany and the administration of "Greater Berlin,"
and have reached the following agreement:

1. In the Preamble of the Protocol of 12th September, 1944, add the words "and Provisional Government of the French Republic" in the enumeration of the participating Governments.

2. In Article 1 of the above-mentioned Protocol, substitute "four" for "three" in the words "three zones," "three Powers" and "three Powers."

3. In the first paragraph of Article 2 of the above-mentioned Protocol, add "and the French Republic" in the enumeration of the participating Powers; substitute "four" for "three" in the words "three zones" and "three zones."

. . . .

7. In the paragraph of Article 2 of the above-mentioned Protocol which relates to the joint occupation of "Greater Berlin," insert "and the French Republic" in the enumeration of the participating Powers; substitute the word "four" for the words "the following three."

8. In Article 3 of the above-mentioned Protocol, substitute "four" for "three" before the word "zones."

9. In Article 4 of the above-mentioned Protocol, substitute "four" for "three" before the word "Powers."

10. In Article 5 of the above-mentioned Protocol, substitute "four" for "three" before the word "Commandants."

11. In Article 6 of the above-mentioned Protocol, substitute "quadruplicate" for "triplicate"; add "French" in the enumeration of the languages; substitute "The three texts" for the words "Both texts."

The above text of the Agreement between the Governments of the United States of America, the Union of Soviet Socialist Republics and the United Kingdom and the Provisional Government of the French Republic regarding Amendments to the Protocol of 12th September, 1944, on the zones of occupation in Germany and the administration of "Greater Berlin" has been prepared and unanimously adopted by the European Advisory Commission at a meeting held on 26th July, 1945.

Representative of the
Government of the
United States of
America on the
European Advisory
Commission:
JOHN G. WINANT

Representative of the
Government of the
Union of Soviet Socialist
Republics on the
European Advisory
Commission:
G. SAKSIN

Representative of the
Government of the
United Kingdom on
the European Advisory
Commission:
RONALD I. CAMPBELL
Lancaster House, London, S.W. 1
26th July, 1945.

Representative of the
Provisional Government
of the French Republic
on the European
Advisory Commission:
R. MASSIGLI

Annex 8

DRAFT AGREEMENT ON CONTROL MACHINERY IN GERMANY SUBMITTED BY SOVIET DELEGATION TO EAC AUGUST 26, 1944

1. Supreme authority in Germany will be exercised in its plenitude by the Commanders-in-Chief of the armed forces of the U.S.S.R., the U.K. and the U.S.A., each in his own zone of occupation.

2. Each Commander-in-Chief will have attached to him military representatives of the other two Commanders-in-Chief for liaison duties.

3. To ensure uniformity of action by the Commanders-in-Chief, and to secure the settlement of important problems common to the whole of Germany, namely the principal political and economic problems, e.g. trade, industry, transport, displaced persons, etc.; the chief military problems; and also in order to control the German Government and its central organs, the three Commanders-in-Chief will constitute a Control Council.

The German central Government and the German central organs will operate under the direction of the Control Council, and will be responsible to it for complicance with any demands made.

Meetings of the Control Council will be convened at least once in ten days and, if necessary, at any time on the initiative of any Commander-in-Chief. Decisions of the Control Council must be unanimous. The Chairmanship of the Control Council will be held in rotation.

4. A permanent 'Co-ordinating Committee' will be set up under the Control Council, consisting of representatives of the three Commanders-in-Chief not below General Officer's rank. The structure of the committee should be determined accordingly.

5. The duties of the 'Co-ordinating Committee' will include:-
   (a) implementing the decisions of the Control Council;
   (b) day-to-day supervision and control of the activities of the corresponding organs of the German Government and central institutions;
   (c) co-ordination of current problems which call for uniform measures in all three zones;
   (d) preliminary examination and preparation for the Control Council of all questions submitted by individual Commanders-in-Chief.

6. An Inter-Allied 'Governing Authority' (Komendatura) will be set up to administer the City of Berlin, consisting of three commandants, one from each Power. The Inter-Allied 'Komendatura' will be headed by a Chief Commandant, whose duties will be carried out by each Commandant in turn.

A Technical Staff will be set up under the Inter-Allied 'Komendatura' consisting of personnel of the three Allied Powers and organized to serve the purpose of controlling the activities of the local organs of Berlin responsible for various municipal services.

The Inter-Allied 'Komendatura' of 'Greater Berlin' will be subordinate to the Control Council.

7. The Allied organs for the control and administration of Germany outlined above will operate during the first period of the occupation of Germany immediately following surrender, that is, the period when Germany is carrying out the basic requirements of unconditional surrender.

8. The question of the Allied organs required for carrying out the functions of control and administration in Germany in the second period will be the subject of a separate agreement between the Governments of the U.S.S.R., the U.K. and the U.S.A.

Annex 9

AGREEMENT ON CONTROL MACHINERY IN GERMANY
NOVEMBER 14, 1944

The Governments of the United States of America, the United Kingdom of Great Britain and Northern Ireland and the Union of Soviet Socialist Republics have reached the following Agreement with regard to the organisation of the Allied control machinery in Germany in the period during which Germany will be carrying out the basic requirements of unconditional surrender:-

Article 1.

Supreme authority in Germany will be exercised, on instructions from their respective Governments, by the Commanders-in-Chief of the armed forces of the United States of America, the United Kingdom and the Union of Soviet Socialist Republics, each in his own zone of occupation, and also jointly, in matters affecting Germany as a whole, in their capacity as members of the supreme organ of control constituted under the present Agreement.

Article 2.

Each Commander in Chief in his zone of occupation will have attached to him military, naval and air representatives of the other two Commanders-in-Chief for liaison duties.

Article 3.

(a) The three Commanders-in-Chief, acting together as a body, will constitute a supreme organ of control called the Control Council.

(b) The functions of the Control Council will be:-

(i) to ensure appropriate uniformity of action by the Commanders-in-Chief in their respective zones of occupation;

(ii) to initiate plans and reach agreed decisions on the chief military, political, economic and other questions affecting Germany as a whole, on the basis of instructions received by each Commander-in-Chief from his Government;

(iii) to control the German central administration, which will operate under the direction of the Control Council and will be responsible to it for ensuring compliance with its demands;

(iv) to direct the administration of 'Greater Berlin' through appropriate organs.

(c) The Control Council will meet at least once in ten days; and it will meet at any time upon request of any one of its members. Decisions of the Control Council shall be unanimous. The chairmanship of the Control Council will be held in rotation by each of its three members.

(d) Each member of the Control Council will be assisted by a political adviser, who will, when necessary, attend meetings of the Control Council. Each member of the Control Council may also, when necessary, be assisted at meetings of the Council by naval or air advisers.

Article 4.

A permanent Co-ordinating Committee will be established under the Control Council, composed of one representative of each of the three Commanders-in-Chief, not below the rank of General Officer or the equivalent rank in the naval or air forces. Members of the Co-ordinating Committee will, when necessary, attend meetings of the Control Council.

Article 5.

The duties of the Co-ordinating Committee, acting on behalf of the Control Council and through the Control Staff, will include:-

(a) the carrying out of the decisions of the Control Council;

(b) the day-to-day supervision and control of the activities of the German central administration and institutions;

(c) the co-ordination of current problems which call for uniform measures in all three zones;

(d) the preliminary examination and preparation for the Control Council of all questions submitted by individual Commanders-in-Chief.

Article 6.

(a) The members of the Control Staff, appointed by their respective national authorities, will be organized in the following Divisions:-

Military; Naval; Air; Transport; Political; Economic; Finance; Reparation, De-

ANNEXES

liveries and Restitution; Internal Affairs and Communications; Legal; Prisoners of War and Displaced Persons; Man-power.

Adjustments in the number and functions of the Divisions may be made in the light of experience.

(b) At the head of each Division there will be three high-ranking officials, one from each Power. The duties of the three heads of each Division, acting jointly, will include:-

(i) exercising control over the corresponding German Ministries and German central institutions;

(ii) acting as advisers to the Control Council and, when necessary, attending meetings thereof;

(iii) transmitting to the German central administration the decisions of the Control Council, communicated through the Co-ordinating Committee.

(c) The three heads of a Division will take part in meetings of the Co-ordinating Committee at which matters affecting the work of their Division are on the agenda.

(d) The staffs of the Divisions may include civilian as well as military personnel. They may also, in special cases, include nationals of other United Nations, appointed in their personal capacity.

Article 7.

(a) An Inter-Allied Governing Authority (Komendatura) consisting of three Commandants, one from each Power, appointed by their respective Commanders-in-Chief, will be established to direct jointly the administration of the 'Greater Berlin' area. Each of the Commandants will serve in rotation, in the position of Chief Commandant, as head of the Inter-Allied Governing Authority.

(b) A Technical Staff, consisting of personnel of each of the three Powers, will be established under the Inter-Allied Governing Authority, and will be organised to serve the purpose of supervising and controlling the activities of the local organs of 'Greater Berlin' which are responsible for its municipal services.

(c) The Inter-Allied Governing Authority will operate under the general direction of the Control Council and will receive orders through the Co-ordinating Committee.

Article 8.

The necessary liaison with the Governments of other United Nations chiefly interested will be ensured by the appointment by such Governments of military missions (which may include civilian members) to the Control Council, having access, through the appropriate channels, to the organs of control.

Article 9.

United Nations' organisations which may be admitted by the Control Council to operate in Germany will, in respect of their activities in Germany, be subordinate to the Allied control machinery and answerable to it.

Article 10.

The Allied organs for the control and administration of Germany outlined above will operate during the initial period of the occupation of Germany immediately following surrender, that is, the period when Germany is carrying out the basic requirements of unconditional surrender.

Article 11.

The question of the Allied organs required for carrying out the functions of control and administration in Germany in a later period will be the subject of a separate

Agreement between the Governments of the United States of America, the United Kingdom and the Union of Soviet Socialist Republics.

The above text of the Agreement on Control Machinery in Germany between the Governments of the United States of America, the United Kingdom and the Union of Soviet Socialist Republics has been prepared and unanimously adopted by the Representatives of the United States of America, the United Kingdom and the Union of Soviet Socialist Republics on the European Advisory Commission at a meeting held on 14th November, 1944, and is now submitted to their respective Governments for approval.

For the Representative of the Government of the United States of America on the European Advisory Commission:	Representative of the Government of the United Kingdom on the European Advisory Commission:	Representative of the Government of the Union of Soviet Socialist Republics on the European Advisory Commission:
PHILIP E. MOSELY	WILLIAM STRANG	F. GUSEV

LANCASTER HOUSE, LONDON, S.W. 1
14th November, 1944

Annex 10

PARAGRAPH FOR INCLUSION IN COVERING REPORT TO AMENDING AGREEMENT TO PROTOCOL ON ZONES OF OCCUPATION
SUBMITTED BY FRENCH DELEGATION TO EAC
JULY 9, 1945

The Commission has further been informed that a French contingent is already in Berlin and will remain there until this question has been finally settled.

In these circumstances the Commission before submitting to Governments recommendations for the delimitation of the French sector, would like to receive information on the physical conditions prevailing in Berlin which it at present lacks and to be notified of any recommendations which might be formulated by the Allied Representatives on the spot.

DRAFT LAST PARAGRAPH OF COVERING REPORT TO AMENDING AGREEMENT TO PROTOCOL ON ZONES OF OCCUPATION
SUBMITTED BY AMERICAN DELEGATION TO EAC JULY 2, 1945.
DISCUSSED AT EAC MEETING OF JULY 9, 1945

In view of the physical conditions prevailing in the area of 'Greater Berlin,' the Commission has not attempted, in Article 7 of the present Agreement, to delineate an area in 'Greater Berlin' to be occupied by forces of the French Republic. The Commission recommends that the four Governments instruct their respective Commanders-in-Chief in Germany, acting jointly, to determine the area in 'Greater Berlin' to be assigned to occupation by forces of the French Republic.

Annex 11

DRAFT OF LAST PARAGRAPH OF COVERING REPORT TO
AMENDING AGREEMENT TO PROTOCOL ON
ZONES OF OCCUPATION
SUBMITTED BY SOVIET DELEGATION TO EAC JULY 11, 1945

In view of the physical conditions prevailing in the area of 'Greater Berlin,' the Commission has not attempted, in Article 7 of the present Agreement, to delineate an area in 'Greater Berlin' to be occupied by forces of the French Republic. The Commission recommends that the question of determining the boundaries of the French area of occupation in 'Greater Berlin,' which area, in consequence of the Soviet zone of the City having undergone greater destruction, will be formed out of the American and British areas in 'Greater Berlin,' should be referred to the Control Council for consideration.

FINAL VERSION OF LAST PARAGRAPH OF
COVERING REPORT TO AMENDING AGREEMENT TO
PROTOCOL ON ZONES OF OCCUPATION APPROVED
BY EAC ON JULY 27, 1945

In view of the physical conditions prevailing in the area of 'Greater Berlin,' the Commission in the drafting of Article 7 of the present Agreement did not attempt to delimit the area in 'Greater Berlin' to be occupied by the armed forces of the French Republic. The Commission recommends that the question of the delimitation of the French area in 'Greater Berlin,' which will have to be allotted from the American and British areas of 'Greater Berlin' as a consequence of the greater destruction in the Soviet area of the City, should be referred to the Control Council in Berlin for consideration.

Annex 12

THE QUADRIPARTITE AGREEMENT ON BERLIN
OF SEPTEMBER 3, 1971

The Governments of the United States of America, the French Republic, the Union of Soviet Socialist Republics, and the United Kingdom of Great Britain and Northern Ireland, represented by their Ambassadors, who held a series of meetings in the building formerly occupied by the Allied Control Council in the American Sector of Berlin,

Acting on the basis of their quadripartite rights and responsibilities, and of the corresponding wartime and postwar agreements and decisions of the Four Powers, which are not affected,

Taking into account the existing situation in the relevant area,

Guided by the desire to contribute to practical improvements of the situation,

Without prejudice to their legal positions,

Have agreed on the following:

PART I
General Provisions

1. The four Governments will strive to promote the elimination of tension and the prevention of complications in the relevant area.
2. The four Governments, taking into account their obligations under the Charter of the United Nations, agree that there shall be no use or threat of force in the area and that disputes shall be settled solely by peaceful means.
3. The four Governments will mutually respect their individual and joint rights and responsibilities, which remain unchanged.
4. The four Governments agree that, irrespective of the differences in legal views, the situation which has developed in the area, and as it is defined in this Agreement as well as in the other agreements referred to in this Agreement, shall not be changed unilaterally.

PART II
Provisions relating to the Western Sectors of Berlin

A. The Government of the Union of Soviet Socialist Republics declares that transit traffic by road, rail and waterways through the territory of the German Democratic Republic of civilian persons and goods between the Western Sectors of Berlin and the Federal Republic of Germany will be unimpeded; that such traffic will be facilitated so as to take place in the most simple and expeditious manner; and that it will receive preferential treatment.

Detailed arrangements concerning this civilian traffic, as set forth in Annex I, will be agreed by the competent German authorities.

B. The Governments of the French Republic, the United Kingdom and the United States of America declare that the ties between the Western Sectors of Berlin and the Federal Republic of Germany will be maintained and developed, taking into account that these Sectors continue not to be a constituent part of the Federal Republic of Germany and not to be governed by it.

Detailed arrangements concerning the relationship between the Western Sectors of Berlin and the Federal Republic of Germany are set forth in Annex II.

C. The Government of the Union of Soviet Socialist Republics declares that communications between the Western Sectors of Berlin and areas bordering on these Sectors and those areas of the German Democratic Republic which do not border on these Sectors will be improved. Permanent residents of the Western Sectors of Berlin will be able to travel to and visit such areas for compassionate, family, religious, cultural or commercial reasons, or as tourists, under conditions comparable to those applying to other persons entering these areas.

ANNEXES

The problems of the small enclaves, including Steinstücken, and of other small areas may be solved by exchange of territory.

Detailed arrangements concerning travel, communications and the exchange of territory, as set forth in Annex III, will be agreed by the competent German authorities.

D. Representation abroad of the interests of the Western Sectors of Berlin and consular activities of the Union of Soviet Socialist Republics in the Western Sectors of Berlin can be exercised as set forth in Annex IV.

PART III
Final Provisions

This Quadripartite Agreement will enter into force on the date specified in a Final Quadripartite Protocol to be concluded when the measures envisaged in Part II of this Quadripartite Agreement and in its Annexes have been agreed.

DONE at the building formerly occupied by the Allied Control Council in the American Sector of Berlin, this 3rd day of September, 1971, in four originals, each in the English, French and Russian languages, all texts being equally authentic.

For the Government of the French Republic: /s/ Jean Sauvagnargues

For the Government of the Union of Soviet
Socialist Republics: /s/ Pyotr A. Abrasimov

For the Government of the United Kingdom
of Great Britain and Northern Ireland: /s/ Roger Jackling

For the Government of the United States
of America: /s/ Kenneth Rush

ANNEX I
Communication from the Government of the Union of Soviet Socialist Republics to the Governments of the French Republic, the United Kingdom and the United States of America

The Government of the Union of Soviet Socialist Republics, with reference to Part II (A) of the Quadripartite Agreement of this date and after consultation and agreement with the Government of the German Democratic Republic, has the honor to inform the Governments of the French Republic, the United Kingdom and the United States of America that:

1. Transit traffic by road, rail and waterways through the territory of the German Democratic Republic of civilian persons and goods between the Western Sectors of Berlin and the Federal Republic of Germany will be facilitated and unimpeded. It will receive the most simple, expeditious and preferential treatment provided by international practice.
2. Accordingly,
   (a) Conveyances sealed before departure may be used for the transport of civilian goods by road, rail and waterways between the Western Sectors of Berlin and the Federal Republic of Germany. Inspection procedures will be limited to the inspection of seals and accompanying documents.
   (b) With regard to conveyances which cannot be sealed, such as open trucks, inspection procedures will be limited to the inspection of accompanying

documents. In special cases in which there is sufficient reason to suspect that unsealed conveyances contain either material intended for dissemination along the designated routes or persons or material put on board along these routes, the content of unsealed conveyances may be inspected. Procedures for dealing with such cases will be agreed by the competent German authorities.

(c) Through trains and buses may be used for travel between the Western Sectors of Berlin and the Federal Republic of Germany. Inspection procedures will not include any formalities other than identification of persons.

(d) Persons identified as through travellers using individual vehicles between the Western Sectors of Berlin and the Federal Republic of Germany on routes designated for through traffic will be able to proceed to their destinations without paying individual tolls and fees for the use of the transit routes. Procedures applied for such travellers shall not involve delay.

The travellers, their vehicles and personal baggage will not be subject to search, detention or exclusion from use of the designated routes, except in special cases, as may be agreed by the competent German authorities, where there is sufficient reason to suspect that misuse of the transit routes is intended for purposes not related to direct travel to and from the Western Sectors of Berlin and contrary to generally applicable regulations concerning public order.

(e) Appropriate compensation for fees and tolls and for other costs related to traffic on the communication routes between the Western Sectors of Berlin and the Federal Republic of Germany, including the maintenance of adequate routes, facilities and installations used for such traffic, may be made in the form of an annual lump sum paid to the German Democratic Republic by the Federal Republic of Germany.

3. Arrangements implementing and supplementing the provisions of Paragraphs 1 and 2 above will be agreed by the competent German authorities.

ANNEX II
Communication from the Governments of the
French Republic, the United Kingdom and the
United States of America to the Government of the
Union of Soviet Socialist Republics

The Governments of the French Republic, the United Kingdom and the United States of America, with reference to Part II (B) of the Quadripartite Agreement of this date and after consultation with the Government of the Federal Republic of Germany, have the honour to inform the Government of the Union of Soviet Socialist Republics that:

1. They declare, in the exercise of their rights and responsibilities, that the ties between the Western Sectors of Berlin and the Federal Republic of Germany will be maintained and developed, taking into account that these Sectors continue not to be a constituent part of the Federal Republic of Germany and not to be governed by it. The provisions of the Basic Law of the Federal Republic of Germany and of the Constitution operative in the Western Sectors of Berlin which contradict the above have been suspended and continue not to be in effect.

2. The Federal President, the Federal Government, the *Bundesversammlung*, the *Bundesrat* and the *Bundestag*, including their Committees and *Fraktionen*, as well

ANNEXES

as other state bodies of the Federal Republic of Germany will not perform in the Western Sectors of Berlin constitutional or official acts which contradict the provisions of Paragraph 1.

3. The Government of the Federal Republic of Germany will be represented in the Western Sectors of Berlin to the authorities of the three Governments and to the *Senat* by a permanent liaison agency.

ANNEX III
*Communication from the Government of the
Union of Soviet Socialist Republics to the
Governments of the French Republic,
the United Kingdom and the United States of America*

The Government of the Union of Soviet Socialist Republics, with reference to Part II (C) of the Quadripartite Agreement of this date and after consultation and agreement with the Government of the German Democratic Republic, has the honour to inform the Governments of the French Republic, the United Kingdom and the United States of America that:

1. Communications between the Western Sectors of Berlin and areas bordering on these Sectors and those areas of the German Democratic Republic which do not border on these Sectors will be improved.
2. Permanent residents of the Western Sectors of Berlin will be able to travel to and visit such areas for compassionate, family, religious, cultural or commercial reasons, or as tourists, under conditions comparable to those applying to other persons entering these areas. In order to facilitate visits and travel, as described above, by permanent residents of the Western Sectors of Berlin, additional crossing points will be opened.
3. The problems of the small enclaves, including Steinstücken, and of other small areas may be solved by exchange of territory.
4. Telephonic, telegraphic, transport and other external communications of the Western Sectors of Berlin will be expanded.
5. Arrangements implementing and supplementing the provisions of Paragraphs 1 to 4 above will be agreed by the competent German authorities.

ANNEX IV
*A. Communication from the Governments of the
French Republic, the United Kingdom and the
United States of America to the Government of the
Union of Soviet Socialist Republics*

The Governments of the French Republic, the United Kingdom and the United States of America, with reference to Part II (D) of the Quadripartite Agreement of this date and after consultation with the Government of the Federal Republic of Germany, have the honour to inform the Government of the Union of Soviet Socialist Republics that:

1. The Governments of the French Republic, the United Kingdom and the United States of America maintain their rights and responsibilities relating to the representation abroad of the interests of the Western Sectors of Berlin and their permanent residents, including those rights and responsibilities concerning matters of security and status, both in international organizations and in relations with other countries.

2. Without prejudice to the above and provided that matters of security and status are not affected, they have agreed that:
   (a) The Federal Republic of Germany may perform consular services for permanent residents of the Western Sectors of Berlin.
   (b) In accordance with established procedures, international agreements and arrangements entered into by the Federal Republic of Germany may be extended to the Western Sectors of Berlin provided that the extension of such agreements and arrangements is specified in each case.
   (c) The Federal Republic of Germany may represent the interests of the Western Sectors of Berlin in international organizations and international conferences.
   (d) Permanent residents of the Western Sectors of Berlin may participate jointly with participants from the Federal Republic of Germany in international exchanges and exhibitions. Meetings of international organizations and international conferences as well as exhibitions with international participation may be held in the Western Sectors of Berlin. Invitations will be issued by the *Senat* or jointly by the Federal Republic of Germany and the *Senat*.
3. The three Governments authorize the establishment of a Consulate General of the USSR in the Western Sectors of Berlin accredited to the appropriate authorities of the three Governments in accordance with the usual procedures applied in those Sectors, for the purpose of performing consular services, subject to provisions set forth in a separate document of this date.

B. *Communication from the Government of the Union of Soviet Socialist Republics to the Governments of the French Republic, the United Kingdom and the United States of America*

The Government of the Union of Soviet Socialist Republics, with reference to Part II (D) of the Quadripartite Agreement of this date and to the communication of the Governments of the French Republic, the United Kingdom and the United States of America with regard to the representation abroad of the interests of the Western Sectors of Berlin and their permanent residents, has the honour to inform the Governments of the French Republic, the United Kingdom and the United States of America that:

1. The Government of the Union of Soviet Socialist Republics takes note of the fact that the three Governments maintain their rights and responsibilities relating to the representation abroad of the interests of the Western Sectors of Berlin and their permanent residents, including those rights and responsibilities concerning matters of security and status, both in international organizations and in relations with other countries.
2. Provided that matters of security and status are not affected, for its part it will raise no objection to:
   (a) The performance by the Federal Republic of Germany of consular services for permanent residents of the Western Sectors of Berlin.
   (b) In accordance with established procedures, the extension to the Western Sectors of Berlin of international agreements and arrangements entered into by the Federal Republic of Germany provided that the extension of such agreements and arrangements is specified in each case.

ANNEXES

    (c) The representation of the interests of the Western Sectors of Berlin by the Federal Republic of Germany in international organizations and international conferences.

    (d) The participation jointly with participants from the Federal Republic of Germany of permanent residents of the Western Sectors of Berlin in international exchanges and exhibitions, or the holding in those Sectors of meetings of international organizations and international conferences as well as exhibitions with international participation, taking into account that invitations will be issued by the *Senat* or jointly by the Federal Republic of Germany and the *Senat*.

3. The Government of the Union of Soviet Socialist Republics takes note of the fact that the three Governments have given their consent to the establishment of a Consulate General of the USSR in the Western Sectors of Berlin. It will be accredited to the appropriate authorities of the three Governments, for purposes and subject to provisions described in their communication and as set forth in a separate document of this date.

NOTES

Chapter One

1. Philip Mosely records that, "A further factor favorable to making Berlin the seat of Allied authority was that any proposal to create a new capital, especially one situated in a western zone, seemed bound to meet with unrelenting Soviet opposition." Philip E. Mosely, "The Occupation of Germany: New Light on How the Zones Were Drawn," *Foreign Affairs* 28 (1950), p. 587.

2. There are two published articles which record the history of the negotiations in outline form. These are Philip E. Mosely, "The Occupation of Germany: New Light on How the Zones Were Drawn," *Foreign Affairs* 28 (1950), pp. 580–604; and William M. Franklin, "Zonal Boundaries and Access to Berlin," *World Politics* 16 (1963), pp. 1–31.

Chapter Two

1. Karl Loewenstein, "The Allied Presence in Berlin: Legal Basis," *Foreign Policy Bulletin*, vol. 38, no. 11, p. 81.

2. Ernst Dauerlein, *Die Einheit Deutschlands* (Frankfurt, 1961), vol. I, p. 36.

3. "Summary of the Proceedings of the Fourth Session of the Tripartite Conference, October 22, 1943," in U.S. Department of State, Historical Office, *Foreign Relations of the United States, 1943*, Vol. I-General (Washington, 1963), p. 605. Hereafter cited as *F. R. U. S., 1943–I*.

4. *Ibid.*, p. 606.

5. *Ibid.*, pp. 607–608.

6. "Summary of the Proceedings of the Fifth Session of the Tripartite Conference, October 23, 1943," in *F. R. U. S., 1943–I*, pp. 620–621.

7. *Ibid.*

8. See Philip E. Mosely, "The Occupation of Germany: New Light on How the Zones Were Drawn," *Foreign Affairs* 28 (1950), p. 581.

9. *Ibid.*

10. *Ibid.*

11. *Ibid.*

12. George F. Kennan, *Memoirs 1925–1950* (Boston, 1967), pp. 164–165.

13. *Ibid.*, p. 165; For Cordell Hull's ideas see his telegram to the American Ambassador in London, December 23, 1943, in *F. R. U. S., 1943–I*, p. 812.

14. *F. R. U. S., 1943–I*, p. 664.

15. *Ibid.*

16. *Ibid.*

17. *Ibid.*

18. William Lord Strang, *Home and Abroad* (London, 1956), p. 202.

19. *F. R. U. S., 1943–I*, pp. 756–757.

20. Mosely, *op. cit.*, p. 582.

21. Strang, *op. cit.*, p. 203.

22. *Ibid.*

23. For a discussion of the British committee system see General Sir Leslie Hollis, *One Marine's Tale* (London, 1956), p. 6.

24. Kennan, *op. cit.*, pp. 165–166.

25. William M. Franklin, "Zonal Boundaries and Access to Berlin," *World Politics* 16 (1963), p. 2.

26. Robert E. Sherwood, *Roosevelt and Hopkins: An Intimate History* (New York, 1948), pp. 714–715.

27. Quoted in Cordell Hull, *The Memoirs of Cordell Hull* (New York, 1948), II, pp. 1284–1285.

28. The Interdivisional Committee was commonly known as the CAC-Country and Area Committee for Germany. The complete files of the committee are located in the archives of the Department of State. For a brief account of the work of the committee see Harley Notter, *Postwar Foreign Policy Preparation 1939–1945*, Department of State Publication 3580 (Washington, 1949), pp. 176–177.

29. Mosely, *op. cit.*, p. 586; Notter, *op. cit.*, p. 177.

30. Mosely, *op. cit.*, p. 586.

31. Mosely, *op. cit.*, p. 583.

32. Jean Edward Smith, *The Defense of Berlin* (Baltimore, 1963), p. 20; Mosely, *op. cit.*, pp. 584–585.

33. See Henry L. Stimson and McGeorge Bundy, *On Active Service in Peace and War* (New York, 1947), p. 55.

34. Ray S. Cline, *Washington Command Post: The Operations Division*, Office of the Chief of Military History, Department of the Army (Washington, 1951), pp. 323–326.

35. Mosely, *op. cit.*, pp. 584–585.

36. *Ibid.*, p. 585.

37. Kennan, *op. cit.*, p. 165.

38. For an account of this complicated and inexpeditious procedure see Cline, *op. cit.*, pp. 324–325.

39. Franklin, *op. cit.*, p. 1.

40. Sherwood, *op. cit.*, pp. 721–724, 755, 757, 774–775.

41. Smith, *op. cit.*, pp. 17–18; see also John L. Snell, *Dilemma in Germany* (New Orleans, 1959), p. 72.

42. *F. R. U. S., 1943–I*, p. 810.

43. Mosely, *op. cit.*, p. 582. In a memorandum to the author, August 30, 1970, Mosely states that it is possible that the telegram to Winant was approved by James F. Dunn and never seen by Secretary Hull.

44. Kennan, *op. cit.*, p. 166.

45. *Ibid.*

46. Strang, *op. cit.*, p. 205.

47. Files of the United States Delegation to the European Advisory Commission, Department of State decimal file 740.00119 EAC/101. Washington: The National Archives.

48. *Ibid.*

49. Strang, *op. cit.*, p. 204.

50. Mosely, *op. cit.*, p. 582.

51. Strang, *op. cit.*, pp. 204–205.

52. Strang, *op. cit.*, p. 206.

Chapter Three

1. Robert E. Sherwood, *Roosevelt and Hopkins: An Intimate History* (New York, 1948), pp. 711, 713.
2. *Ibid.*, p. 711.
3. Philip E. Mosely, "The Dismemberment of Germany: The Allied Negotiations from Yalta to Potsdam," *Foreign Affairs* 28 (1950), p. 487.
4. *Ibid.*
5. The first paper, entitled "Germany: Partition," was issued August 17, 1943, and was a policy memorandum based on an "H-document" for briefing Secretary Hull in connection with the First Quebec Conference. The second paper, entitled "The Political Reorganization of Germany," was issued September 23, 1943, and was prepared by the Country and Area Committee—Germany. Texts of these papers found in Harley A. Notter, *Postwar Foreign Policy Preparation 1939–1945*, Department of State Publication 3580 (Washington, 1950), pp. 554–560.
6. *Ibid.*, p. 559.
7. A full account of the military plans developed during 1943 is found in Sir Frederick Morgan, *Overture to Overlord* (Garden City, New York, 1950).
8. See Maurice Matloff, *Strategic Planning for Coalition Warfare, 1943–44* (Washington, 1959), p. 226.
9. William M. Franklin, "Zonal Boundaries and Access to Berlin," *World Politics* 16 (1963), p. 7.
10. *Ibid.*
11. Cordell Hull, *The Memoirs of Cordell Hull* (New York, 1948), II, p. 1233.
12. *Ibid.*, pp. 1233–1234.
13. See Philip E. Mosely, "The Occupation of Germany: New Light on How the Zones Were Drawn," *Foreign Affairs* 28 (1950), pp. 580–581, hereafter cited as Mosely, "Occupation of Germany." Also Philip E. Mosely, "The Dismemberment of Germany: The Allied Negotiations from Yalta to Potsdam," *Foreign Affairs* 28 (1950), p. 489, hereafter cited as Mosely, "Dismemberment of Germany."
14. The document is reproduced in U.S. Department of State, *Foreign Relations of the United States, 1943*, Volume I-General, Department of State Publication 7585 (Washington, 1963), pp. 720–723, hereafter cited as *F. R. U. S., 1943–I*. A discussion of the American proposals appears in Hull, *op. cit.*, II, pp. 1284–1287.
15. *F. R. U. S., 1943–I*, p. 721.
16. Franklin, *op. cit.*, p.4.
17. Sir Llewellyn Woodward, *British Foreign Policy in the Second World War* (London, 1962), pp. 443–445.
18. Winston S. Churchill, *Triumph and Tragedy* (Boston, 1953), pp. 507–508; Woodward, *op. cit.*, pp. 445–448, 465–470.
19. Mosely, "Occupation of Germany," *op. cit.*, p. 589; also Franklin, *op. cit.*, p. 8.
20. Franklin, *op. cit.*, pp. 8–9.
21. *Ibid.*, p. 9.
22. U.S. Department of State, Historical Office, *Foreign Relations of the United States, The Conferences at Cairo and Tehran, 1943*, Department of State Publication 7187 (Washington, 1961), p. 253. Hereafter cited as *Conferences at Cairo and Tehran, 1943*.
23. Matloff, *op. cit.*, p. 341.

NOTES

24. Minutes of the President's Meeting With the Joint Chiefs of Staff, November 19, 1943, 2 p.m., Admiral's Cabin, U.S.S. 'Iowa,' in *The Conferences at Cairo and Tehran, 1943, op. cit.*, p. 254.

25. *Ibid.*

26. Franklin, *op. cit.*, p. 10.

27. *The Conferences at Cairo and Tehran, 1943, op. cit.*, p. 253.

28. *Ibid.*, p. 254.

29. *Ibid.*, pp. 254–255.

30. The map is printed in Matloff, *op. cit.*, facing p. 341.

31. Franklin, *op. cit.*, p. 11.

32. Jean Edward Smith, *The Defense of Berlin* (Baltimore, 1963), p. 17.

33. Matloff, *op. cit.*, p. 491.

34. Sumner Welles, *The Time for Decision* (New York, 1944), pp. 336–364. In a written memorandum to the author, August 30, 1970, Philip E. Mosely noted that in the chapter on partition Sumner Welles simply paraphrased a State Department study in favor of partition and made no mention of an opposing memo written at the same time, about November, 1942. See also Sumner Welles, *Seven Decisions That Shaped History* (New York, 1950), p. 204; also Sherwood, *op. cit.*, pp. 797–798.

35. Sherwood, *op. cit.*, pp. 797–798; Mosely, "Dismemberment of Germany," *op. cit.*, p. 490; *Conferences at Cairo and Tehran, 1943, op. cit.*, pp. 596–604.

36. Smith, *op. cit.*, p. 18.

37. The document, as revised, is reproduced in *Conferences at Cairo and Tehran, 1943*, pp. 786–787.

38. *Ibid.*, p. 787.

39. Franklin, *op. cit.*, p. 12.

40. *Conferences at Cairo and Tehran, 1943, op. cit.*, p. 688.

41. Sir Frederick Morgan, *Overture to Overlord* (Garden City, N.Y., 1950), p. 250. Quoted in Franklin, *op. cit.*, p. 12.

42. Mosely, "The Occupation of Germany," *op. cit.*, p. 587.

43. *Ibid.* William Franklin states that "there seems to be no documentary evidence that this perceptive plan was ever pushed by the Department of State or was ever formally proposed in the Working Security Committee." Franklin, *op. cit.*, p. 16.

Chapter Four

1. Telegram from Hull to Winant, Department of State lot file 52 M 64, files of the United States Political Adviser to the American Delegation to the European Advisory Commission, section 144–I. The records pertaining to the work of the American Delegation to the European Advisory Commission are in Washington, D.C., in the custody of the Department of State. There are two divisions of these records: the decimal files, which are official State Department documents relating to the work of the American Delegation, EAC, located at the National Archives; and the lot files, which are the files of the United States Political Adviser to the American Delegation to the EAC, located at a Federal Records Center. The particular decimal file frequently cited in this book is 740.00119 EAC, located at the National Archives. The lot file frequently cited is 52 M 64, located at a Federal Records Center and serviced by the Department of State. Access to these files was arranged with the permission of the Historical Office of the Department of State. The re-

search was carried out under the guidance of Dr. Arthur Kogan, Chief, Research Guidance and Review Division, now Special Assistant to the Director of the Historical Office.

2. Telegram from Winant to Secretary of State, January 13, 1944, Department of State lot file 52 M 64. Penciled note at top reads "Draft—not sent."

3. See Philip E. Mosely, "The Occupation of Germany: New Light on How the Zones Were Drawn," *Foreign Affairs* 28 (1950), p. 584.

4. U.S. Department of State, Historical Office, *Foreign Relations of the United States, 1944*, Volume I-General, Department of State Publication 8138 (Washington, 1966), pp. 112–113. Hereafter cited as *F. R. U. S., 1944–I*.

5. These papers are reproduced in *F. R. U. S., 1944–I*, pp. 112–159, together with map showing British proposal for zones of military occupation.

6. William M. Franklin, "Zonal Boundaries and Access to Berlin," *World Politics* 16 (1963), p. 13.

7. *F. R. U. S., 1944–I*, p. 112.

8. *Ibid.*, p. 152.

9. Dept. of State decimal file 740.00119 EAC/80.

10. Dept. of State decimal file 740.00119 EAC/74.

11. The document is printed in *F. R. U. S., 1944–I*, pp. 173–179. Professor Smith states that the Soviet proposal delineated the actual city boundaries of Berlin. Jean Edward Smith, *The Defense of Berlin* (Baltimore, 1963), p. 21. A reading of the version printed in *Foreign Relations* plus two identical versions found in the State Department files shows, however, that this is not the case.

12. Mosely, *op. cit.*, p. 591.

13. Dept. of State decimal file 740.00119 EAC/180.

14. *F. R. U. S., 1944–I*, p. 173.

15. *Ibid.*, p. 180.

16. Quoted in Franklin, *op. cit.*, pp. 14–15.

17. Telegram: Stettinius to Winant, in *F. R. U. S., 1944–I*, pp. 183–184.

18. See Franklin, *op. cit.*, p. 15.

19. *F. R. U. S., 1944–I*, pp. 188–189.

20. Franklin, *op. cit.*, p. 17.

21. Mosely, *op. cit.*, p. 591; Smith, *op. cit.*, p. 22. Smith's account is based upon an article in the *Saturday Evening Post*. Albert L. Warner, "Our Secret Deal Over Germany," *Saturday Evening Post*, August 2, 1952, pp. 66–68. Mosely at this time was a member of the Working Security Committee. In a written memorandum to the author, August 30, 1970, Mosely explained that on the map received in London accompanying the proposal the zonal lines came close to Berlin so that the boundaries, as half-drawn, only seemed to converge at Berlin. The Civil Affairs Division representatives, junior to Mosely at the time, could neither explain nor clarify matters.

22. The document, together with maps, is reproduced in *F. R. U. S., 1944–I*, pp. 195–196.

23. See Mosely, *op. cit.*, p. 591; Franklin, *op. cit.*, pp. 17–18; Smith, *op. cit.*, p. 22.

24. *F. R. U. S., 1944–I*, p. 208.

25. George F. Kennan, *Memoirs 1925–1950* (Boston, 1967), p. 169.

26. *Ibid.*, p. 171.

27. *F. R. U. S., 1944–I*, p. 211.

NOTES 197

28. See Franklin, *op. cit.*, p. 19; Mosely, *op. cit.*, pp. 592–593.
29. Smith, *op. cit.*, pp. 24–25.
30. Lucius D. Clay, *Decision in Germany* (Garden City, N. Y., 1950), p. 15. In a memorandum to the author Mosely states that General Clay wrote his account mainly on the basis of hearsay insofar as it concerned events and decisions prior to his appointment to Germany in 1945.
31. Written memorandum from Mosely to the author, August 30, 1970.
32. For a full account see Mosely, *op. cit.*, pp. 592–593.
33. *F. R. U. S., 1944–I*, p. 231.
34. Dept. of State lot file 52 M 64, Section 144–I.
35. *Ibid.*
36. *F. R. U. S., 1944–I*, p. 239.
37. General Meyer's Notes of Informal Meeting of EAC Held June 30, 1944, Dept. of State lot file 52 M 64, Section-EAC meetings.
38. Telegram from Winant to Secretary of State, Dept. of State decimal file 740.00119 EAC/7–344.
39. General Meyer's Notes of Informal Meeting of EAC Held July 4, 1944, Dept. of State lot file 52 M 64, Section 301.2–I.
40. *F. R. U. S., 1944–I*, p. 240.
41. *Ibid.*, pp. 240–241.
42. General Meyer's Notes of Informal Meeting of EAC Held July 10, 1944, Dept. of State lot file 52 M 64, Section 301.2–I.
43. Memorandum: Meyer to Winant, Dept. of State lot file 52 M 64, Section 144–I.
44. General Meyer's Notes of Informal Meeting of EAC Held July 12, 1944, Dept. of State lot file 52 M 64, Section 301.2–I.
45. Dept. of State lot file 52 M 64, Section 144–I.
46. General Meyer's Notes of Informal Meeting of EAC Held July 17, 1944, Dept. of State lot file 52 M 64, Section 301.2–I.
47. There was an extended argument over the use of the word "auxiliary" to precede the word "contingents" in Article 4, the article which provided for token small-power participation in the military occupation of Germany. The argument threatened to cause considerable delay to agreement on the zones protocol but was finally settled at the July 27th meeting.
48. Telegram from Winant to Secretary of State, July 27, 1944, Dept. of State decimal file 740.00119 EAC/7–2744.
49. Minutes of the Seventh Formal Meeting printed in *F. R. U. S., 1944–I*, pp. 252–261.
50. General Meyer's Notes of Informal Meeting of EAC Held July 27, 1944, Dept. of State lot file 52 M 64, Section 301.2–I.
51. Ambassador Winant appointed Mr. J. D. Beam and Dr. Mosely, who served as Chairman of the subcommittee. British members of the Committee were Mr. C. O'Neill and Major Filmer, a map expert. Soviet members were Mr. Saksin, Mr. Ivanov, and Mr. Marchenko.
52. *F. R. U. S., 1944–I*, p. 262.
53. General Meyer's Notes of Informal Meeting of EAC Held July 31, 1944, Dept. of State lot file 52 M 64, Section 301.2–I.

54. See Cordell Hull, *The Memoirs of Cordell Hull* (New York, 1948), II, p. 1613. See also the memorandum from Undersecretary of State Stettinius to Secretary of State Hull in *F. R. U. S., 1944–I*, p. 264.

55. Henry L. Stimson and McGeorge Bundy, *On Active Service in Peace and War* (New York, 1947), p. 568.

56. Forrest C. Pogue, *The Supreme Command* (Washington, 1954), p. 350.

57. *Ibid.*, pp. 350–351.

58. Stimson and Bundy, *op. cit.*, p. 569, 575.

59. *F. R. U. S., 1944–I*, pp. 331–332.

60. General Meyer's Notes of Informal Meeting of EAC Held September 11, 1944, Dept. of State lot file 52 M 64, Section 301.2–I.

61. Winston S. Churchill, *Triumph and Tragedy* (Boston, 1953), p. 156.

62. See Fleet Admiral William D. Leahy, *I Was There: The Personal Story of the Chief of Staff to Presidents Roosevelt and Truman, Based on His Notes and Diaries Made at the Time* (New York, 1950), pp. 262–263; Mosely, *op. cit.*, pp. 596–597; Stimson and Bundy, *op. cit.*, p. 576; Smith, *op. cit.*, pp. 27–28; Franklin, *op. cit.*, p. 21.

63. The amendments to be incorporated in the protocol were drawn up in a memorandum by the Combined Chiefs of Staff which was approved by Roosevelt and Churchill. The document, C.C.S. 320/27, was transmitted to Winant by the State Department on September 20. Text printed in *F. R. U. S., 1944–I*, pp. 340–341.

64. Philip E. Mosely, "The Dismemberment of Germany: The Allied Negotiations from Yalta to Potsdam," *Foreign Affairs* 28 (1950), p. 491.

65. *F. R. U. S., 1944–I*, p. 344.

66. *Ibid.*, p. 343.

67. This is confirmed by a written memorandum from Mosely to the author August 30, 1970. Mosely states that the assumption pleased the U.S. Delegation, because it would give the United States control of Tempelhof Airdrome.

68. *F. R. U. S., 1944–I*, p. 348.

69. It is possible that this telegram was never actually cabled to the State Department. In the files it is placed together with another telegram bearing a handwritten note in the margin "not sent." The substance of the two telegrams is similar. In a memorandum to the author, Mosely notes that these are probably two drafts of the same cable, and that the one quoted in the text was in all probability actually cabled to Washington. Dept. of State lot file 52 M 64, Section 144–I.

70. *Ibid.*

71. Meyer met with Lieutenant General Bedell Smith, Chief of Staff of SHAEF; Major General Hilldring of the Civil Affairs Division of the War Department; and Brigadier General Julius Holmes, Deputy Chief of the G-5 (Civil Affairs) Division of SHAEF. *F. R. U. S., 1944–I*, p. 354.

72. *F. R. U. S., 1944–I*, pp. 349–351.

73. *Ibid.*, pp. 352–354.

74. *Ibid.*, pp. 358–359.

75. See Hull, *op. cit.*, II, pp. 1619–1622; Stimson and Bundy, *op. cit.*, p. 572; Mosely, "The Occupation of Germany," *op. cit.*, p. 596; Smith, *op. cit.*, p. 29.

76. Smith, *op. cit.*, p. 29.

77. Dept. of State decimal file 740.00119 EAC/10–2144. Original not underlined.

78. Mosely, "The Occupation of Germany," *op. cit.*, p. 596. Winant's trip was probably related more to politics than to EAC business. While in the United States, he did a considerable amount of traveling, speaking, and campaigning on behalf of Roosevelt's reelection. He also lobbied heavily for postwar lend-lease to Britain, and this probably helped him to avoid a head-on clash with Morgenthau over German policy.

79. *F. R. U. S., 1944–I*, p. 384. The telegram was drafted and dispatched by Mosely, even though it was stamped with the name of the American chargé in London, Mr. Gallman.

80. Mosely, "The Occupation of Germany," *op. cit.*, p. 597.

81. Written memorandum from Mosely to the author, January 27, 1970.

82. *F. R. U. S., 1944–I*, pp. 391–392.

83. Mosely, "The Occupation of Germany," *op. cit.*, p. 598.

84. *F. R. U. S., 1944–I*, p. 392.

85. Mosely, "The Occupation of Germany," *op. cit.*, p. 598.

86. General Meyer's Notes of Informal Meeting of EAC Held December 7, 1944, Dept. of State lot file 52 M 64, Section 301.2–IV.

87. Interview with Philip E. Mosely, New York City, April 26, 1969; Memorandum from Mosely to the author, August 30, 1970.

88. See Franklin, *op. cit.*, p. 22. For text of the agreements see U.S. Department of State, Historical Office, *Foreign Relations of the United States, The Conferences at Malta and Yalta, 1945* (Washington, 1955), pp. 198–201.

89. Franklin, *op. cit.*, p. 23; Mosely, "The Occupation of Germany," *op. cit.*, p. 599.

90. Edward R. Stettinius, *Roosevelt and the Russians: The Yalta Conference* (Garden City, N.Y., 1949), p. 56.

91. Franklin, *op. cit.*, p. 23; *Conferences at Malta and Yalta*, pp. 201, 498.

92. See the memorandum prepared for the Secretary of State on December 26, 1944, by the Division of Central European Affairs in *F. R. U. S., 1944–I*, pp. 425–426.

93. *F. R. U. S., 1944–I*, p. 422. The memorandum was written by Mr. James W. Riddleberger, Chief of the Division of Central European Affairs, and addressed to Mr. James C. Dunn, Director of the Office of European Affairs, and Mr. H. Freeman Matthews, the Deputy Director.

Chapter Five

1. The French memorandum was first circulated in the EAC on December 27, 1944. It was printed and distributed as an official EAC document on December 29 and was taken up as EAC business for the first time at the meeting of January 2. The complete text of the document entitled "Germany: Terms of Surrender and Machinery for Their Enforcement," is printed in U.S. Department of State, Historical Office, *Foreign Relations of the United States, 1944*, Volume I-General, Department of State Publication 8138 (Washington, 1966), pp. 427–429. Hereafter cited as *F. R. U. S., 1944–I*.

2. *Ibid.*, p. 427.

3. *Ibid.*, p. 428.

4. See Winant's telegram of January 2 to the State Department in U.S. Department of State, Historical Office, *Foreign Relations of the United States, 1945*, Volume III-European Advisory Commission, Austria, Germany, Department of State Publication 8364 (Washington, 1968), p. 161. Hereafter cited as *F. R. U. S., 1945–III.*

5. *Ibid.*, p. 162.

6. *Ibid.*

7. Interview with Philip E. Mosely, New York City, April 26, 1969.

8. The two other meetings were held January 9 and 29, 1945. General Meyer's Notes of EAC Meetings, Dept. of State lot file 52 M 64, Section 301.2–IV.

9. Interview with Philip E. Mosely, New York City, April 26, 1969.

10. *Ibid.*

11. *Ibid.*

12. See Edward R. Stettinius, Jr., *Roosevelt and the Russians: The Yalta Conference* (Garden City, N.Y., 1949), pp. 126–129, 298–299, 344–345; also Philip E. Mosely, "The Occupation of Germany: New Light on How the Zones Were Drawn," *Foreign Affairs* 28 (1950), p. 599; Jean Edward Smith, *The Defense of Berlin* (Baltimore, 1963), pp. 29–30; Robert Sherwood, *Roosevelt and Hopkins* (New York, 1948), pp. 858–861.

13. U.S. Department of State, Historical Office, *Foreign Relations of the United States, The Conferences at Malta and Yalta, 1945* (Washington, 1955), p. 978.

14. Interview with Philip E. Mosely, New York City, April 26, 1969.

15. Stettinius, *op. cit.*, p. 88, 289.

16. *F. R. U. S., The Conferences at Malta and Yalta, 1945*, p. 978.

17. See Philip E. Mosely, "The Dismemberment of Germany: The Allied Negotiations from Yalta to Potsdam," *Foreign Affairs* 28 (1950), p. 492.

18. Interview with Philip E. Mosely, New York City, April 26, 1969; private letters were sent in both directions by courier.

19. *F. R. U. S., 1945–III*, p. 182.

20. *Ibid.*, p. 184, footnote 61.

21. *Ibid.*, p. 185.

22. Charles de Gaulle, *The War Memoirs of Charles de Gaulle, Vol. II-Salvation* (New York, 1960), pp. 7, 53–55, 57, 62, 95.

23. *F. R. U. S., 1945–III*, p. 189.

24. *Ibid.*, p. 202.

25. *Ibid.*

26. General Meyer's Notes of Informal Meetings of EAC, Month of April, Dept. of State lot file 52 M 64, Section 301.2–IV.

27. *F. R. U. S., 1945–III*, pp. 236–237.

28. Written memorandum from Philip E. Mosely to the author, August 30, 1970.

29. General Meyer's Notes of Informal Meetings of EAC, Month of May, Dept. of State lot file 52 M 64, Section 301.2–IV.

30. Dept. of State lot file 52 M 64, Section 144–IV.

31. *Ibid.*

32. Text printed in *F. R. U. S., 1945–III*, p. 319.

33. The story of these extra-meeting negotiations is difficult to trace. The relevant folder (144–III) covering negotiations on zones of occupation from January 1 to April 30 is missing from the State Department's EAC lot files. The best account

NOTES

is found in the *F. R. U. S., 1945–III* volume in various telegrams and memoranda from p. 247 to p. 363. It is possible that additional material relating to extra-meeting negotiations on Berlin is contained in the missing file.

34. See text of a Joint Chiefs of Staff memorandum to the Secretary of State, transmitted to Winant by Acting Secretary Grew on April 28 in *F. R. U. S., 1945–III*, p. 247.

35. *F. R. U. S., 1945–III*, p. 297.

36. This point is emphasized in a memorandum by James Riddleberger, Chief of the Division of Central European Affairs in the State Department in *F. R. U. S., 1945–III*, pp. 320–321. The memorandum contains notes on a conversation on May 31, 1945, between Riddleberger and Armand Berard, Counselor of the French Embassy, and is not addressed to any specific person.

37. Mosely, "The Occupation of Germany," *op. cit.*, p. 600. See also Murphy's cable to State Department of June 27 in *F. R. U. S., 1945–III*, pp. 345–346.

38. Mosely, "The Occupation of Germany," *op. cit.*, p. 600.

39. De Gaulle states, somewhat inaccurately, "I myself had determined the territories we would control. . . . " See Charles de Gaulle, *op. cit.*, p. 233.

40. *F. R. U. S., 1945–III*, p. 363.

41. Mosely, "The Dismemberment of Germany," *op. cit.*, p. 493.

42. *F. R. U. S., 1945–III*, p. 206.

43. Quoted in telegram from Stettinius to Winant in *F. R. U. S., 1945–III*, p. 221; also quoted in Mosely, "The Dismemberment of Germany," *op. cit.*, p. 494.

44. Mosely, "The Dismemberment of Germany," *op. cit.*, p. 494.

45. *Ibid.*, p. 495.

46. *Ibid.*, pp. 496–497.

47. *F. R. U. S., 1945–III*, p. 317, footnote 7.

48. Mosely, "The Dismemberment of Germany," *op. cit.*, p. 498.

49. Mosely, "The Occupation of Germany," *op. cit.*, p. 602; see also Harry S. Truman, *Year of Decisions* (Garden City, N.Y., 1955), pp. 298–305; Winston S. Churchill, *Triumph and Tragedy* (Boston, 1953), pp. 507–519, 572–574, 601–604, 673–674.

50. *F. R. U. S., 1945–III*, p. 232.

51. *Ibid.*, pp. 235–236.

52. Interview with Philip E. Mosely, New York City, April 26, 1969. See also Mosely's statements in "The Occupation of Germany," *op. cit.*, p. 602.

53. U. S. Department of State, Historical Office, *Foreign Relations of the United States, The Conference of Berlin (Potsdam), 1945*, Volume I, Department of State Publication 7015 (Washington, 1960), pp. 6–7.

54. General Meyer's Notes of EAC Meeting Held May 29, 1945, Dept. of State lot file 52 M 64, Section 301.2–V.

55. *F. R. U. S., 1945–III*, pp. 316–317.

56. Lucius D. Clay, *Decision in Germany* (Garden City, N.Y., 1950), p. 21.

57. See Eisenhower's telegram of June 6 to the Joint Chiefs of Staff in *F. R. U. S., 1945–III*, pp. 328–329.

58. *Ibid.*, p. 331.

59. *Ibid.*, p. 329.

60. *Ibid.*, pp. 333–334.

61. *Ibid.*, p. 326.
62. *Ibid.*, p. 132. See also Fleet Admiral William D. Leahy, *I Was There: The Personal Story of the Chief of Staff to Presidents Roosevelt and Truman, Based on His Notes and Diaries Made at the Time* (New York, 1950), pp. 349–350; Lieutenant General Walter Bedell Smith, *My Three Years in Moscow* (New York, 1950), pp. 21–22; Churchill, *op. cit.*, pp. 604–609.
63. *F. R. U. S., 1945–III*, pp. 133–134.
64. *Ibid.*, pp. 134–135.
65. *Ibid.*, p. 136.
66. *Ibid.*, p. 137.
67. *F. R. U. S., The Conference of Berlin (Potsdam)*, I, p. 107.
68. Clay, *op. cit.*, pp. 30–31.
69. *F. R. U. S., 1945–III*, p. 132.
70. *Ibid.*
71. *Ibid.*, p. 232.
72. Written memorandum from Philip E. Mosely to the author, August 30, 1970.
73. The author could not find in the EAC files any clue as to which delegation originally made this suggestion or when the suggestion was made. It was reported to the State Department by Winant in a telegram dated June 28. See *F. R. U. S., 1945–III*, p. 347.
74. *Ibid.* There is no definite answer as to which delegation proposed the wording of this paragraph. However, the author concludes that the American delegation submitted the wording, since Winant, in his telegram of June 30, asks whether he may recede "to my orig draft leaving open question redivision Berlin." *Ibid.*, p. 362.
75. *F. R. U. S., 1945–III*, pp. 347–348.
76. *Ibid.*, p. 352.
77. General Meyer's Notes of Informal Meeting of EAC Held June 29, 1945, Dept. of State lot file 52 M 64, Section 301.2–VII.
78. General Meyer's Notes of Informal Meeting of EAC Held June 30, 1945, Dept. of State lot file 52 M 64, Section 301.2–VII.
79. General Meyer's Notes of Informal Meeting of EAC Held July 2, 1945, Enclosure, Dept. of State lot file 52 M 64, Section 301.2–VII.
80. General Meyer's Notes of Informal Meeting of EAC Held July 6, 1945, Dept. of State lot file 52 M 64, Section 301.2–VII.
81. *Ibid.*
82. General Meyer's Notes of Informal Meeting of EAC Held July 4, 1945, Dept. of State lot file 52 M 64, Section 301.2–VII. Not underlined in the original.
83. General Meyer's Notes of Informal Meeting of EAC Held July 6, 1945, Dept. of State lot file 52 M 64, File 301.2–VII.
84. *Ibid.*
85. Interview with Philip E. Mosely, New York City, April 26, 1969.
86. Mosely, "The Occupation of Germany," *op. cit.*, p. 601.
87. General Meyer's Notes of Informal Meeting of EAC Held July 9, 1945, at 11:45, Dept. of State lot file 52 M 64, Section 301.2–VII.
88. General Meyer's Notes of Informal Meeting of EAC Held July 9, 1945, at 20:30, Dept. of State lot file 52 M 64, Section 301.2–VII.

89. *Ibid.*, Enclosure to Minutes of July 9.
90. General Meyer's Notes of Informal Meeting of EAC Held July 9, 1945, at 20:30, Dept. of State lot file 52 M 64, Section 301.2–VII.
91. F. R. U. S., *The Conference of Berlin (Potsdam)*, I, pp. 600–601.
92. General Meyer's Notes of Informal Meeting of EAC Held July 12, 1945, Dept. of State lot file 52 M 64, Section 301.2–VII.
93. *Ibid.*, Enclosure to Minutes of July 12.
94. Interview with Philip E. Mosely, New York City, April 26, 1969.
95. General Meyer's Notes of Informal Meeting of EAC Held July 12, 1945, Dept. of State lot file 52 M 64, Section 301.2–VII.
96. F. R. U. S., *The Conference of Berlin (Potsdam)*, I, pp. 602–603.
97. Mosely, "The Occupation of Germany," *op. cit.*, p. 601.
98. See Clay, *op. cit.*, pp. 27–29; see also Frank Howley, *Berlin Command* (New York, 1950), pp. 57–59.
99. Mosely, "The Occupation of Germany," *op. cit.*, p. 601.
100. F. R. U. S., *The Conference of Berlin (Potsdam)*, II, p. 1001.
101. *Ibid.*, p. 1002.
102. Memorandum for the Ambassador (Winant) Regarding Physical Conditions in Berlin and the French Sector, July 19, 1945, Dept. of State lot file 52 M 64, Section 144–IV.
103. *Ibid.*
104. Interview with Philip E. Mosely, New York City, April 26, 1969.
105. General Meyer's Notes of Informal Meeting of EAC Held July 23, 1945, Dept. of State lot file 52 M 64, Section 301.2–VII.
106 F. R. U. S., *1945–III*, p. 364, footnote 34.
107. *Ibid.*, p. 365.
108. Mosely, "The Occupation of Germany," *op. cit.*, p. 602.
109. Minutes of the First Meeting of the Control Council for Germany, Held at Berlin, July 30, 1945, F. R. U. S., *1945–III*, pp. 366–367.
110. Protocol of the Proceedings of the Berlin Conference, F. R. U. S., *The Conference of Berlin (Potsdam)*, II, pp. 1478–1481.
111. General Meyer's Notes of Informal Meetings of EAC, Month of August, Dept. of State lot file 52 M 64, Section 301.2–VII.

Chapter Six

1. Interview with Philip E. Mosely, New York City, April 26, 1969.
2. William M. Franklin, "Zonal Boundaries and Access to Berlin," *World Politics* 16 (1963), p. 25.
3. Text in U.S. Department of State, Historical Office, *Foreign Relations of the United States, The Conferences at Malta and Yalta, 1945* (Washington, 1955), p. 124.
4. William Lord Strang, *Home and Abroad* (London, 1956), p. 215.
5. *Ibid.*, p. 216.
6. Franklin, *op. cit.*, p. 24.
7. *Ibid.*
8. *Ibid.*
9. Philip E. Mosely, "The Occupation of Germany: New Light on How the Zones Were Drawn," *Foreign Affairs* 28 (1950), p. 603.

10. *Ibid.*
11. Interview with Philip E. Mosely, New York City, April 30, 1969.
12. Mosely, "The Occupation of Germany," *op. cit.*, p. 603.
13. Edward R. Stettinius, *Roosevelt and the Russians: The Yalta Conference* (Garden City, N.Y., 1949), pp. 37–38.
14. Quoted in Herbert Feis, *Churchill, Roosevelt, and Stalin: The War They Waged and the Peace They Sought* (Princeton, 1957), p. 533.
15. U.S. Department of State, Historical Office, *Foreign Relations of the United States, 1945, Volume III: European Advisory Commission; Austria; Germany*, Department of State Publication 8364 (Washington, 1968), p. 189. Hereafter cited as *F. R. U. S., 1945–III*.
16. Franklin, *op. cit.*, p. 27.
17. *F. R. U. S., 1945–III*, p. 188.
18. Franklin, *op. cit.*, p. 27. In a written memorandum to the author, August 30, 1970, Mosely states that he has no recollection that the EAC was informed of this action. It is possible that some military person consulted General Meyer, but if so, it is probable, though not certain, that Mosely would have known about it, since General Meyer always dealt with Winant and Mosely in a very open and cooperative way.
19. *F. R. U. S., 1945–III*, p. 333.
20. Mosely, *op. cit.*, pp. 603–604. Copies of most EAC telegrams with military significance were also sent regularly to Ambassador Murphy at SHAEF.
21. Telegram printed in *F. R. U. S., 1945–III*, pp. 135–136.
22. *Ibid.*, p. 137.
23. Quoted in Harry S. Truman, *Year of Decisions* (Garden City, N. Y., 1955), pp. 306–307.
24. Lucius D. Clay, *Decision in Germany* (Garden City, N. Y., 1950), p. 24.
25. Complete notes of this meeting are printed in *F. R. U. S., 1945–III*, pp. 353–361. The notes were transmitted to the State Department by the U.S. Political Adviser for Germany, Robert Murphy, in a letter of April 7, 1948. The notes were identified by General Parks as his own in a memorandum of April 1, 1948, to General Alfred M. Gruenther, then Director of the Joint Staff of the Joint Chiefs of Staff. The memorandum transmitted a copy of the notes to General Gruenther. The following paragraphs are based on the notes as printed in the *Foreign Relations* volume.
26. Clay, *op. cit.*, pp. 25, 26.
27. Clay probably means that no official record or tripartitely agreed minutes were made. Quite obviously the rather complete notes taken by General Parks constitute a "record" of the meeting.
28. Clay, *op. cit.*, p. 26.
29. *Ibid.*, p. 25.
30. *Ibid.*, p. 26.
31. *Ibid.*
32. Strang, *op. cit.*, p. 217.
33. Mosely, *op. cit.*, p. 604.
34. *Ibid.*
35. Strang, *op. cit.*, p. 217.

36. *Ibid.*
37. *F. R. U. S., 1945–III*, pp. 158–159.
38. Franklin, *op. cit.*, p. 31.
39. Written memorandum from Philip E. Mosely to the author, August 30, 1970.
40. *F. R. U. S., 1945–III*, p. 1577.
41. *Ibid.*, pp. 1577–1579.
42. The members of the Coordinating Committee were Army General Sokolovsky, U.S.S.R. (Chairman); Lieutenant General Clay, U.S.; Lieutenant General Robertson, U.K.; Lieutenant General Koeltz, France.
43. *F. R. U. S., 1945–III*, p. 1580.
44. *Ibid.*, pp. 1580–1581.
45. *Ibid.*, pp. 1582–1583.
46. See the Letter from the Foreign Minister of the German Democratic Republic to the Deputy Foreign Minister of the Soviet Union, September 20, 1955, confirming these arrangements in U.S. Department of State, Historical Office, *Documents on Germany, 1944–1959*, Committee on Foreign Relations, U.S. Senate (Washington, 1961), p. 158.
47. *Documents on Germany, 1944–1959, op. cit.*, the entries for March 6–22, 1951, p. 470, and for October 23, 1952, p. 478.
48. Wolfgang Heidelmeyer and Guenter Hindrichs, eds., *Documents on Berlin 1943–1963* (Munich, 1963), p. 304.
49. *F. R. U. S., 1945–III*, p. 353, footnote 66.

Chapter Seven

1. U. S. Department of State, Historical Office, *Foreign Relations of the United States, 1944*, Volume I-General (Washington, 1966), p. 152.
2. William Lord Strang, *Home and Abroad* (London, 1956), p. 215.
3. Secret Protocol of the Moscow Conference in U.S. Department of State, Historical Office, *Foreign Relations of the United States, 1943*, Volume I-General (Washington, 1963), pp. 751, 757.
4. George F. Kennan, *Memoirs 1925–1950* (Boston, 1967), p. 172.
5. *Ibid.*
6. *Ibid.*, pp. 173–174.
7. *Ibid.*
8. Jean Edward Smith, *The Defense of Berlin* (Baltimore, 1963), pp. 24, 32, 33.
9. Quoted in Kennan, *op. cit.*, p. 171.
10. See Smith, *op. cit.*, p. 32.

Chapter Eight

1. Marshal Vasili I. Chuikov, *The Fall of Berlin*, trans. by Ruth Kisch (New York, 1968), pp. 195–246. Chuikov was the Commander of the Soviet Eighth Guards Army, which was the elite corps chosen to carry out the storming of Berlin. In writing of his talks with the German General Krebs during the last days of the war, Chuikov states, "Here Krebs had said a little too much, and thereby confirmed

our guesses and suppositions. The real truth was in his words about Hitler having given orders that all units of Germany's armed forces should be transferred 'from there,' that is from the west, to Berlin, to the Eastern front against us, thus opening the way to the troops of the Western powers." Chuikov, *op. cit.*, p. 229.

2. Walter L. Dorn, "The Debate Over American Occupation Policy in Germany in 1944–1945," *Political Science Quarterly* 72 (1957), p. 488.

3. *Ibid.*, p. 489.

4. *Time* Magazine, September 13, 1971, p. 30.

BIBLIOGRAPHY

I. Archives and Private Papers

U.S. Department of State, Historical Office. Complete Files of the American Delegation to the European Advisory Commission. Decimal Files, 740.00119 EAC—The National Archives, Washington. Lot Files, Lot 52 M 64—The State Department, Washington.

Winant, John Gilbert. The Papers of John Gilbert Winant, U.S. Ambassador to the Court of St. James During World War II. Microfilm. Columbia University Library.

II. Official Publications and Documents Collections

Befehle des Obersten Chefs der Sowjetischen Militärverwaltung in Deutschland. Aus dem Stab der Sowjetischen Militärverwaltung in Deutschland, Sammelheft 1, 1945. Berlin: Verlag der Sowjetischen Militärverwaltung in Deutschland, 1946.

Berlin Senat. *Berlin: Kampf um Freiheit und Selbstverwaltung, 1945-1946.* Berlin: Heinz Spitzing Verlag, 1961.

Cline, Ray S. *Washington Command Post: The Operations Division.* Office of the Chief of Military History, Department of the Army. Washington: Government Printing Office, 1951.

Federal Republic of Germany. Bundesministerium für Gesamtdeutsche Fragen. *Die Sowjetische Besatungszone Deutschlands in den Jahren 1945-1954.* Bonn, 1956.

Federal Republic of Germany, Ministry of All-German Affairs. *The Soviet Zone of Germany.* Cologne, 1960.

Gablentz, Otto Martin von der, ed. *The Berlin Question in Its Relation to World Politics 1944-1963.* Documents and Reports of the Research Institute of the German Society for Foreign Affairs, Bonn, Vol. 19. Munich: R. Oldenbourg Verlag, 1964.

German Information Center, New York. *Berlin: Crisis and Challenge.* New York, 1962.

Great Britain. *Berlin and the Problem of German Reunification.* London: British Information Services, 1961.

Great Britain. *Selected Documents on Germany and the Question of Berlin, 1944-1961.* Cmnd. 1552. London: H. M. Stationery Office, 1961.

Heidelmeyer, Wolfgang, and Hindrichs, Guenter, eds. *Documents on Berlin 1943-1963.* Issued under the auspices of the Research Institute of the German Society for Foreign Affairs, Bonn. Munich: R. Oldenbourg Verlag, 1963.

Hillgruber, Andreas. *Berlin Dokumente 1944-1961.* Darmstadt: Stephan Verlagsgesellschaft, MBH, 1961.

Matloff, Maurice. *Strategic Planning for Coalition Warfare, 1943-1944.* Office of the Chief of Military History, Department of the Army. Washington: Government Printing Office, 1959.

Notter, Harley A. *Postwar Foreign Policy Preparation 1939-1945.* Department of State. Washington: Government Printing Office, 1949.

Oppen, Beate Ruhm von. *Documents on Germany Under Occupation 1945-1954.* London: Oxford University Press, 1955.

Plischke, Elmer. *Berlin: Development of Its Government and Administration*. Historical Division, Office of the U.S. High Commissioner for Germany. Bonn, 1952.

Pogue, Forrest C. *The Supreme Command*. Office of the Chief of Military History, Department of the Army. Washington: Government Printing Office, 1954.

Rottmann, Joachim von. *Der Viermächte-Status Berlins*. Zweite, durchgesehene Auflage. Bonn/Berlin: Bundesministerium für Gesamtdeutsche Fragen, 1959.

Union of Soviet Socialist Republics. *Stalin's Correspondence with Churchill, Attlee, Roosevelt, and Truman, 1941–1945*. New York: E. P. Dutton and Co., 1958.

Union of Soviet Socialist Republics. *The Tehran, Yalta, and Potsdam Conferences: Documents*. Moscow: Progress Publishers, 1969.

U.S. Congress. Senate. Committee on Foreign Relations. *Report on Berlin in a Changing Europe*. 88th Cong., 1st sess. Washington: Government Printing Office, 1963.

U.S. Department of State. Historical Office. *Documents on Germany, 1944–1961*. Committee on Foreign Relations, U.S. Senate, 86th Cong., 1st sess. Washington: Government Printing Office, 1961.

U.S. Department of State. Historical Office. *Foreign Relations of the United States: Conference on Berlin (Potsdam) 1945*. 2 vols. Washington: Government Printing Office, 1960.

U.S. Department of State. Historical Office. *Foreign Relations of the United States: Conferences at Cairo and Tehran, 1943*. Washington: Government Printing Office, 1961.

U.S. Department of State. Historical Office. *Foreign Relations of the United States: Conferences at Malta and Yalta, 1945*. Washington: Government Printing Office, 1955.

U.S. Department of State. Historical Office. *Foreign Relations of the United States: Diplomatic Papers, 1943*. Volume I-General. Washington: Government Printing Office, 1963.

U.S. Department of State. Historical Office. *Foreign Relations of the United States: Diplomatic Papers, 1944*. Volume I-General. Washington: Government Printing Office, 1966.

U.S. Department of State. Historical Office. *Foreign Relations of the United States: Diplomatic Papers, 1945*. Volume III-European Advisory Commission, Austria, Germany. Washington: Government Printing Office, 1968.

U.S. Department of State. *Occupation of Germany, Policy and Progress, 1945–1946*. Washington: Government Printing Office, 1947.

U.S. Department of State. *The Soviet Note on Berlin: An Analysis*. Department of State Publication 6757. Washington: Government Printing Office, 1959.

U.S. Department of State. *Toward the Peace, Documents*. Washington: Government Printing Office, 1945.

U.S. Office of Military Government for Germany. *Military Government Information Bulletin*. Berlin, 1945–1949.

U.S. Office of Military Government for Germany. *Official Gazette of the Control Council*. Berlin, 1945–1948.

U.S. Office of Military Government, U.S. Sector, Berlin. *A Four Year Report-July 1, 1945–September 1, 1949*. Berlin, 1949.

Western European Union. Assembly. General Affairs Committee. Eighth Ordinary Session. *Berlin 1944–1962*. Brief on the Berlin question prepared by Mr. A. Molter, Rapporteur. Paris, 1962.

BIBLIOGRAPHY

Woodward, Sir Llewellyn. *British Foreign Policy in the Second World War*. London: H. M. Stationery Office, 1962.

III. Books and Memoirs

Albrecht, Gunter. *Berlin im Blickpunkt der Welt*. Berlin: Deutscher Zentralverlag, 1959.

Association of the Bar of the City of New York. *The Issues in the Berlin-German Crisis*. Background Papers and Proceedings of the First Hammarskjöld Forum Organized by the Association of the Bar of the City of New York, Lyman M. Tondel, Jr., ed. Dobbs Ferry, N.Y.: Oceana Publications, Inc., 1963.

Bathurst, M. E., and Simpson, J. L. *Germany and the North Atlantic Community: A Legal Survey*. Published under the auspices of the London Institute of World Affairs. London: Stevens and Sons Limited, 1956.

Campbell, John C., and the Research Staff of the Council on Foreign Relations. *The United States in World Affairs 1945–1947*. New York: Harper and Brothers (for the Council on Foreign Relations), 1947.

Chuikov, Marshal Vasili I. *The Fall of Berlin*. Translated by Ruth Kisch. New York: Holt, Rinehart and Winston, 1968.

Churchill, Winston S. *Triumph and Tragedy*. Boston: Houghton Mifflin, 1953.

Clauss, Max Walter. *Der Weg nach Jalta: President Roosevelt's Verantwortung*. Heidelberg: Vowinkel, 1952.

Clay, Lucius D. *Decision in Germany*. Garden City, N.Y.: Doubleday and Co., 1950.

Deane, John R. *The Strange Alliance: The Story of Our Efforts at Wartime Cooperation With Russia*. New York: Viking Press, 1947.

de Gaulle, General Charles. *The War Memoirs of Charles de Gaulle*. New York: Simon and Schuster, 1959–1960.

Dennett, Raymond, and Johnson, Joseph E., eds. *Negotiating With the Russians*. Boston: World Peace Foundation, 1951.

Dauerlein, Ernst. *Die Einheit Deutschlands*. Bd. I: Die Erörterungen und Entscheidungen der Kriegs-und Nachkriegskonferenzen 1941–1949. Frankfurt: A. Metzner, 1961.

Eden, Sir Anthony. *Facing the Dictators: The Memoirs of Anthony Eden, Earl of Avon*. Boston: Houghton Mifflin, 1962.

Eden, Sir Anthony. *Freedom and Order: Selected Speeches, 1939–1946*. London: Faber and Faber, 1947.

Eisenhower, Dwight D. *Crusade in Europe*. Garden City, N.Y.: Doubleday and Co., 1948.

Faust, Fritz. *Das Potsdamer Abkommen und seine völkerrechtliche Bedeutung*. Frankfurt: A. Metzner, 1959.

Feis, Herbert. *Between War and Peace: The Potsdam Conference*. Princeton: Princeton University Press, 1960.

Feis, Herbert. *Churchill, Roosevelt, Stalin: The War They Waged and the Peace They Sought*. Princeton: Princeton University Press, 1957.

Friedmann, Wolfgang. *Allied Military Government in Germany*. London: Stevens and Sons Limited, 1947.

Gottlieb, Manuel. *The German Peace Settlement and the Berlin Crisis.* New York: Paine Whitman, 1960.

Henkin, Louis. *The Berlin Crisis and the United Nations.* New York: Carnegie Endowment for International Peace, 1959.

Howley, Frank (Brigadier General). *Berlin Command.* New York: Putnam's Sons, 1950.

Hubatsch, Walter, ed. *The German Question.* Translated by Salvator Attanasio. New York: Herder Book Center, 1967.

Hull, Cordell. *The Memoirs of Cordell Hull.* 2 vols. New York: Macmillan, 1948.

Kennan, George F. *Memoirs 1925–1950.* Boston: Little, Brown and Company, 1967.

Leahy, Fleet Admiral William D. *I Was There: The Personal Story of the Chief of Staff to Presidents Roosevelt and Truman, Based on His Notes and Diaries Made at the Time.* New York: Whittlesley House, 1950.

Legien, Rudolf. *The Four Power Agreements on Berlin: Alternative Solutions to the Status Quo?* Translated by Trevor Davies. Berlin: Carl Heymanns Verlag, 1960.

McNeill, William Hardy. *America, Britain, and Russia: Their Cooperation and Conflict, 1941–1946.* London: Oxford University Press (for the Royal Institute of International Affairs), 1953.

Martin, Alexander. *Brennpunkt Berlin: 70 Fragen and 70 Antworten zum Berlin-Problem.* Berlin-Ost, 1959.

Meissner, Boris. *Russland, die Westmächte und Deutschland: die sowjetische Deutschlandpolitik, 1943–1953.* Hamburg: Nolke, 1953.

Mezerik, A. G., ed. *Berlin and Germany: Berlin Crisis, Wall, Free City, Separate Treaty, Cold War Chronology.* New York: International Review Service, 1962.

Moltmann, Günter. *Amerikas Deutschlandpolitik im zweiten Weltkrieg: Kriegs-und Friedensziele, 1941–1945.* Heidelberg: C. Winter, 1958.

Montgomery, Viscount. *The Memoirs of Montgomery of Alamein.* Cleveland: World Publishing Company, 1958.

Morgan, Sir Frederick. *Overture to Overlord.* Garden City, N.Y.: Doubleday and Co., 1950.

Morgenthau, Henry J. *Germany Is Our Problem.* New York: Harper and Brothers, 1945.

Mosely, Philip E. *The Kremlin and World Politics.* New York: Random House and Alfred A. Knopf, 1960.

Nettl, J. P. *The Eastern Zone and Soviet Policy in Germany, 1945–1950.* London: Oxford University Press, 1951.

Neumann, William L. *After Victory: Churchill, Roosevelt, Stalin and the Making of the Peace.* New York: Harper and Row, 1967.

Neumann, William L. *Making the Peace, 1941–1945: The Diplomacy of the Wartime Conferences.* Washington: Foundation for Foreign Affairs, 1950.

Pounds, Norman J. G. *Divided Germany and Berlin.* Princeton: Van Nostrand, 1962.

Riklin, Alois. *Das Berlinproblem: Historisch-politische und völkerrechtliche Darstellung des Viermächtestatus.* Abhandlungen des Bundesinstituts zur Erforschung des Marxismus-Leninismus, Band VI. Köln: Verlag Wissenschaft und Politik, 1964.

Robson, Charles B., ed. and trans. *Berlin: Pivot of German Destiny.* Chapel Hill, N. C.: University of North Carolina Press, 1960.

BIBLIOGRAPHY

Rothfels, Hans, ed. *Berlin in Vergangenheit und Gegenwart.* Tübinger Studien zur Geschichte und Politik, Nr. 14. Tübingen: J. C. B. Mohr, 1961.

Rozek, Edward J. *Allied Wartime Diplomacy: A Pattern in Poland.* New York: John Wiley and Sons, 1958.

Schulz, Klaus-Peter. *Berlin Zwischen Freiheit und Diktatur.* Berlin: Staneck, 1962.

Sherwood, Robert E. *Roosevelt and Hopkins: An Intimate History.* New York: Harper and Brothers, 1948.

Smith, Jean Edward. *The Defense of Berlin.* Baltimore: Johns Hopkins Press, 1963.

Smith, Lieutenant General Walter Bedell. *My Three Years in Moscow.* Philadelphia: J. B. Lippincott Co., 1950.

Snell, John L., ed. *The Meaning of Yalta.* Baton Rouge: Louisiana State University Press, 1956.

Snell, John L. *Wartime Origins of the East-West Dilemma over Germany.* New Orleans: Hauser Press, 1959.

Stanger, Roland J., ed. *West Berlin: The Legal Context.* Columbus, Ohio: Ohio State University Press, 1966.

Steiniger, Peter Alfons. *Westberlin: Ein Handbuch zur Westberlinfrage.* Erarbeitet von einem Kollektiv von Mitarbeitern wissenschaftlicher Institut sowie staatlicher und gesellschaftlicher Institutionen unter der Leitung von Prof. Steiniger. Berlin (Ost): Kongress Verlag, 1959.

Stettinius, Edward R. *Roosevelt and the Russians: The Yalta Conference.* Garden City, N.Y.: Doubleday and Co., 1949.

Stimson, Henry L., and Bundy, McGeorge. *On Active Service in Peace and War.* New York: Harper and Brothers, 1950.

Strang, William Lord. *Home and Abroad.* London: Andre Deutsch Limited, 1956.

Strauss, Harold, *The Division and Dismemberment of Germany.* Geneva: Les Presses Savoie, 1952.

Truman, Harry S. *Year of Decisions.* Garden City, N.Y.: Doubleday and Co., 1955.

Warburg, James P. *Germany: Bridge or Battleground.* New York: Harcourt and Brace, 1947.

Welles, Sumner. *The Time for Decision.* New York: Harper and Brothers, 1944.

Wilmot, Chester. *The Struggle for Europe.* New York: Harper and Brothers, 1952.

Winant, John G. *Letters from Grosvenor Square.* Boston: Houghton Mifflin, 1947.

Zink, Harold. *The United States in Germany 1944–1955.* Princeton: Van Nostrand Co., 1957.

IV. Articles

Acheson, Dean G. "On Dealing with Russia: An Inside View." *New York Times Magazine,* April 12, 1959, 27, 88–89.

Bentzien, Joachim. "Die Luftkorridore von und nach Berlin." *Aussenpolitik* 12 (1961), 685–690.

Bishop, J. W. "The Origin and Nature of the Rights of the Western Allies in Berlin," in Roland J. Stanger, ed., *West Berlin: The Legal Context.* Columbus, Ohio: Ohio State University Press, 1966, 23–52.

Castellan, Georges. "La Politique Allemande de l'U.S.S.R., 1941–1945." *Revue d'Histoire de la Deuxième Guerre Mondiale* 6 (Janvier, 1956), 38–54.

Dorn, Walter L. "The Debate over American Occupation Policy in Germany in 1944–1945." *Political Science Quarterly* 72 (1957), 481–501.

Draht, Martin. "Die staatsrechtliche Stellung Berlins." *Archiv des Öffentlichen Rechts* 1 (1957), 27–75.

Faust, Fritz. "Die völkerrechtliche Beurteilung der Berlin-Frage." *Wehrwissenschaftliche Rundschau* 9 (1963), 510–531.

Feis, Herbert. "The Three Who Led." *Foreign Affairs* 27 (1959), 282–292.

Franklin, William M. "Zonal Boundaries and Access to Berlin." *World Politics* 16 (1963), 1–31.

Friedmann, Wolfgang. "Legal and Political Aspects of the Berlin Crisis." *Columbia Society of International Law Bulletin* (1961), 3–8.

Gergh, Hendrik van. "Der Rest, der übrigblieb: Die Deutschlandpläne der Allierten 1945." *Politische Studien* 8 (Juli, 1957), 1–19.

Green, L. C. "The Legal Status of Berlin." *Netherlands International Law Review* 10 (1963), 113–138.

Grewe, Wilhelm G. "Other Legal Aspects of the Berlin Crisis." *American Journal of International Law* 56 (1962), 510–513.

Herder, Gerhard. "Berlin war keine fünfte Besatungszone." *Staat und Recht* 1 (1962), 47–52.

Howley, Frank P. "I've Talked 1600 Hours With the Russians." *Reader's Digest*, May, 1949, 73–78.

Jessup, Philip C. "The Rights of the United States in Berlin." *American Journal of International Law* 43 (1949), 92–95.

Korovin, E. A. "Berlinfrage und Völkerrecht." *Neue Zeit* 2 (1959), 17–19.

Kreutzer, Heinz. "West Berlin: City and State," in Charles B. Robson, ed. and trans., *Berlin: Pivot of German Destiny*. Chapel Hill, N. C.: University of North Carolina Press, 1960, 67–99.

Kröger, Herbert. "Zu einigen Fragen des staatsrechtlichen Status von Berlin." *Deutsche Aussenpolitik* 1 (1958), 10–26.

Lauterpacht, E. "The Position of the Western Powers in Berlin." *International and Comparative Law Quarterly* 8 (1959), 207–212.

Leprette, J. "Le Status de Berlin." *Annuaire Français de Droit International* 1 (1955), 123–127.

Lindner, Gerhard. "Die widerrechtliche Besetzung Westberlins." *Deutsche Aussenpolitik* 3 (1959), 231–255.

Lindner, Gerhard. "Zur Lufthoheit der DDR." *Deutsche Aussenpolitik* 10 (1957), 820–833.

Loewenstein, Karl. "The Allied Presence in Berlin: Legal Basis." *Foreign Policy Bulletin*, vol. 38, no. 11 (1959), 81–84.

Metzger, Stanley D. "The Division of Berlin and of Germany," in Roland J. Stanger, ed., *West Berlin: The Legal Context*. Columbus, Ohio: Ohio State University Press, 1966, 3–22.

Morgenthau, Hans. "The Problem of German Reunification." *Annals of the American Academy of Political and Social Science* 330 (1960), 124–132.

Mosely, Philip E. "Dismemberment of Germany: The Allied Negotiations from Yalta to Potsdam." *Foreign Affairs* 28 (1950), 487–498.

Mosely, Philip E. "Some Soviet Techniques of Negotiation," in Raymond Dennett and Joseph E. Johnson, eds., *Negotiating With the Russians*. Boston: World Peace Foundation, 1951, 271–303.

BIBLIOGRAPHY

Mosely, Philip E. "The Occupation of Germany: New Light on How the Zones Were Drawn." *Foreign Affairs* 28 (1950), 580–604.

Rauschning, Hermann. "Danzig, Berlin, und die deutsche Frage." *Blätter für Deutsche und Internationale Politik* 12 (1961), 1095–1109.

Schüle, Adolf. "Berlin als völkerrechtliches Problem," in Hans Rothfels, ed., *Berlin in Vergangenheit und Gegenwart*. Tübingen: J. C. B. Mohr, 1961, 124–139.

Simpson, J. L. "Berlin: Allied Rights and Responsibilities in the Divided City." *International and Comparative Law Quarterly* 6 (1957), 83–102.

Skowronski, A. "Legal Problems of the Occupation Status of Greater Berlin." *Review of Contemporary Law* 8 (1961), 73–87.

Tunkin, Gregory I. "The Berlin Problem and International Law." *International Affairs* (Moscow), 1959, 36–43.

Wagner, Wolfgang. "Besatzungszonen und Spaltung Deutschlands." *Aussenpolitik* 5 (August, 1954), 496–508.

Warner, Albert L. "Our Secret Deal Over Germany." *Saturday Evening Post*, August 2, 1952, 30, 66, 68.

Wright, Quincy. "Some Legal Aspects of the Berlin Crisis." *American Journal of International Law* 55 (1961), 959–965.

INDEX

Access, zones of occupation, 69–70, 85, 130–139
Agreement on Control Machinery, 122
Air Directorate, 137–138
Airdromes. See Staaken; Tempelhof.
Air lanes, 131, 137–138
Allied Control Council for Germany, 2, 90, 96, 103–104, 111–112, 118, 128, 133–136 *passim*, 138, 147, 153, 155
Antwerp, 26
Armistice Day, 70
Attlee, Clement, 15, 29
Attlee Committee. See British Armistice and Postwar Committee.
Austria, 29, 32, 33, 40, 82, 91, 102–105, 127, 151
Autobahn Ring, 47

Babelsberg, 116
Baden, 29, 31, 85
Balkans, 91
Baltic Sea, 31
Bavaria, 29, 31, 32
Belgium, 26, 30, 31, 141
Berlin: significance of, 1; devastation of, 1–2, 93; division of, by Allied Powers, 3, 29–30, 46–48, 50–51, 57, 80–81; blockade, 3, 139; location of, 119, 141; as enclave, 142; Quadripartite Agreement on, 156
Berlin, airlift, 3
Berlin Wall, 3
Bevin, Ernest, 15
Big Three, 32–33, 106, 163
Bohlen, Charles, 13
Bowman, Isaiah, 17
Bradley, Omar, 131
Brandenburg, 29, 34
Braunschweig, 131
Bremen, 69, 71, 73, 95, 130, 131, 138, 157
Bremerhaven, 69, 71, 73
British Armistice and Postwar Committee, 15, 29–30, 32, 121, 141
British Chiefs of Staff, 32–33
British Foreign Office, 24, 34
British War Cabinet, 29
Brunswick, 29
Bückeburg, 137, 138
Bulgaria, 60
Byrnes, James F., 115, 116

Cabell, C. P., 38, 48, 57
Cairo, 32
Campbell, Ronald, 116, 117
Cate, Benjamin, 166
Chuikov, Vasili I., 157, 205
Churchill, Winston S.: at Tehran, 10; view on postwar collaboration, 12; approves Attlee proposal, 30; view on partitioning, 32, 162; at Cairo, 33; on French occupation of Berlin, 77; on delaying withdrawal, 88–91, 94–95, 129, 157, 158; on postwar order, 96–99; influences Roosevelt, 149; mentioned, 157, 160, 163, 167
Civil Affairs Division, U.S. War Department: role in decision-making, 18–19, 35–36, 41–43, 65, 69, 120–121, 144, 147; defends military interests, 44, 45, 100
Clay, Lucius, 44, 93, 101, 114, 130–135, 166
Cold War, 2, 158
Combined Chiefs of Staff, 32, 149
Committee on Boundaries, 59
Committee on Dismemberment, 79
Copenhagen, 137
COSSAC, 26–27, 30, 32, 33, 34, 36, 37, 38, 41, 42
Council of Foreign Ministers, 118

INDEX

Country and Area Committee, U.S. Department of State: opposes dismemberment, 25–26; proposal on occupation zones, 33–34, 35, 36, 120
Crimea Conference. See Yalta.
Czechoslovakia, 31, 91

Danube River, 95
Dauerlein, Ernst, 10
Declaration Regarding the Defeat of Germany, 88, 92
Declaration of Unconditional Surrender, 83 n.
Deane, John, 130
de Gaulle, Charles, 60, 80, 87, 157
de Leusse, Pierre Marie, 81, 100–102 *passim*
Denmark, 26, 30
Dismemberment: committee, 79, 86–87; proposal discarded, 88; approved by Roosevelt, 148; British attitudes on, 162
Donaldson, E. P., 22
Doeberitz, 48
Dorn, Walter, 158–159
Dunn, James C., 115
Düsseldorf, 26

EAC. See European Advisory Commission.
East Berlin, 3, 48, 154, 164
East German regime, 156
East Prussia, 29, 40, 58
Eden, Anthony: on consultation for postwar problems, 10–11, 13, 16; meeting with Roosevelt, 24; opposes dismemberment, 27; mentioned, 162
Eisenach, 29
Eisenhower, Dwight D., 60, 64, 89, 93, 96, 117, 118, 119
English Channel, 26
European Advisory Commission (EAC): records, 7; created, 10, 13; mandate, 21; meetings, 22, 24, 38; Soviet proposals, 48–49, 111–113; acts on surrender instrument, 58; work halts, 60, 76; signs protocol, 72–73; agrees on control machinery, 72; French zone problems, 75–76; declaration, 88; work jeopardized, 89; French sector problem, 99–101, 105, 114; amends protocol, 117; report, 118; assessment of, 140, 142–144, 148, 150–154 *passim*, 157–158, 168–170

Federal Republic of Germany, 166, 170
Filmer, Major, 59
First Quebec Conference, 26, 27
Flory, Lester D., 94, 137
Foreign Affairs, 34 n.
France, 11, 26, 31, 83
Frankfurt, 95, 130, 132
Franklin, William, 28, 32, 33, 121, 123, 136–137
French Provisional Government, 70, 72
Friedrichshafen, 48
Friedrichshain, 50

Gau Berlin, 46, 47
Geneva, 3
German Democratic Republic, 164, 170
German forces, surrender of, 87
German *Reich*, 1, 2
Germany, dismemberment of. See Dismemberment.
Germany, planned occupation of: American zone, 29; eastern (Soviet) zone, 29; British zone, 29; French zone, 84–86
Gesetzsammlung, 50
Gousev. See Gusev, Fedor T.
Greater Berlin: special occupation zone, 48–53 *passim;* terms of reference, 49; administrative proposal for, 61; dispute over access, 62
Grew, Joseph C., 84
Grigg, James, 15
Gruenewald, 59
Gusev, Fedor T.: Soviet representative, EAC, 14, 23; on division of Berlin, 40, 48; on administering Berlin, 52–58 *passim*, 71; on transit rights, 69–70, 108, 125, 137; on dismemberment, 87; on Control Coun-

cil, 91–92; on French sector, 100, 109–111; inability to maneuver, 143, 159; mentioned, 81, 86, 162

Hamburg, 26, 137, 138
Hannover, 29, 131, 132
Harriman, W. Averell, 60
Herman, Leona, 47 *n*.
Hesse-Darmstadt, 29
Hesse-Nassau, 29
Hill, General, 132
Hilldring, John H., 44
Hitler, Adolf, 1, 58, 164
Holland, 30, 141
Hood, Samuel, 81, 100–111 *passim*, 116
Hopkins, Harry, 16, 31, 60, 73, 77, 88, 93, 129–130, 145
Horst Wessel, 50
Hull, Cordell: attitude on proposed tripartite consultation, 11, 12, 13; relationship with Roosevelt, 20, 27, 28, 30, 31, 67; opposes dismemberment, 27; disapproves Morgenthau Plan, 63; cooperation with Winant, 66; lacks authority, 145
Hungary, 91

Instrument of Unconditional Surrender, 82, 87, 88
Interdivisional Committee on Germany, U.S. Department of State, 17–18
Iowa. See USS *Iowa*.
Iron curtain, 94
Italy, 31

Japan, 89
Joint Chiefs of Staff, United States, 16, 30, 32–33, 37–39 *passim*, 72, 73, 83, 84, 126–128 *passim*, 144, 145, 149, 150
Joint Postwar Committee, Joint Chiefs of Staff, 19

Karlsruhe, 85
Kennan, George F.: on Roosevelt's view of EAC, 12; on limits on Winant's role, 15; criticizes War Department, 19, 144; as adviser to Winant, 20, 38, 43–44; on EAC, 20, 21; on State Department's subordination, 145; confers with Roosevelt, 43, 149
Kennedy, John F., 1
Kennedy, Joseph P., 14
Kerr, Archibald Clark, 60
Kiel Canal, 27
King, Ernest J., 31, 60
Kleist Park, 4
Koeltz, Louis, 117
Koenig, Lieutenant General, 118
Koepenick, 48
Komendatura: established, 48; relationship to control machinery, 51–52, 51 *n*.; administration of Berlin, 55. See also Kommandatura.
Kommandatura: functioning of, 2, 155; original term, 51 *n*.; created by EAC, 155
Kootz, Colonel, 126
Kremlin, 166
Kreuzberg, 50, 59
Khrushchev, Nikita, 3
Kutzevalov, T. F., 137

Lancaster House, 22, 62, 78, 98, 137, 145, 148, 155, 169
Länder, 29
Leahy, William D., 30, 145
Leipzig, 32
Leverich, Henry P., 28
Lichtenberg, 48
Lightner, E. Allen, Jr., 116
London, 11, 37, 74, 134, 155
Löwenstein, Karl, 10
Luxembourg, 30, 31
Lübeck, 26

McCloy, John J., 60, 73, 82, 115
Magdeburg, 131, 132
Malta, 73, 126
Mannheim, 85
Marrakech, 126
Marshall, George C., 30, 31
Massigli, Rene: represents France in EAC, 72; on French zone of occupa-

INDEX

tion, 75–76; assuages de Gaulle, 87; not concerned with access to Berlin, 121–122; debates Gusev, 104; proposes compromise on French sector, 111–112

Mecklenburg, 29

Meyer, Vincent: replaces Wickersham, 38, 47 *n.*; advises Winant, 52; forwards SHAEF's views, 55–56; consults SHAEF, 65

Mitte, 48, 59, 112

Molotov, Vyacheslav M.: attitude on tripartite commission, 11; demands definition of EAC functions, 13; preoccupation with military affairs, 143

Montgomery, Bernard Law, 118

Morgan, Frederick: heads COSSAC, 26; confers with General Marshall, 30; reports on switching occupation zones, 33

Morgenthau, Henry, Jr.: favors dismemberment of Germany, 25; attends Second Quebec Conference, 62; relationship with Roosevelt, 147

Morgenthau Plan: recommended by Roosevelt, 62–63; 147–148; shifting attitudes on, 74; waning influence of, 86; opposition to, 147–148

Moscow Conference. See Tripartite Conference of Foreign Ministers.

Moselle River, 31

Mosely, Philip: comments on EAC, 14; drafts proposal on Germany, 28; on drawing zones, 34 *n.*; proposes corridor, 34; as Winant's adviser, 38, 47 *n.*; on access to Berlin, 45; on Berlin's boundaries, 59; requests instructions, 61; on signing protocols, 70–72; negotiates disputes, 71; on dismemberment, 88; objects to Churchill proposal, 90; on division of Berlin, 107; drafts access plan, 125–126; urges access agreement, 136; mentioned, 18, 143, 152

Murphy, Robert, 85, 139

National Geographic Society, 31, 68, 150

NATO (North Atlantic Treaty Organization), 166

Naziism, 1

Nazi Germany, 161

Nazi Third *Reich*, 163

Netherlands, 26, 33

Neukölln, 83, 84

New York Times, 170

Normandy invasion, 58

North Sea, 30

Norway, 26

OVERLORD, 26, 31

Palewski, Gaston, 85

Pankow, 48

Parks, Floyd L., 96

Poland, 11, 29

Pomerania, 29

Post-Hostilities Planning Committee (U.K.), 15

Potsdam, 47, 59, 115, 117

Potsdam Conference, 94, 111, 114–117

Potsdam Agreement, 160, 169, 170

Prague, 137

Prenzlauerberg, 50

Prussia, 29, 32, 34

QUADRANT, 26

Quadripartite Agreement on Berlin, 1971, 3–5 *passim*, 164–166, 170

Quebec. See Second Quebec Conference.

Rail lines, 131

RANKIN, 26, 27, 30, 140

Red Army, 35, 89, 102

Reinickendorf, 117

Rhineland, 27

Rhine Province, 29

Rhine River, 26, 29

Riddleberger, James, 16

Robertson, Brian H., 138

Roosevelt, Franklin D.: at Tehran, 10; on collaboration with Soviets, 12; on postwar policy, 16; fails to establish jurisdictions, 19; relationship with State Department, 20, 144–145; on

zones of occupation, 30–33 *passim*; proposes American zone, 31, 41, 43, 62; on partitioning Germany, 32; does not support EAC, 41, 42, 67, 143, 159; on American occupation, 60; reelection, 77; on dismemberment, 86; on access problem, 134; favors Morgenthau Plan, 62, 147–148; abilities, 145; objection to postwar agreement, 163; mentioned, 157, 160, 163, 167
Rotterdam, 26
Ruhr, 26, 27, 114

St. James' Palace, 22
Saksin, Georgii F., 111
Saxony, 129
Saxony-Anhalt, 29, 34
Scandinavia, 33
Second Quebec Conference, 61, 62–63, 89
Secret Protocol, Moscow Conference, 13
SHAEF (Supreme Headquarters Allied Expeditionary Forces), 27, 55, 65, 85, 87, 126
Sherwood, Robert, 20
Smith, Jean Edward, 20, 32, 44, 67, 148–149
Smith, Walter Bedell, 65
Sobolev, Arkadii, 80
Sokolovsky, Vasily, 138
Soviet Foreign Ministry, 162
Spandau, 47
Staaken Airdrome (Aerodrome), 48, 49, 52, 54, 57–58
Stalin, Josef: regime, 8; at Tehran, 10; favors weakening of Germany, 32; agrees to French occupation, 77; victory speech, 88; grants Allied mission to Vienna, 95; lacks enthusiasm for EAC, 143, 159; mentioned, 95, 157, 160, 162, 167
Stark, Harold, 38
State-War-Navy Coordinating Committee (SWNCC), 82, 83, 145
Stendal, 131
Stettin, 31

Stettinius, Edward R.: receives memorandum on EAC proposal, 41; disagrees with Roosevelt, 60; as secretary of state, 73; cables Winant, 86; on Churchill proposal, 90; lacks influence, 145; mentioned, 115
Stimson, Henry L., 60
Strang, William: reconciles conflict on EAC, 13; as British representative to EAC, 14, 22; serves on British postwar committee, 15; comments on EAC, 22; issues memorandum on military occupation, 38; attitude on zone boundaries, 40; supports Winant's zones proposal, 54; notes French proposals, 75; supports Winant on control machinery, 92; assigned to Weeks, 116; comments on access to Berlin, 123; presents Attlee Committee proposals, 141; mentioned, 23 *n*., 162
Surrender. See Instrument of Unconditional Surrender.
Switzerland, 26
SWNCC. See State-War-Navy Coordinating Committee.

Tehran Conference, 10, 14, 30, 32
Tempelhof Airdrome (Aerodrome), 48, 50, 57, 84
Territorial Studies Committee, U.S. Department of State, 17
Thuringia, 29, 129
Transit, rights of: British zone, 73; Austria, 102–103
Treaty of Cooperation, 170
Treptow, 48, 83
Tripartite Conference of Foreign Ministers (Moscow Conference): negotiations on Berlin, 7; agreement on EAC, 10–11, 142; delegates, 28; American commitments, 146; mentioned, 68, 158, 161
Truman, Harry S.: on Allied troop withdrawal, 88–91, 129; on postwar order, 96–99 *passim*; proposals on access to Berlin and Vienna, 129–130, 134; mentioned, 157

INDEX

United Nations, 12, 89, 163, 166

United States Air Transport Command, 48

United States Department of State: formation of postwar policy, 16; uninformed on Attlee Committee proposals, 36; views on zones protocol, 53; chronic quarrel with War Department, 143; failures, 146; reason for WSC, 152

United States Department of the Treasury, 147

United States Department of War: postwar policies, 16; attitude toward EAC, 18-19; safeguards military interests, 55, 135; quarrels with State Department, 144

United States Embassy, Paris, 85

United States 2nd Armored Division, 96

USS *Iowa*, 30, 33, 38, 149

Versailles, 85

Vienna: occupation zones, 94-95, 102-105 *passim*; access negotiations, 107-108, 127, 136-137, 151

Vyshinsky, Andrey, 12

Warsaw, 137

Warsaw Pact, 166

Wedding, 117

Weeks, Ronald, 114, 115, 117, 130, 132, 133, 135, 139

Weissensee, 48, 80, 81

Welles, Sumner, 25

West Berlin, 1, 156, 164

Westmark, 29

Westphalia, 29

Wickersham, Cornelius W., 38, 43

Williamson, Charles G., 38, 57, 84

Wilmersdorf, 59

Winant, John G.: U.S. representative to EAC, 14, 20-21, 22; encounters difficulties, 15-19 *passim*, 35-40 *passim*, 63-66, 146-147; communications with Washington, 17-18, 44, 51, 52-53, 69, 85-88 *passim*, 121, 125; staff, 38; agrees on occupation zones, 45; proposes new boundary for Berlin area, 47; urges flexibility, 53; takes protocol to Quebec, 62; views Berlin as fourth zone, 68; urges zones protocol ratification, 73; relations with Stettinius, 77; objects to Churchill proposal, 90; advocates control machinery, 92; agrees on withdrawal, 98; debates French sector problem, 113; raises Western access question, 121; links withdrawal with Berlin entry, 130; defense of, 145-146; disagrees with Roosevelt, 150; mentioned 33, 67, 91, 123, 125, 151, 162, 165

Working Security Committee: established, 17-18; procedures, 18-20 *passim*; inability to instruct Winant, 41; confusion in, 41-42; replaced by SWNCC, 82; purpose, 144; deadlock, 146; mentioned, 35

WSC. See Working Security Committee.

Württemberg, 29, 31, 85

Yalta Conference: grants French occupation in Germany, 77-78; omits mention of Berlin, 78; contributes to EAC paralysis, 78-79; creates confusion, 86; examines access problem, 126; displeasure with EAC, 146; agreement violated, 164; mentioned, 76, 164

Yugoslavia, 11

Zehlendorf, 59, 83

Zhukov, Georgi K.: decision on occupation forces, 93; meets with Clay and Weeks, 101, 114, 130-133; supplies information on Soviet sector, 112; at Control Council, 118; mentioned, 96

Zonal occupation: draft on, 46; redraft on, 46-47; Soviet proposal for, 48